I0890541

International Criminal Justice *in bello*?

International Humanitarian Law Series

VOLUME 34

Editors-in-Chief
H.E. Judge Sir Christopher Greenwood
Professor Timothy L.H. McCormack

Editorial Advisory Board
Professor Georges Abi-Saab
H.E. Judge George H. Aldrich
Madame Justice Louise Arbour
Professor Ove Bring
Professor Antonio Cassese
Professor John Dugard
Professor Dr. Horst Fischer
Dr. Hans-Peter Gasser
Professor Leslie C. Green
H.E. Judge Geza Herczegh
Professor Frits Kalshoven
Professor Ruth Lapidoth
Professor Gabrielle Kirk McDonald
H.E. Judge Theodor Meron
Captain J. Ashley Roach
Professor Michael Schmitt
Professor Jiří Toman

The International Humanitarian Law Series is a series of monographs and edited volumes which aims to promote scholarly analysis and discussion of both the theory and practice of the international legal regulation of armed conflict.
The series explores substantive issues of International Humanitarian Law including,

- protection for victims of armed conflict and regulation of the means and methods of warfare
- questions of application of the various legal regimes for the conduct of armed conflict
- issues relating to the implementation of International Humanitarian Law obligations
- national and international approaches to the enforcement of the law and
- the interactions between International Humanitarian Law and other related areas of international law such as Human Rights, Refugee Law, Arms Control and Disarmament Law, and International Criminal Law.

The titles published in this series are listed at brill.nl/ihul

International Criminal Justice *in bello*?

The ICC between Law and Politics in Darfur and Northern Uganda

by

Dr. Philipp Kastner LL.M.

MARTINUS NIJHOFF PUBLISHERS

LEIDEN • BOSTON
2012

This book is printed on acid-free paper.

Library of Congress Cataloging-in-Publication Data

Kastner, Philipp.
International criminal justice in bello? / The ICC between law and politics in Darfur and Northern Uganda / by Dr. Philipp Kastner.
p. cm. -- (International humanitarian law series ; v. 34)
Includes bibliographical references and index.
ISBN 978-90-04-19312-3 (hardback : alk. paper)
1. International Criminal Court. 2. International criminal courts--Political aspects. 3. Sudan--History--Darfur Conflict, 2003- 4.
Uganda--History--1979- I. Title.
KZ7312.K37 2012
341.6--dc23

2011038309

ISSN 1389-6776
ISBN 978 9004 19312 3

Copyright 2012 by Koninklijke Brill NV, Leiden, The Netherlands.
Koninklijke Brill NV incorporates the imprints BRILL, Global Oriental, Hotei Publishing, IDC Publishers, Martinus Nijhoff Publishers and VSP.

All rights reserved. No part of this publication may be reproduced, translated, stored in a retrieval system, or transmitted in any form or by any means, electronic, mechanical, photocopying, recording or otherwise, without prior written permission from the publisher.

Authorization to photocopy items for internal or personal use is granted by Koninklijke Brill NV provided that the appropriate fees are paid directly to The Copyright Clearance Center, 222 Rosewood Drive, Suite 910, Danvers MA 01923, USA.
Fees are subject to change.

Table of Contents

Preface

This book is based on my doctoral thesis that I submitted in July 2009 to the Faculty of Law of the University of Innsbruck, Austria.

My special thanks go to Elisabeth Roy Trudel for our invaluable discussions throughout the drafting process of this thesis and her constructive comments on the final version. I would also like to thank the University of Innsbruck for the financial support that I received in form of a doctoral scholarship.

I would like to note that some of my preliminary work on the role of the International Criminal Court in the Darfur conflict was submitted as an LL.M. thesis to the Faculty of Law of McGill University, Montreal, and published in the ILSA Journal of International and Comparative Law in 2007 (14:1).

Montreal (Quebec), Canada
Philipp Kastner

List of Acronyms

AMIS	African Union Mission in Sudan
ARLPI	Acholi Religious Leaders Peace Initiative
AU	African Union
DPA	Darfur Peace Agreement
DRC	Democratic Republic of the Congo
ICC	International Criminal Court
ICTR	International Criminal Tribunal for Rwanda
ICTY	International Criminal Tribunal for the former Yugoslavia
IDP	Internally displaced person
ILC	International Law Commission
JEM	Justice and Equality Movement
LRA	Lord's Resistance Army
NATO	North Atlantic Treaty Organization
NCP	National Congress Party
NGO	Non-governmental organization
NRF	National Redemption Front
ONUMOZ	United Nations Operation in Mozambique
OTP	Office of the Prosecutor
PDF	Popular Defense Force
RUF	Revolutionary United Front
SCSL	Special Court for Sierra Leone
SLA/M	Sudan Liberation Army/Movement
SPLA/M	Sudan People's Liberation Army/Movement
TRC	Truth and Reconciliation Commission
UN	United Nations
UNAMID	African Union – United Nations Hybrid Operation in Darfur
UNMIL	United Nations Mission in Liberia
UNMIS	United Nations Mission in Sudan
UPDF	Uganda People's Defence Force

Introduction

The recent developments since the 1990s in the field of international justice have shown that the installation of international criminal tribunals is inherently related to international politics. Both *ad hoc* tribunals for the Former Yugoslavia and Rwanda, which were created by the United Nations Security Council to deal with war crimes, crimes against humanity and genocide in the Balkans and in Rwanda, have significantly advanced international criminal justice but must, at the same time, be considered a substitute to a more effective involvement of the international community.

The rise of international criminal justice that was launched with the installation of the *ad hoc* tribunals manifested itself in another major step in 1998 when the Rome Statute[1] was adopted. It established the International Criminal Court (ICC), which became functional in 2002 following the 60th ratification of its statute. Although this institution was set up as a permanent and independent court with fundamental principles guaranteeing the independence of judges and the Prosecutor, it has, similar to the *ad hoc* tribunals, also been politically exploited.[2] This book examines why and how such exploitation has become possible by focusing on the legal framework regulating the decisions of the Court and other critical players, above all ICC States Parties and the Security Council. When necessary for a better understanding of the legal issues, these decisions will also be put into their political context.

---

1 *Rome Statute of the International Criminal Court*, 17 July 1998, UN Doc. A/CONF.183/9.

2 It should be noted at the outset that this premise relates to the position of the Court in the framework of international relations and is not meant to impinge on the fairness of the proceedings themselves, including those of a politically highly sensitive trial of a (former) head of state.

It will be argued that the ICC has been used in politically opportune situations, on the one hand by States Parties, on the other hand by the Security Council, in order to reach other goals – of political nature – than the one of advancing international criminal justice. The Security Council and governments of ICC States Parties have been exercising political pressure through the channel of international criminal justice, considering the exercise of such pressure the crucial function of the ICC. It seems that fighting impunity itself has only been a secondary concern. Although the ICC must be committed to taking every possibility to putting an end to impunity world-wide, as it has been trying to do since 2002, it should, at the same time, avoid becoming a political tool manipulated by States Parties and the Security Council. This argument does not question the ICC as an institution or the usefulness of international criminal justice *per se* but rather aims to critically analyze the current regime of the Rome Statute and certain decisions formally made on the basis of the Statute.

The first chapter will outline the conceptual framework that distinguishes the ICC from the *ad hoc* tribunals and the increasing impact that international criminal justice therefore has on ongoing armed conflicts. As we have witnessed since the beginning of the 1990s, international criminal justice institutions can have significant effects on the peace process and the reconciliation of transitional societies in post-conflict periods. In addition to that, the ICC represents a new opportunity given its strong potential to influence ongoing armed conflicts. Two conflicts, namely the one in northern Uganda and the one in Darfur, will serve as examples to illustrate this impact.

It is important to understand the roots of these conflicts as well as the complex relationship between the different warring parties in order to examine the impact of the ICC on the key players of these conflicts, as will be shown in the second chapter. Although the nature of the conflicts in northern Uganda and in Darfur and the way ICC jurisdiction has been triggered are fundamentally different, many key issues regarding the ICC involvement are similar in the two situations.

The third chapter will analyze the referrals to the ICC Prosecutor of the two situations. The political motivations behind the referrals will be compared to the objectives set forth in the Rome Statute, with a particular emphasis to the validity of so-called self-referrals. An examination of the selection of cases by the Prosecutor as well as their admissibility according to article 17 of the Rome Statute will shed light on the amplification of the political character of the Court. In this context, it will be analyzed to what extent the prosecutorial strategy itself has been guided and shaped by a faithful interpretation of the prescriptive provisions of the Rome Statute or rather by political reasoning.

The effects of the involvement of the ICC, and in particular of the prosecutorial strategy regarding the selection of cases, on the two conflicts will be studied in the fourth chapter. It will be argued that this considerable impact, which is largely consistent with the expected outcome of the referring authority, does not always correspond to the objectives stipulated in the Rome Statute. Politically valuable effects of the ICC involvement, such as increasing the political pressure on key players, and problematic aspects, such as endangering the conclusion of a peace agreement or the deployment of a peacekeeping mission, will be addressed.

Prosecutorial discretion and possible limits to it will be analyzed in the fifth chapter. Both general rules of international criminal law and specific provisions of the Rome Statute, in particular the reference to the interests of the victims, will be taken into account. The result of the analysis will be applied to the discretion of the ICC Prosecutor in the two situations of northern Uganda and Darfur. It will be studied to what extent the prosecutorial discretion as to whether to indict political and military leaders makes the Prosecutor an active player that exercises significant pressure on key players of the conflict. While the ICC should not be dominated by political issues, the important direct and indirect political effects of its involvement cannot be ignored. Potential risks should therefore be taken into account by an international prosecutor. Finally, solutions within the legal framework governing the Court to render it – as much as possible – independent from the political will of States Parties and the Security Council will be discussed.

Chapter 1

The conceptual framework – international criminal justice and armed conflicts

1.1. *Ad hoc* tribunals providing *ex post facto* justice

International criminal justice has evolved rapidly since the beginning of the 1990s. Nearly fifty years after the International Military Tribunals set up in Nuremberg and Tokyo, which prosecuted crimes committed during World War II, the international community revived the creation of judicial bodies to deal with genocide, crimes against humanity and war crimes, the core crimes under international law. The International Criminal Tribunal for the former Yugoslavia (ICTY) was created by a Chapter VII Security Council resolution in 1993 to face genocide, crimes against humanity and war crimes committed during the war in Bosnia and Herzegovina.[3] The Security Council followed the same approach a year later to deal with the genocide in Rwanda by installing the International Criminal Tribunal for Rwanda (ICTR).[4]

The two *ad hoc* tribunals were intended to target specific situations, with their scope being limited both in time and space. The tribunals have produced an important amount of case law, thus advancing international criminal law significantly. They were, however, ineffective or else came too late to influence the conflicts whilst the atrocities were being committed: The ICTR was established several months after the genocidal outbreak in Rwanda; the ICTY was established during the conflict in Bosnia and Herzegovina but did not have the desired impact of diminishing mass atrocities in the conflict itself. In fact, both tribunals can be considered a substitute to a more effective involvement of the international community, such as more stringent diplomatic pressure or a military intervention. The

3 S/RES/827 (1993).

4 S/RES/955 (1994).

tribunals presented themselves as a financially and politically inexpensive way of responding to demands of the international community to act.[5]

Recent developments in the field of international criminal justice include the establishment of so-called hybrid or internationalized tribunals, which are made up of national and international judges. The Special Court for Sierra Leone (SCSL) was created in 2002[6] to deal with the crimes committed during the brutal civil war in Sierra Leone; the trial of its most notorious suspect, former Liberian president Charles Taylor, started in June 2007. In Kosovo, East Timor and Cambodia, international judges have also been supporting local courts in delivering international criminal justice. The creation of a permanent institution in the form of the ICC illustrates this rather recent but rapidly increasing awareness of the necessity to fight impunity for international crimes.

1.2. Limited effectiveness of *ad hoc* tribunals

It is difficult to assess the success of the *ad hoc* tribunals, as no generalized standards exist to measure success or effectiveness in this field.[7] Yet one of the objectives of the tribunals must be to restore international peace and security, since both the ICTY and the ICTR were established by the Security Council using its Chapter VII powers. The ICTY has been criticized for not fulfilling these expectations, particularly due to its inability to arrest and try senior officials while the conflict was still going on.[8] Only

5 Steven D. Roper & Lilian A. Barria, *Designing Criminal Tribunals, Sovereignty and International Concerns in the Protection of Human Rights* (Aldershot: Ashgate, 2006) at 22; on the preference of states for tribunals to the detriment of a peacekeeping or military intervention because of costs, see Thomas W. Smith, "Moral Hazard and Humanitarian Law: The International Criminal Court and the Limits of Legalism" (2002) 39 International Politics 175 at 184.

6 On the basis of Security Council Resolution 1315 (2000), the Secretary General negotiated an agreement between the United Nations and the government of Sierra Leone to establish the Special Court for Sierra Leone.

7 Roper & Barria, *supra* note 5 at 83.

8 Hideaki Shinoda, "Peace-Building by the Rule of Law: An Examination of Intervention in the Form of International Tribunals" (2002) 7 International Journal of Peace Studies 41.

eight arrests were made by the end of 1996. Moreover, most of those who were indicted until 2000 were lower-rank officials.[9]

More general critics of prosecutions argue that criminal trials are – to be very short – selective and politicized and that they prevent social and ethnic reconciliation.[10] The *ad hoc* tribunals have also been criticized for not meeting their goals:

> "Criminal tribunals in places such as Rwanda and the former Yugoslavia were supposed to bring justice to oppressed peoples. Instead, they have squandered billions of dollars, failed to advance human rights, and ignored the wishes of the victims they claim to respect. It's time to abandon the false hope of international justice."[11]

The well-known "peace versus justice" debate has been a central issue for international criminal justice and its critics since the beginning of the 1990s. The basic argument made by advocates of international criminal justice is that justice is a necessary element to achieve peace and that justice can only be fully accomplished if those who are allegedly most responsible for the crimes committed are brought before a competent tribunal. The legitimacy of international or internationalized tribunals is based on the belief that the international community must react if domestic judicial systems are unable or unwilling to indict perpetrators of core crimes under international law. Moreover, it should be recalled that these crimes are "of concern to the international community as a whole", as stipulated in the preamble of the Rome Statute, which endorses the possibility of an involvement of the international community.

Opponents of prosecutions argue that indictments complicate peace negotiations and prolong conflicts and ongoing violence, as amnesties are sometimes considered a necessary prerequisite to make political and

---

9 Roper & Barria, *supra* note 5 at 86.

10 See e.g. Dominic McGoldrick, "Legal and Political Significance of a Permanent ICC" in Dominic McGoldrick, Peter Rowe & Eric Donnelly, eds., *The Permanent International Criminal Court, Legal and Policy Issues* (Portland: Hart, 2004) 453 at 457; for an in-depth analysis of trials and truth commission as well as the issues of vengeance and reparations, see generally Martha Minow, *Between Vengeance and Forgiveness, Facing History after Genocide and Mass Violence* (Boston: Beacon Press, 1998).

11 Helena Cobban, "Think Again: International Courts" *Foreign Policy* (March/April 2006) [Cobban, "Think Again"].

military leaders come to the negotiating table and accept a peace agreement. Moreover, conventional criminal prosecutions – no matter whether national, international or internationalized ones – are criticized for not acknowledging the particular realities of the respective conflict and for impeding the potential success of other, allegedly more effective mechanisms of holding individuals accountable and bringing about reconciliation in a post-conflict society. This question is highly contentious, both in theory and practice, as will be illustrated by the debate on the possible use of traditional justice mechanisms in Northern Uganda.

The issue of reconciliation has also shaped the discussion over the effectiveness of international criminal tribunals, as reconciliation of war-torn societies is a necessary precondition for lasting peace. Regarding Bosnia, for instance, the need to reconcile Bosnian Serbs, Croats and Muslims, who had lived together for centuries, was widely recognized when the ICTY was established.[12] With respect to Rwanda, the objective of national reconciliation was even specifically mentioned in Security Council Resolution 955 and became therefore an integral part of the ICTR's mandate. As mentioned above, the success of the contribution of the two tribunals to the reconciliation of Hutus and Tutsis in Rwanda as well as the different groups in Bosnia is difficult to evaluate. Some analysts have argued that the ICTR has exercised a moderating influence and that revenge killings in the region would have been far greater without the establishment of the ICTR.[13] Promoters of international criminal justice also argue that the trials have helped to bring about truth, a necessary precondition to achieve reconciliation. Others, however, deny that the ICTR has had any significant impact on reducing the horrors[14] or claim that the end of violent conflict in the Balkans is chiefly a product of international troops, and not of the ICTY.[15]

The effectiveness of international criminal tribunals has been compared to other mechanisms, such as truth and reconciliation commissions

---

12 See Payam Akhavan, "The Yugoslav Tribunal at a Crossroads: The Dayton Peace Agreement and Beyond" (1996) 18:2 Hum. Rts. Q. 259 at 264 [Akhavan, "The Yugoslav Tribunal"].

13 Payam Akhavan, "Beyond Impunity: Can International Criminal Justice Prevent Future Atrocities?" (2001) 95 A.J.I.L. 7 at 23 [Akhavan, "Beyond Impunity"].

14 Adam Roberts, "Implementing the Laws of Wars in Late 20th-Century Conflicts, Part II" (1998) 29:3 Security Dialogue 265 at 274.

15 Cobban, "Think Again", *supra* note 11.

(TRCs), which were installed in many countries emerging from violent conflict over the last decades with varied success. TRCs have been combined with amnesties in different forms. However, while conditional amnesties, especially for low-level perpetrators, are still tolerated to a certain extent, the international legal community increasingly disapproves of blanket amnesties for grave crimes. The most prominent example that has frequently served as a model for other TRCs is certainly the South African post-Apartheid TRC. One of the most remarkable recent ones is the TRC in Sierra Leone due to its complementary character to the SCSL. Regarding the impact of TRCs on post-conflict societies, Helena Cobban, a scholar and veteran journalist, has come to the conclusion that the TRC in South Africa, which granted conditional amnesties, and the absence of any individual accountability in Mozambique have delivered much better results than, for instance, prosecutions before the international criminal tribunal in Rwanda.[16] Moreover, it seems difficult to establish a general rule by linking situations that are hardly comparable. The effects of individual accountability mechanisms cannot be the same for a post-genocidal society like Rwanda, where the genocidal outburst lasted a few months, and in South Africa where a decades-long policy of apartheid was followed by a negotiated regime change. Furthermore, an isolated assessment of accountability mechanisms in post-conflict societies cannot be comprehensive since numerous factors may affect the relative success or failure of a justice mechanism. In addition to the particularities of every situation of armed conflict, the broader context, such as the presence of democratic institutions, the socio-economic situation, the involvement of third states and of the international community more generally, must not be overlooked. In general, trials, TRCs and amnesty programs are more likely to have a better outcome when they are supported by political reforms, a strong institutional system and a relatively good or rapidly recovering economic situation. The paradigm that "trials work best when they are needed least"[17] can be extended to other mechanisms; weak democratic structures will always lower the potential for positive effects of any mechanism.

---

16 Helena Cobban, *Amnesty after Atrocity? Healing Nations after Genocide and War Crimes* (Boulder, Colo.: Paradigm Publishers, 2007) at 194 [Cobban, *Amnesty after Atrocity?*].

17 Jack Snyder & Leslie Vinjamuri, "Trials and Errors, Principle and Pragmatism in Strategies of International Justice" (2004) 28:3 International Security 5 at 20.

Another important rationale of international criminal justice is deterrence. In the history of states, holding criminals individually accountable has been an efficient and valuable instrument of national jurisdictions to deter future crimes. Ideally, the same logic would also apply to international criminal tribunals. Since international criminal law is still in its nascent stage, its importance and the credibility of its institutions are still emerging. With the establishment of the ICTY, the Security Council wanted to send the message to other perpetrators of genocide, crimes against humanity and war crimes that the international community would no longer tolerate impunity for such crimes.[18] Yet in the context of large-scale crimes, specific deterrence is even more difficult to ascertain than in the context of ordinary crimes.[19] The Srebrenica massacre of an estimated 8,000 Bosniak boys and men at a moment when the ICTY was already fully operational is a gloomy illustration of the tribunal's insignificant impact on the ongoing atrocities in Bosnia. Moreover, although the immediate effect of international criminal justice institutions on human rights violators in other countries is difficult to measure, it seems evident that neither the ICTY nor the ICTR have influenced the behavior of political and military leaders in Sierra Leone, Chechnya, East Timor, Darfur and numerous other situations of armed conflict.[20] While there is therefore scant evidence for direct deterrent effects of international indictments and prosecutions on future criminals, it cannot be denied that the potential long-term effects of international trials to discourage future offenders are substantial. The absence of any such trials and their potential threat for perpetrators of core crimes would necessarily lead to a dangerous climate of impunity. In the specific context of the "peace versus justice" debate regarding the

18 See similarly Akhavan, "The Yugoslav Tribunal", *supra* note 12 at 264.

19 See e.g. Payam Akhavan, "Justice in The Hague, Peace in the Former Yugoslavia? A Commentary on the United Nations War Crimes Tribunal" (1998) 20:4 Hum. Rts. Q. 737 at 750 [Akhavan, "Justice in The Hague"]; Akhavan emphasizes the contribution of the ICTY to general deterrence, by transforming the political culture of the international community, over its contribution to specific deterrence; see *ibid.* at 748; on the problems of both specific and general deterrence in the context of international criminal justice, see David Wippman, "Atrocities, Deterrence, and the Limits of International Justice" (1999) 23 Fordham Int'l L.J. 473 at 476, 486; for a very critical view that prosecutions deter future atrocities, see Cobban, "Think Again", *supra* note 11.

20 See also Snyder & Vinjamuri, *supra* note 17 at 20, who focus on the tribunals' effect on altering the calculations of combatants in conflicts world-wide.

SCSL, John Prendergast of the International Crisis Group argued that "[t]he precedent of removing an indictment against Taylor would be disastrous for years to come in encouraging impunity and making a mockery of attempts at establishing accountability for crimes against humanity throughout the world."[21] According to Payam Akhavan, former legal advisor to the Prosecutor of the ICTY and ICTR,

> "the ICTY will help internalize the expectation that individuals, irrespective of their official position, may be held liable for violations of international humanitarian law. [...] Over time, this will contribute significantly to deterrence through the transformation of the political culture of the former Yugoslavia and the international community as a whole."[22]

At the same time, it has been pointed out that the international community should only insist on holding individuals accountable "if the benefits of accountability over the long term are likely to outweigh the costs on the short term of prolonging an ongoing conflict."[23] This decision will, in practice, turn out to be very complicated, since the long-term benefits of deterrence are very difficult to predict and will often be too abstract for victims suffering in a conflict that could have ended more quickly without insisting on prosecutions. As we will see, the pertinence of this discussion is evident in the context of the involvement of the ICC in northern Uganda and Darfur.

Regarding the urgent need to respond to mass atrocities in Bosnia, it must be concluded that the ICTY was established as a rather illusionary substitute to a military intervention since "it seemed that the tribunal was more an instrument for appeasing a troubled conscience that yearned for absolution from responsibility."[24] Even though it furthered international

---

21 John Prendergast, cited in Somini Sengupta, "Besieged Liberian" *New York Times* (11 July 2003).

22 Akhavan, "Justice in The Hague", *supra* note 19 at 748.

23 Nick Grono & Caroline Flintoft, "Negotiating Justice to Understand Accountability", Expert Paper for Workshop 6 – Negotiating Justice", Nuremberg Conference: Building a Future on Peace and Justice (25 June 2007), online: International Crisis Group <http://www.crisisgroup.org/home/index.cfm?id=4912>.

24 Akhavan, "Justice in the Hague", *supra* note 19 at 744; see also Smith, *supra* note 5 at 185.

criminal law significantly by creating an important amount of case law, it had, unfortunately, only minimal effects on the conflict itself. While its positive impact on reconciling Balkan's war-torn societies is also controversial, the ICTY has, at least, stigmatized several war criminals and thus helped to remove them from the political scene.[25] As for the conflict in Rwanda, the ICTR can be considered as another rather poor attempt of the international community to set things right months after the genocidal outburst. One must conclude that the ICTR, due to its institutional limits, could only provide *ex post facto* justice, while hoping that it might have a deterrent effect on future *genocidaires*.

Trying to reduce a major deficiency of the *ad hoc* tribunals, the architects of the hybrid tribunals have sought to bring international justice closer to the people and increase its immediate effects on the respective societies. Even though these efforts have a considerable potential to positively influence domestic legal systems in need of international support, thus increasing both the level of deterrence and the possibility of reconciliation, it is unrealistic to expect that this type of criminal justice institution will ever have the potential to influence an ongoing armed conflict itself. In addition to the fact that both purely international and hybrid tribunals are very costly and are therefore unlikely to be installed on a regular basis, their establishment will always remain time-consuming and dependent on the political will of various players, including the respective governments and the (permanent) members of the Security Council. Therefore, expecting that such tribunals will have an immediate impact on future ongoing conflicts does not seem realistic. The ICC, as a permanent institution, has this potential.

1.3. The imminent capacity of a permanent court to influence ongoing armed conflicts

The ICC is special for a number of reasons. First, unlike the previous international criminal tribunals, it is not a body installed by a Security Council resolution and therefore a sub-organ of the Security Council but a treaty-based institution. The ICC is the outcome of an international treaty, which was negotiated and concluded between sovereign states. Therefore, its democratic legitimacy cannot seriously be challenged.[26] As a suprana-

25 See Akhavan, "Beyond Impunity", *supra* note 13 at 9.

26 Kingsley Chiedu Moghalu, *The Politics of War Crimes Trials* (Westport, C.T.: Praeger Security International, 2006) at 135, arguing that unanimity has never been the basis for democratic legitimacy.

tional authority, the ICC can also assume jurisdiction over nationals of non-States Parties in certain cases.[27] At the same time, the ICC does not have direct jurisdiction over the crimes committed. Since its jurisdiction is marked by the principle of complementarity, the Court serves as an "international jurisdictional safety net"[28], which unfolds only when national jurisdictions are unable or unwilling to deal with core crimes.[29]

Second, the mechanisms triggering jurisdiction of the ICC for specific situations are unprecedented. While the two *ad hoc* tribunals were based on Security Council resolutions and have a temporarily and geographically limited mandate, the ICC can exercise jurisdiction on three grounds, as stipulated in article 13 of the Rome Statute. First, a State Party may refer a situation to the Prosecutor (article 13(a) with further details set forth in article 14). This mechanism was originally conceived as an inter-state complaint, as will be analyzed further below. Second, the Security Council, acting under Chapter VII of the UN Charter, may refer a situation to the Prosecutor (article 13(b)). In such a case, the ICC will have its greatest similarity to the *ad hoc* tribunals. Third, the Prosecutor may initiate investigations on its own initiative (article 13(c) with further details set forth in article 15). These so-called *proprio motu* powers, a very controversial topic in the drafting process of the Rome Statute,[30] are among the most important innovations of the ICC and were intended to ensure the political independence of the Court in fighting impunity for core crimes. It is precisely when neither States Parties nor the Security Council are willing to act that the ICC will probably be most needed to address impunity.[31]

---

27 Madeleine H. Morris, "Democracy, Global Governance and the International Criminal Court" in Ramesh Thakur & Peter Malcontent, eds., *From Sovereign Impunity to International Accountability* (Tokyo: United Nations Press, 2004) 187 at 189.

28 M. Cherif Bassiouni, "The ICC – *Quo Vadis*?" (2006) 4 Journal of International Criminal Justice 421 at 422.

29 Article 17 of the Rome Statute.

30 See e.g. Morten Bergsmo, Catherine Cissé & Christopher Staker, "The Prosecutor of the Nuremberg and Tokyo Tribunals, the ICTY and the ICTR, and the ICC Compared" in Louise Arbour *et al.*, eds., *The Prosecutor of a Permanent International Criminal Court* (Freiburg im Breisgau: edition iuscrim, 1998) 121 at 141.

31 The question why the *proprio motu* powers of the Prosecutor have not yet been used will be discussed below, c. 3.2.

Third, the ICC has no proper enforcement mechanisms and must therefore rely on the cooperation of the States Parties to the Rome Statute. Contrary to the ICTY and the ICTR, the ICC is not a UN body or sub-organ of the Security Council; it only concluded a relationship agreement with the UN. As a result, its jurisdiction cannot be expected to be enforced by the Security Council on a regular basis. Regarding its global effectiveness, the ICC will have to undergo a difficult test whether it can create deterrence without the direct capacity of enforcement. It has persuasively been pointed out that "deterrence depends on the predictable ability to enforce the law coercively, which often falls short in countries where abuses take place."[32] Only in case of a Security Council referral to the ICC Prosecutor, along with a clear obligation for the territorial state and possibly all UN member states to cooperate with the ICC, the Court might resume a similar function as the ICTY and the ICTR as a Chapter VII enforcement organ, which can also rely on the coercive powers of the Security Council.

Fourth, the ICC is also special for its permanent character. Security Council resolutions or agreements with the governments involved, as in the case of the ICTY, the ICTR and the SCSL, are not necessary to activate the ICC. Specific situations will not have to be dealt with by the establishment of *ad hoc* tribunals, which have shown to have many political and legal difficulties,[33] are very costly, and, most importantly, in order to have a realistic impact on an ongoing conflict, take precious time to become functional. The ICC has, therefore, the potential to shift the delivery of post-conflict justice towards in-conflict justice. It has a novel capacity to react immediately[34] and influence armed conflicts by stigmatizing

32 Snyder & Vinjamuri, *supra* note 17 at 11.

33 For more information, see McGoldrick, *supra* note 10 at 454.

34 On the difficulties for the ICC to conduct investigations and prosecutions without delay, see Bassiouni, *supra* note 28 at 423. The possibility for the OTP to start investigations on its own initiative, according to article 15(1) of the Rome Statute, is an important asset for the ICC in order to act politically independent from the Security Council and states parties; on the relationship between the ICC and the Security Council, see below, c. 5.5. On the fact that the ICC has shown to be the slowest international criminal institution so far, see William Schabas, "Prosecutorial Discretion v. Judicial Activism at the International Criminal Court" (2008) 6 Journal of International Criminal Justice 731 at 736-748 [Schabas, "Prosecutorial Discretion"] at 758.

those who are most responsible for genocide, crimes against humanity and war crimes while the conflict is still going on. Since the ICC's objective is to target those most responsible for the crimes committed, in other words political and military leaders, an ICC involvement and possibly indictments against key leaders are likely to alter significantly the dynamics of an ongoing conflict.

Thanks to its permanent character, the ICC also adds to the capacity of deterrence of international criminal justice more generally. The ICC will be far more effective, in a global sense, than *ad hoc* tribunals can be in providing a deterrent effect. The ICTY and the ICTR have shown that the international community is concerned with genocide, crimes against humanity and war crimes and attempts to find ways to end impunity. Yet it is unlikely that costly *ad hoc* tribunals will be established through Security Council resolutions for every situation where such crimes are not being dealt with effectively by national criminal systems. Before 2002, international criminal law remained an abstract notion in many parts of the world. Now, an international criminal court exercises a permanent threat for perpetrators of core crimes.

While deterring perpetrators of future crimes has been an important objective of international criminal justice, specific deterrence will probably become at least as important due to the regime of the ICC. International criminal justice, thanks to the Court's permanent character and its capacity to react faster, can now have a deterrent effect on those fighting in the middle of a conflict situation over which the ICC has assumed jurisdiction. Political and military leaders can be expected to be more careful in making their decisions once the Prosecutor's role has switched from a rather theoretical danger to a concrete, imminent threat.

Furthermore, because the ICC exercises a direct influence on national systems to act due to the principle of complementarity, it is realistic to believe that the mere presence of the ICC will augment the number of national prosecutions in the future[35] and thus increase the long-term potential of global deterrence. As an example, the ICC threat has been

35 See also Parliamentarians for Global Action, "A Deterrent International Criminal Court - The Ultimate Objective", (6-7 December 2004), online: Parliamentarians for Global Action <http://www.pgaction.org/uploadedfiles/deterrent%20paper%20for%20NZ_panel%201_.pdf> at 2. The ICC will, however, have difficulty in building a true threat for perpetrators worldwide due to its lack of coercive enforcement mechanisms; see below, c. 5.6.

used in the case of Kenya to call for a national tribunal, which should try politicians and businessmen involved in the 2007-2008 post-election violence. In November 2008, the Kenyan Commission of Inquiry announced that it might hand over a list of ten suspects to the ICC Prosecutor if a national court was not established in the near future.[36]

Besides these particularities, the Court already faces similar criticism as the *ad hoc* tribunals and finds itself in the middle of a discussion over justice versus peace, individual accountability mechanisms versus amnesties or pardons, trials versus TRCs or traditional forms of justice. Since targeting political and military leaders of warring parties unavoidably influences peace negotiations, international indictments can certainly be a destabilizing factor. These are issues the ICC is even more susceptible to due to its potential ability to interfere into (nearly) any ongoing armed conflict. In this context, two of the most controversial and complex situations – both from a legal and political perspective – are the conflicts in northern Uganda and in Darfur, Sudan.

36 "EU in Kenya Poll Tribunal Threat" *BBC News* (18 November 2008), online: BBC News <http://news.bbc.co.uk/go/pr/fr/-/2/hi/africa/7736011.stm>. See also International Criminal Court, "Address to the Assembly of States Parties by Mr Luis Moreno-Ocampo" (14 November 2008), online: International Criminal Court <http://www2.icc-cpi.int/NR/rdonlyres/50F9D0FA-33A0-48B3-942E-4CFF88CA3A27/0/ICCASPASP7StatementProsecutor.pdf> at 2 [ICC, "Address to the ASP"]. Despite efforts of the Kenyan government, the establishment of such a tribunal was not approved by the Kenyan parliament. As a result, the Commission of Inquiry communicated the results of its investigation to the ICC Prosecutor.

Chapter 2

The factual framework – the conflicts in northern Uganda and Darfur

This chapter intends to shed light on the causes and complex nature of the armed conflicts in northern Uganda and Darfur. A comprehensive understanding of the actions and motivations of the key actors is necessary in order to assess the reasoning behind the referrals to the ICC Prosecutor, to identify those individuals who bear the greatest responsibility for crimes which have not been investigated or prosecuted at the national level, as well as to evaluate the role of the ICC and its – at least potential – contribution to bring about and ensure lasting peace in the two situations.

Clearly, the two conflicts are very different in nature. While the conflict in northern Uganda basically opposes an armed movement, that has lost its popular base and has become notorious for terrorizing civilians since the 1980s, and the Ugandan army, the Darfurian rebel movements have mostly fought for relatively clear defined political goals against the central government and have largely been trying to protect the civilian population against attacks from the Sudanese army and its proxy militias.

In addition to the factual differences that will be further explored below, ICC jurisdiction was triggered in a different way, with the stance of the respective territorial state *vis-à-vis* the ICC being fundamentally divergent. In the situation of northern Uganda, the Ugandan government referred the situation to the ICC Prosecutor. It was therefore widely expected that Kampala would fully cooperate with the ICC. In the situation of Darfur, a Security Council resolution triggered ICC jurisdiction, while the Sudanese government has, as expected, continuously refused any cooperation with the ICC.

Despite these differences, the ICC faces similar challenges in the two situations, in particular with respect to the danger of political exploitation of international criminal justice, the potential impact of the ICC's involvement on peace negotiations and on humanitarian action, and the scope of prosecutorial discretion in the light of article 53 of the Rome Statute. Moreover, it is interesting to note at this point that the two conflicts also have one important factual link, with the government of Sudan being a significant player that is directly or indirectly implicated in both situations.

2.1. The conflict in northern Uganda

2.1.1. Origins of "the world's most neglected humanitarian catastrophe"[37]

The origins of the conflict lie in the struggle between the National Resistance Army of the current Ugandan President, Yoweri Museveni, and the then-government of Uganda. The consequences of this struggle are to an important extent responsible for the decades-long tensions in the trans-border region of northern Uganda and southern Sudan. After Museveni had overthrown President Tito Okello in 1986, many of the former government fighters sought refuge in northern Uganda. Acholi[38] soldiers, who had made up large parts of the former national army, also found refuge in the neighboring region of southern Sudan. They could count on the Sudanese Acholi population, which was mostly hostile to the agenda and activities of the Sudanese People's Liberation Army (SPLA) and therefore welcomed the influx of Ugandan Acholi fighters as valuable support.[39]

Another factor, which significantly determined the character of the conflict, was the Islamic government of Sudan. Khartoum considered the

---

37 In the words of Jan Egeland, former Under Secretary-General for Humanitarian Affairs and Emergency Relief Coordinator; cited in International Crisis Group, "Northern Uganda: Seizing the Opportunity for Peace" (26 April 2007), online: International Crisis Group <http://www.crisisgroup.org/home/index.cfm?id=4791> at 1 [ICG, "Northern Uganda: Seizing the Opportunity for Peace"]. This part will focus on the events from 1986 onwards, which was a decisive time for the formation of the LRA. For the earlier history of northern Uganda, including the long-term effects of forced mass displacements in the region and the construction of the Acholi as a distinct population group in the 19th and early 20th century, see Tim Allen, *Trial Justice, The International Criminal Court and The Lord's Resistance Army* (London: International African Institute, 2006) at 25. Allen also provides a good account of the political development in Uganda after the independence; *ibid.* at 28.

38 The Acholi are one of the peoples living in northern Uganda.

39 Allen, *supra* note 37 at 30. For more information on the Sudanese war between the North and the South, see below, c. 5.1.2.

1986 regime change in Uganda as a threat and began to support Ugandan rebel groups, mainly in northern Uganda. One of these groups was the Holy Spirit Movement, headed by the self-declared prophetess Alice Auma Lakwena.[40] After the defeat of the movement by the Ugandan army, a man named Joseph Kony, claiming to be a relative of Alice Auma Lakwena and to possess similar spiritual powers, assembled the remainders of the movement and founded the Lord's Resistance Army (LRA), which developed into the most important rebel group in northern Uganda. The LRA was for a long time supported by the Sudanese government, evidently in exchange for Uganda's support for the SPLA. In the 1990s, the LRA was one of the proxy militia forces through which the Sudanese government was fighting the war in the south,[41] which led to the rather incongruent fact that an Islamist regime was supporting a fundamentally Christian group.

The political goals of the LRA, as proclaimed by Joseph Kony, were the overthrow of the Museveni government and the establishment of a society built on the Ten Commandments in Uganda. However, it quickly became evident that the LRA did not only lack a coherent political agenda, but also did not have any popular support in northern Uganda.[42] While the LRA also fought and still fights government forces, its primary target have been civilians, who have been terrorized by the LRA. Over the years, about 100,000 civilians have been killed and up to 1.5 million have been displaced; tens of thousands of children, sometimes as young as six years old, have been abducted, abused and turned into sex slaves and forcibly recruited as child soldiers, with abducted children representing up to 85% of the armed forced of the LRA; the LRA also became notorious for cutting hands, lips and ears and for pillaging and burning villages.[43]

---

40 Payam Akhavan, "The Lord's Resistance Army Case: Uganda's Submission of the First State Referral to the International Criminal Court" (2005) 99 A.J.I.L. 403 at 406 [Akhavan, "The LRA Case"]. For more information on the history of the LRA, see Allen, *supra* note 37 at 25.

41 Allen, *supra* note 37 at 49.

42 Akhavan, "The LRA case", *supra* note 40 at 407.

43 For more information on the atrocities committed by the LRA, see UN Commission on Human Rights, "Report of the United Nations High Commissioner for Human Rights on the mission undertaken by her Office, pursuant to Commission resolution 2000/60, to assess the situation on the ground with regard to the abduction of children from northern Uganda", UN Doc. E/CN.4/2002/86 (9 November 2001) at paras. 15-19 [Commission on Human Rights, "Report of the UNHCHR"]; Human Rights Watch,

Despite this undoubtedly long list of manifest breaches of international humanitarian law and international human rights law committed by the LRA, it should be noted that some political demands voiced by the LRA in recent years do correspond to those of the local Acholi population. Political and economic equality between the (poorer) northern and the (richer) southern part of the country and the end of government violence and repression figure among the most important demands of the Acholi, who have to some extent recognized the importance of the negotiations between the Ugandan government and the LRA and the opportunity to assert their political agenda more strongly through the channels of the LRA.[44]

While the LRA has manifestly committed numerous grave violations of international humanitarian and human rights law, the government of Uganda is not an innocent actor in this conflict either. The Acholi have also suffered under the counterinsurgency campaign by the government: as early as in 1991, civilians were massacred for alleged rebel support.[45] Moreover, to shield the civilian population from LRA attacks, the government created so-called "protected villages", a very controversial step which, in reality, displaced even more civilians without increasing their security. Around 80 per cent of the population of the northern districts Gulu, Kitgum and Pader were forced to move to these camps, where the security level for the civilians continued to be low.[46] Human rights organ-

---

"Stolen Children" (March 2003), online: Human Rights Watch <http://www.hrw.org/reports/2003/uganda0303/uganda0403.pdf>; Akhavan, "The LRA case", *supra* note 40 at 408; UN Security Council, "Security Council Presidential Statement Demands Release of Women, Children by Lord's Resistance Army, Expeditious Conclusion of Peace Process", UN Doc. SC/8869 (16 November 2006), online: United Nations <http://www.un.org/News/Press/docs/2006/sc8869.doc.htm>; International Criminal Court, "Background Information on the Situation in Uganda" (29 January 2004), online: International Criminal Court <http://www.icc-cpi.int/library/press/pressreleases/Uganda_200401_EN.doc>.

44 Adam Branch, "Uganda's Civil War and the Politics of ICC Intervention" (2007) 21:2 Ethics & International Affairs 179, online: Wiley InterScience <http://www3.interscience.wiley.com/journal/117999022/abstract> at 191 [Branch, "Uganda's Civil War"]. Also, in the 2006 presidential elections those regions which have suffered most in the conflict voted against President Museveni.

45 *Ibid.* at 181.

46 Allen, *supra* note 37 at 53.

izations, such as the International Crisis Group, have denounced these "over-crowded, unsanitary, and dangerous internally displaced persons' camps where millions of northern Ugandans have been forced to live."[47] It has been convincingly argued that this forced displacement for "security reasons" constitutes a violation of international humanitarian law and international human rights law, for which members of the Ugandan army and government should be held individually accountable, possibly before the ICC. "The continuing internment of over a million people without military necessity and without adequate protection and aid constitutes a grave violation of the laws of war and certainly falls within the ICC's temporal jurisdiction."[48]

2.1.2. Decades between violence and peace negotiations

In the 1990s, the conflict went on with varying intensity, including periods of relative absence of violence. Over a long time, the LRA benefited from Khartoum's support and found a safe harbor in southern Sudan, from where it launched its incursions into northern Uganda. Several military advances by the government were replied by increased LRA violence, while attempts of peace negotiations did not produce any significant results. "Operation North", a military advance initiated by the government in 1991, led to a particularly violent reaction of the LRA. Civilians who were suspected of collaborating with the government were maimed or killed. Typical punishments carried out by the LRA were the amputation of limbs and the cutting of lips, noses and ears.[49]

In 1994, promising peace talks were held for the first time since the beginning of the conflict. The Minister of State for Pacification of Northern Uganda and chief negotiator with the LRA for many years, Betty Bigombe, negotiated and attained a ceasefire. However, after a rather inconsiderate ultimatum to the rebels proclaimed by Museveni, the vio-

47 International Crisis Group, "Conflict History: Uganda", online: International Crisis Group <http://www.crisisgroup.org/home/index.cfm?action=conflict_search&l=1&t=1&c_country=111> [ICG, "Conflict History: Uganda"].

48 Branch, "Uganda's Civil War", *supra* note 44 at 181. On the responsibility of humanitarian agencies, see Adam Branch, "Against Humanitarian Impunity: Rethinking Responsibility for Displacement and Disaster in Northern Uganda" (2008) 2:2 Journal of Intervention and Statebuilding 151.

49 See Allen, *supra* note 37 at 47.

lence recommenced.[50] Museveni had argued, as he has since done on many occasions, that lengthy peace negotiations would only allow the LRA to gather its forces and build up its military strength.[51]

After emphasizing the military option for several years, the government of Uganda restarted in 1999 to seriously consider peace efforts and passed an amnesty act, which came into force in early 2000 despite some opposition of President Museveni, who stated publicly that the Act should not apply to LRA commanders.[52] The Amnesty Act offered amnesty to all Ugandans who had been engaged in acts of rebellion against the government since 1986.[53] In the words of one of the most important Ugandan non-governmental organizations working in this field, the Refugee Law Project, the Act "seeks to balance the more immediate needs of resolving conflict with the long-term demands of justice."[54] Although the Act enjoyed broad support in Uganda, it bears a very controversial issue by providing a quasi-unconditional amnesty without any mechanism to establish the truth about past crimes or leave the door open to hold certain individuals accountable. Article 3(2) of the Act reads: "A person [...] shall not be prosecuted or subjected to any form of punishment for the participation in the war or rebellion for any crime committed in the cause of the war or armed rebellion."[55] The law has also been criticized by human rights organizations as a barrier to victims who could claim reparations against the LRA before national courts.[56]

---

50 *Ibid.* at 48.

51 *Ibid.*; see also for an analysis of additional reasons why Museveni withdraw his support for Bigombe's negotiating strategy.

52 See *ibid.* at 74.

53 In addition to the LRA, numerous other armed groups have fought against Museveni's government since 1986. The Ugandan non-governmental organization Refugee Law Project lists 22; see Refugee Law Project, "Whose Justice? Perceptions of Uganda's Amnesty Act 2000: The Potential for Conflict Resolution and Long-Term Reconciliation" (February 2005), online: Refugee Law Project <http://www. refugeelawproject.org/resources/papers/workingpapers/RLP.WP15.pdf> at note 11.

54 *Ibid.* at 4.

55 *The Amnesty Act, 2000*, available online: Website of International Humanitarian Law <http://www.wihl.nl/finals/Uganda/UG.%20T-TR.Agreement%20on%20Amnesty%20Commission.pdf>. See also below, c. 4.1.2.2.

56 Amnesty International, "Left to Their Own Devices, The Continued Suffering of Victims of the Conflict in Northern Ugandan and the Need for

In 2003 and 2004, the amnesty offer was accepted by a relatively large number of LRA fighters but not by the senior commanders of the LRA.[57] By the end of January 2005, nearly 15,000 former rebel fighters had reported to the Amnesty Commission, the institution established to implement the Act.[58] Interestingly, traditional and religious leaders have had an important impact on encouraging amnesty and forgiveness,[59] in addition to their considerable role in the peace negotiations. In particular the Catholic Church, well-respected in the country, played a major role in convincing the government to adopt the Amnesty Act and in promoting the idea of forgiveness among NGOs and the local council system.[60] This position explains, at least to a certain extent, the rather harsh opposition of the traditional and religious leaders to the ICC, as will be further discussed below.

In 2002, shortly after the adoption of and directly opposed to the purpose of the Amnesty Act, the government launched operation "Iron Fist" with the goal of definitely defeating the LRA on the battlefield. The operation gave rise to even more violent attacks by the LRA and displaced even more persons in the region.[61] During the operation, the Ugandan army pursued the LRA also into Sudanese territory, fighting side by side with the SPLA.[62] It is worth noting that these operations on Sudanese territory had been agreed to by the Sudanese government, despite its continued and manifest political interest in supporting the LRA. This concession to Kampala can be explained by the fact that, in 2002, Khartoum had already been exposed to heavy international pressure following the assassination attempt of Hosni

---

Reparations" (17 November 2008), online: Amnesty International <http://www.amnesty.org/fr/library/info/AFR59/009/2008/en> at 8 [AI, "Left to Their Own Devices"].

57 Allen, *supra* note 37 at 75.

58 Refugee Law Project, *supra* note 53 at 7.

59 The two terms should not be understood to be mutually exclusive or necessarily distinct, in particular in the Ugandan context. In the Lwo language, for instance, the terms "amnesty", "forgiveness", "reconciliation", etc. are not conceptually different; see Allen, *supra* note 37 at 131.

60 Allen, *supra* note 37 at 137. For an excellent account of the importance of the Christian ethic of forgiveness and redemption in the context of the South African TRC, see Richard A. Wilson, "Reconciliation and Revenge in Post-Apartheid South Africa: Rethinking Legal Pluralism and Human Rights" (2000) 41:1 Current Anthropology 75 at 80.

61 ICG, "Conflict History: Uganda", *supra* note 47.

62 Allen, *supra* note 37 at 50.

Mubarak and the bombings of the embassies of the United States in Kenya and Tanzania in 1998, presumably carried out by Osama bin Laden, who had found a safe harbor in Sudan.[63] While Khartoum facilitated operation "Iron Fist", the politics made in Washington also played a considerable role. The United States had added the LRA on its list of terrorist organizations after September 11, 2001 and provided logistical support to the Ugandan government to carry out "Iron Fist."[64] Despite these favorable circumstances in which the operation took place, it could not eradicate the LRA and must ultimately be considered a failure, since the leaders escaped. Although hundreds of members of the LRA were killed, most of them were abductees and distant from the LRA leadership.[65]

In the course of the second Iron Fist campaign in 2004, the LRA was, however, more and more weakened by the government forces, and several LRA commanders deserted and accepted the amnesty offer.[66] Nevertheless, at the time of writing, the LRA is still far from being defeated. Violence and abductions, although at a much smaller scale than in previous years, continued even after the heavy military losses that the LRA underwent in 2004. As a consequence, the LRA continued its tactic of withdrawing and re-gathering its forces in inaccessible regions. Since southern Sudan was not a safe haven any more, the LRA moved its camps into the neighboring Democratic Republic of the Congo (DRC), in a remote area near Garamba National Park, in late 2005 and early 2006.[67]

Peace talks between the LRA and the Ugandan government resumed in Juba, South Sudan, in July 2006. The potential of this process was enhanced by the government of South Sudan, a key player in the region, which took the lead in mediating the peace process.[68] In August 2006, a

---

63 *Ibid.* at 51.

64 *Ibid.*

65 *Ibid.*

66 ICG, "Conflict History: Uganda", *supra* note 47.

67 See e.g. UN Security Council, "Report of the Secretary-General pursuant to resolutions 1653 (2006) and 1663 (2006)", UN Doc. S/2006/478 (26 June 2006) online: United Nations <http://daccessdds.un.org/doc/UNDOC/GEN/N06/415/40/PDF/N0641540.pdf?OpenElement> at para. 2 [UN SC, "Report of the Secretary-General pursuant to resolutions 1653 and 1663"].

68 For more information on the peace talks, see International Crisis Group, "Peace in Northern Uganda?" (13 September 2006), online: International Crisis Group <http://www.crisisgroup.org/home/index.cfm?id=4374&l=1> at 2-5. See also Resolve Uganda, "Seizing the Second Chance: Peace on

Cessation of Hostilities Agreement was signed, with very positive consequences: no attacks or abductions occurred in the following months,[69] and nearly 300,000 IDPs returned to their villages.[70]

In spite of these encouraging developments, the talks turned out to be more and more difficult and came to a standstill at a certain point, with the question of justice clearly remaining the biggest obstacle to the continuation of the process.[71] Although the Ugandan government promised that it would try to have the ICC indictments "withdrawn" – an impossible request under the Rome Statute – once an agreement was reached, the LRA leaders made a withdrawal of the arrest warrants a precondition for engaging in a peace agreement. As a result, an annex to the original June 2007 Agreement on Accountability and Reconciliation was signed on 19 February 2008,[72] providing for domestic judicial proceedings instead of trials before the ICC. According to article 7 of the annex, "[a] special division of the High Court of Uganda shall be established to try individuals who are alleged to have committed serious crimes during the conflict."[73] Moreover, an additional agreement, signed shortly after, stipulates that after the signing of the final peace agreement the government would request the Security Council to defer the investigations and prosecutions of the ICC in northern Uganda.[74]

---

the Horizon for Uganda?" (26 April 2007), online: Resolve Uganda <http://www.resolveuganda.org/seizing-the-second-chance> [Resolve Uganda, "Seizing the Second Chance"].

69 Resolve Uganda, "Seizing the Second Chance", *supra* note 68.

70 Resolve Uganda, "The Peace Process Must Live On: Juba's Lessons and Its Legacy" (June 2008), online: Resolve Uganda <https://salsa.democracyinaction.org/o/2241/images/Resolve%20Uganda%20Policy%20Brief%20June%202008.pdf> [Resolve Uganda, "The Peace Process Must Live On"].

71 For more information, see Resolve Uganda, "Seizing the Second Chance", *supra* note 68.

72 For more information on the agreement and its annex, see Amnesty International, "Uganda: Agreement and Annex on Accountability and Reconciliation Falls Short of a Comprehensive Plan to End Impunity" (March 2008), online: reliefweb <http://www2.reliefweb.int/rw/RWFiles2008.nsf/FilesByRWDocUnidFilename/LRON-7CTEZN-full_report.pdf/$File/full_report.pdf> [AI, "Agreement and Annex on Accountability"].

73 *Annexure to the Agreement on Accountability and Reconciliation* (19 February 2008), available at <http://www.iccnow.org/documents/Annexure_to_agreement_on_Accountability_signed_today.pdf>.

74 Security Council Report, "Uganda/LRA, Update Report No.1" (11 April

2.1.3. Continued instability and violence

Since its move to Garamba National Park in northeastern DRC, the LRA has largely been absent on Ugandan territory. However, the situation cannot be considered stable, as killings of civilians and abductions continue in neighboring countries.[75] During the year of 2008, the LRA abducted almost 500 children in southern Sudan, DRC and the Central African Republic, as estimated by the ICC Prosecutor.[76]

According to a report of the UN Secretary-General,

> "[d]espite its reduced numbers, [the LRA] presents a real threat to the rule of law and adds to the existing security problems in the Great Lakes region, which are compounded, inter alia, by the breakdown of local authority and law enforcement mechanisms." [...] Furthermore, LRA remains a violent criminal group with a severe disruptive capacity against the civilian population within its reach, humanitarian convoys in the area and personnel of the United Nations Mission in the Democratic Republic of the Congo (MONUC), UNMIS and other United Nations programmes, funds and agencies operating in the Great Lakes region.[77]

The LRA has also clashed with the SPLA in southern Sudan,[78] where growing prospects of a new instability make it possible that the LRA restore its old ties with the government of Sudan.[79] Moreover, the peace

---

2008), online: Security Council Report <http://www.securitycouncilreport.org/site/c.glKWLeMTIsG/b.4018489/>.

75 UN Security Council, "Additional report of the Secretary-General on children and armed conflict in Uganda", UN Doc. S/2008/409 (23 June 2008).

76 ICC, "Address to the ASP", *supra* note 36 at 6. Moreover, as reported by human rights organizations, numerous other human rights violations, including unlawful killings, have been committed in the three countries; see AI, "Left to Their Own Devices", *supra* note 56 at 33, note 1.

77 UN SC, "Report of the Secretary-General pursuant to resolutions 1653 and 1663", *supra* note 67 at paras. 5 and 7.

78 Joe Wacha, "Kony Meeting Request Raises Hopes" *Institute for War & Peace Reporting* (21 August 2008), online: Institute for War & Peace Reporting <http://www.iwpr.net/?p=acr&s=f&o=346316&apc_state=henh> [Wacha, "Kony Meeting Request"].

79 Resolve Uganda, "The Peace Process Must Live On", *supra* note 70.

negotiations have still not been finalized, although repeated reports in the first half of 2008 suggested that Kony had requested to meet with peace negotiators and planned to come to Juba to sign the final peace accord.[80] Some analysts believed that officials in Kampala, Kinshasa and Juba started to make plans for another military offensive against the LRA instead.[81] Nevertheless, over the summer 2008, chances for a signing of the peace deal seemed to increase. According to the special envoy of the United Nations for the LRA-affected areas, Joaquim Chissano, the agreement could be signed soon; the outstanding arrest warrants issued by the ICC would not hamper the peace process.[82]

However, "Operation Lightning Thunder", a joint operation launched by Uganda, the DRC and South Sudan in December 2008 to defeat the LRA and arrest its leaders provoked the LRA to retaliate against the civilian population by killing over 500.[83] In 2009, LRA violence continued unabated; in a four-day campaign in December 2009, for instance, the LRA killed over 300 civilians and abducted at least 250 in northeastern DRC.[84] At the time of writing, the final peace agreement has not been signed, and Kony is still hiding in the bush of Garamba National Park.

2.2. The conflict in Darfur

2.2.1. Origins of the conflict

The current armed conflict between the government of Sudan and rebel groups in Darfur started in 2003. The Sudan Liberation Army/Movement (SLA/M)[85] and the Justice and Equality Movement (JEM) turned against

80 Wacha, "Kony Meeting Request", *supra* note 78.

81 Resolve Uganda, "The Peace Process Must Live On", *supra* note 70.

82 Wacha, "Kony Meeting Request", *supra* note 78.

83 Human Rights Watch, "DR Congo: LRA Slaughters 620 in 'Christmas Massacre'" (17 January 2009), online: Human Rights Watch <http://www.hrw.org/en/news/2009/01/17/dr-congo-lra-slaughters-620-christmas-massacres>.

84 Human Rights Watch, "DR Congo: Lord's Resistance Army Rampage Kills 321" (28 March 2010), online: Human Rights Watch <http://www.hrw.org/en/news/2010/03/28/dr-congo-lord-s-resistance-army-rampage-kills-321>.

85 The SLA is the military arm of the political faction SLM. On the relationship between the SLA/M and the JEM, see Res Publica, "The Darfur Resistance, *Who They Are, What They Want, and What They Need to Create*

the Sudanese government, which had continued the British colonial administration's policy of neglecting the region.[86] This deliberate underdevelopment of Darfur, an independent sultanate for centuries before being annexed to the Anglo-Egyptian Condominium in 1916, had already led to tensions before and was particularly criticized during the devastating, but foreseeable famine of 1984, which cost the life of around 100,000 people.[87] Darfur of the late 1990s has been described as an "increasingly marginalized, violent and frustrated place".[88]

In addition to this policy of marginalization, the ever-present cleavage between farmers and herdsmen, which had largely become equivalent to a distinction of Africans versus Arabs in the mid-twentieth century, was increasingly exploited. It has been pointed out that although these cattle and camel nomads claim Arab origins and speak Arabic, they are ethnically the product of intertribal marriage with their African neighbors since their arrival in the 16th and 17th century.[89] In short, the distinction does not appear to be grounded on biological or ethnic reasons but largely on a different lifestyle.[90]

The draughts of the 1970s and 1980s multiplied the incidents between sedentary agriculturalists and cattle-raising nomads, which did not, however, necessarily correspond to the Arab-African dichotomy.[91] The Arab-Islamist government of Sudan added a new dimension to the difference between nomadic and sedentary lifestyles in Darfur by emphasizing the ideological and racist definition of "Arab" and *zuruq* (black) more and more.[92] In the late 1980s, nearly all Arab groups, influenced by this new pro-

---

a New Sudan", online: Res Publica <http://www.darfurgenocide.org/ResPublicaDarfurTripReport.pdf> at 18.

86 For more information on the British administration of the province, see Julie Flint & Alex de Waal, *Darfur, A Short History of a Long War* (London: Zed Books, 2005) at 12.

87 Gérard Prunier, *Darfur, The Ambiguous Genocide* (Ithaca, N.Y.: Cornell University Press, 2005) at 56 [Prunier, *The Ambiguous Genocide*].

88 *Ibid.* at 81.

89 Robert O. Collins, "Disaster in Darfur: Historical Overview" in Samuel Totten & Eric Markusen, *Genocide in Darfur, Investigating the Atrocities in the Sudan* (New York: Routledge, 2006) 3 at 3.

90 Prunier, *The Ambiguous Genocide*, *supra* note 87 at 5.

91 Jérôme Tubiana, "Le Darfour, un conflit pour la terre?" (2006) 101 Politique africaine 111 at 113 [Tubiana, "Le Darfour, un conflit pour la terre?"].

92 Collins, *supra* note 89 at 9. On the genealogical constructs of Sudanese

Arab ideology propagated by the governments of Libya and Sudan, united themselves to fight the Fur.[93] At that time, the infamous term *Janjaweed* also came up for the first time, referring to Arab militiamen on horseback. It should be noted that they are not a popular representation of the Arab tribes in Darfur,[94] as has sometimes been suggested, but can be considered as armed bandits and sometimes proxy militias that were tolerated or even supported by the government because of their Arab correlation.[95]

Another aggravating factor was the introduction of automatic weapons in the 1980s into the region, which gradually buried traditional forms of settling disputes over land ownership and access to water wells, another major source of the conflict.[96] The persistent availability of these weapons significantly added to the danger of an escalation of frequent but originally not highly dangerous disputes. In fact, some commentators explain the ethnic cleansing chiefly with a fight over land: "il s'agit de vider des espaces de leurs habitants, et c'est bel et bien une guerre pour le contrôle de la terre qui semble se dérouler."[97] Even of true to a certain extent, such claims have been viciously exploited by the government of Sudan who has been presenting the whole conflict as a low-level, inter-ethnic dispute over land. According to Alex de Waal, a social anthropologist and one of the most renowned experts of the situation in Darfur, the dichotomy between Africans and

---

"Arabs" and the "African" identity, the latter being adopted by the SLM/A similar to that of the SPLA, which reproduced a polarized discourse, see Ruth Iyob & Gilbert M. Khadiagala, *Sudan, The Elusive Quest for Peace* (Boulder, Colo.: Lynne Rienner Publishers, 2006) at 31.

93 Tubiana, "Le Darfour, un conflit pour la terre?", *supra* note 91 at 113. Darfur literally means "land of the Fur".

94 Prunier compares the *Janjaweed* to the Rwandan Interahamwe, who were not a natural expression of the Hutu in Rwanda either; Prunier, *The Ambiguous Genocide*, *supra* note 87 at 97.

95 *Ibid.* at 97.

96 Collins, *supra* note 89 at 6. The easy availability of weapons was largely due to the war in southern Sudan and the use of Darfur as a basis for Chadian rebels, who, supported by Libya, launched their attacks from Darfur; see "Report of the International Commission of Inquiry on Darfur Pursuant to Security Council Resolution 1564 of 18 September 2004", UN Doc. S/2005/60 (Geneva, 25 January 2005) at para. 58 [UNCOI].

97 ["It is about emptying the spaces from their inhabitants, and it is really a war over controlling the land that seems to take place."] Tubiana, "Le Darfour, un conflit pour la terre?", *supra* note 91 at 112.

Arabs is "historically bogus, but disturbingly powerful".[98] Yet SLA members have expressed their will to reconcile with the *Janjaweed* under the condition that their leaders are brought to justice.[99] As Khamis Abakir, one of the SLA commanders, expressed it, "[o]ur problem is not with the Arabs. It is with the government."[100] In short, the facts that members of the two groups have intermarried in the past and that they are all Muslim and mostly speak Arabic[101] are strong indicators for a largely political construction of the Arab-African distinction that has been increasingly exploited.

2.2.2. *Escalation in 2003*

On February 26, 2003, the constant, low-level violence in Darfur[102] suddenly erupted. About three hundred members of the SLA seized the town of Golu, killed two hundred government soldiers and proclaimed their political demands, the most important of which were that Khartoum address the uneven development and socio-economic marginalization of Darfur as well as the separation of religion and politics.[103] The Sudanese government decided to fight the insurrection, assuming that it would be able to solve the conflict before it could affect the fragile peace process with the South.[104] However, victories of the SLA in Western Darfur rapidly showed that the Sudanese army was incompetent and insufficiently prepared. As a matter of fact, the Sudanese government could in this situation not fully rely on

98 Alex De Waal, "Who are the Darfurians? Arab and African Identities, Violence and External Engagement" (2005) 104:415 African Affairs 181 at 197.

99 *Ibid.*

100 Cited in Flint & de Waal, *supra* note 86 at 70.

101 René Lemarchand, "Unsimplifying Darfur" (2006) 1:1 Genocide Studies and Prevention 1 at 5.

102 Prunier speaks of an "undeclared sporadic war"; see Gérard Prunier, "Darfur's Sudan Problem", openDemocracy (15 September 2006), online: opendemocracy <http://www.opendemocracy.net/democracy-africa_democracy/darfur_conflict_3909.jsp>.

103 Collins, *supra* note 89 at 9. The SLA's manifesto largely resembles the SPLA's vision of a united, but decentralized Sudan; according to Flint & de Waal, senior SPLA members coauthored the political declaration of the SLA; see Flint & de Waal, *supra* note 86 at 82.

104 Prunier, *The Ambiguous Genocide*, *supra* note 87 at 97. For the North-South peace process, see below, c. 5.1.2.

its army, which was largely made up of Darfurians and would therefore have to fight its "own" people.

As a result, Khartoum responded by rearming the already existing *Janjaweed* militias[105] and by recruiting mercenaries from Libya, Chad, and other countries.[106] Although not a new practice, since the government had increasingly armed Arab tribes and their militias and disarmed non-Arab tribes with the purpose of intensifying the ethnic divide throughout the 1990s,[107] this major sponsorship was decisive in setting off wide-spread atrocities in Darfur. In addition, *Janjaweed* fighters were partly incorporated into the Sudanese army through an associated group called the Popular Defense Force (PDF).[108] They received weapons, official army uniforms, and were paid and trained by government officials. They have been described as an "ad hoc unit of Sudan's army".[109]

Usman Tar, an expert in African peace studies, explains why the *Janjaweed* were ready to take up arms against the insurgents and the civilians in Darfur:

> "Janjaweed militias have seemingly cashed in on their strategic positions as agents of the Sudanese government, perhaps with the tacit approval of the latter, to vent their racial/ethnic anger and hatred on rival African communities with whom they have clashed for decades over economic resources and ethnic/racial differences."[110]

---

105 For more information on the origins of the *Janjaweed*, see Prunier, *The Ambiguous Genocide*, *supra* note 87 at 97.

106 UNCOI, *supra* note 96 at para. 68.

107 Armin Mekki Medani, *Crimes Against International Humanitarian Law in Sudan, 1989-2000* (Cairo: Dar El Mostaqbal El Arabi, 2001) at 204. For more details on the attacks of Arab militias on hundreds of Masalit villages in 1997 and 1998, see *ibid.* at 206.

108 Flint & de Waal, *supra* note 86 at 102. The PDF emerged in the 1980s, its members being associated with the Muslim Brotherhood; see also Pablo Castillo, "Rethinking Deterrence: The International Criminal Court in Sudan" (2007) 13 UNISCI Discussion Papers 167 at 172.

109 Usman Tar, "Counter-Insurgents or Ethnic Vanguards? Civil Militia and State Violence in the Darfur Region, Western Sudan" in David J. Francis, ed., *Civil Militia, Africa's Intractable Security Menace?* (Hants: Ashgate, 2005) 134 at 145.

110 *Ibid.*

Khartoum's decision to recruit Arab militias was not a novelty in its fight in peripheral regions in Sudan. As early as in 1985, Baggara militias, known as *Murahaliin*, were recruited to fight against the SPLA in the South and to terrorize civilians suspected of supporting the SPLA.[111] The government also armed Arab tribes to sponsor a brutal ethnic-cleansing campaign in the Nuba Mountains in the 1990s.[112]

Since the increased level of violence in Darfur, government troops and *Janjaweed* militias have been fighting the local insurgencies, above all the SLA, which had grown to a force of approximately 11,000 men in 2005 compared to a few hundred in 2001.[113] The JEM, albeit much smaller, could rely on the military and political experience of its leaders, some of them having been part of the central government.[114] Although several ceasefire agreements were negotiated and concluded, the fighting has never stopped.

Despite the assertion of important political demands, the main issue of the conflict became the targeting of the civilian population of Darfur by the Sudanese army and the *Janjaweed*. A presence of rebels in Darfurian villages has visibly been irrelevant for the attackers; a general fear that civilians from the Fur, Zaghawa and Masalit tribes might join the rebels or give them foodstuff and shelter has resulted in the destruction of hundreds of villages. Numerous atrocities that manifestly amount to crimes against humanity and war crimes, have been reported: persecution, murder, rape, intentional attacks on civilians and civilian property, pillaging, and other crimes within the jurisdiction of the ICC[115] have led to the death of at

111 Flint & de Waal, *supra* note 86 at 24; see also Belachew Gebrewold, "Civil Militia and Militarisation of Society in the Horn of Africa" in David J. Francis, ed., *Civil Militia, Africa's Intractable Security Menace?* (Hants: Ashgate, 2005) 189 at 201.

112 Lucian Niemeyer, *Africa, the Holocausts of Rwanda and Sudan* (Albuquerque: University of New Mexico Press, 2006) at 435.

113 Flint & de Waal, *supra* note 86 at 85.

114 For more information on the two main pillars of the JEM, one being its link to the Islamist movement, the other its tribal component due to its close relation to the Kobe branch of the Zaghawa, see *ibid.* at 89.

115 See International Criminal Court, "Fourth Report of the Prosecutor of the International Criminal Court, Mr. Luis Moreno Ocampo, to the UN Security Council Pursuant to UNSCR 1593 (2005)" (14 December 2006), online: International Criminal Court <http://www.icc-cpi.int/library/organs/otp/OTP_ ReportUNSC4-Darfur_English.pdf> at 4 [ICC, "Fourth Report of the Prosecutor"]. The debate whether genocide has been committed became a key question for Western governments and in the Western media to measure

least 200,000 people and to the displacement of two and a half million.[116]

---

the degree of violence and possibly justify a humanitarian intervention. This debate, however, does not serve the interests of the hundreds of thousands of victims for whom it makes little difference whether they are being targeting with genocidal intent or "only" persecuted; it is worth noting that the outcome of crimes against humanity can be worse than genocide. The rather specific question of the offenders' intent should be solved by a judicial institution. It has been argued that the "use of the "G-word" in the Darfur crisis has neither helped galvanize broad international support for action to stop the killings nor forced the Sudanese government to halt its campaign of ethnic cleansing;" see Martin Mennecke, "What's in a Name? Reflections on Using, Not Using, and Overusing the "G-Word"" (2007) 2:1 Genocide Studies and Prevention 57 at 60; Gareth Evans, the President of the International Crisis Group, has argued that using the term genocide in the Darfur case can be "unproductive, non-productive, and even counterproductive," see Don Cheadle & John Prendergast, *Not on Our Watch, The Mission to End Genocide in Darfur and Beyond* (New York: Hyperion, 2007) at 2; on the genocide debate, see also William A. Schabas, "Darfur and the 'Odious Scourge': The Commission of Inquiry's Findings on Genocide" (2005) 18 Leiden J. Int'l L. 871 [Schabas, "Darfur and the 'Odious Scourge'"]; Scott Strauss, "Darfur and the Genocide Debate" (2005) 84 Foreign Affairs 123; Jerry Fowler, "A New Chapter of Irony: The Legal Definition of Genocide and the Implications of Powell's Determination" in Samuel Totten & Eric Markusen, *Genocide in Darfur, Investigating the Atrocities in the Sudan* (New York: Routledge, 2006) 127. On the social impact of applying the term genocide, see William F.S. Miles, "Labeling "Genocide" in Sudan: A Constructionist Analysis of Darfur" (2006) 1:3 Genocide Studies and Prevention 251.

116 UN Office for the Coordination of Humanitarian Affairs, "Darfur Humanitarian Profile No. 30" (1 January 2008) online: OCHA <http://www.unsudanig.org/docs/DHP%2030%20-%201%20January%202008%20-%20narrative.pdf > [OCHA, "Darfur Humanitarian Profile No. 30"]; Human Rights Watch, "Q & A: Crisis in Darfur", online: Human Rights Watch <http://hrw.org/english/docs/2004/05/05/darfur8536.htm>; "Q&A: Sudan's Darfur Conflict" *BBC News* (15 November 2007) online: BBC <http://news.bbc.co.uk/2/hi/africa/3496731.stm>. The estimated numbers vary a lot. Other sources estimate that up to 400,000 have died; see Save Darfur Coalition, "Background" (25 October 2006) online: SaveDarfur <http://www.savedarfur.org>. According to the ICC Prosecutor, government and militia forces have killed at least 35,000 in attacks on villages; see ICC, "Eighth Report of the Prosecutor of the International Criminal Court, Mr. Luis Moreno Ocampo, to the UN Security Council Pursuant to UNSCR 1593 (2005)" (3 December 2008), online: International Criminal Court <http://www.icc-

Because of these brutal attacks on civilians, which have often been carried out in villages without any rebel presence and without any legitimate military necessity,[117] the rebels have enjoyed growing support among the population and have had no difficulty in finding new recruits who want to resist the Sudanese army and government.[118]

Although Khartoum hesitates to admit any link with the *Janjaweed* and usually labels them "armed bandits,"[119] many sources show that the government has been arming, training and funding the militias, as well as coordinating the attacks on civilians.[120] Victims describe a typical pattern in which most of the attacks on their villages were carried out by the Sudanese army, which first launched aerial attacks, followed by the militias, who attacked the villages on horseback and camels.[121] According to various reports, the violence, including indiscriminate and disproportionate air strikes by the Sudanese army, has continued throughout the years of 2007 and 2008.[122]

---

cpi.int/library/organs/otp/8thUNSCreportsenttoUN-ENG.pdf> at para. 43 [International Criminal Court, "Eighth Report of the Prosecutor"].

117 ICC, "Eighth Report of the Prosecutor", *supra* note 116 at paras. 33-34.

118 Res Publica, *supra* note 85 at 12.

119 UNCOI, *supra* note 96 at para. 117.

120 *Ibid.* at para. 111; Human Rights Watch, "Entrenching Impunity, Government Responsibility for International Crimes in Darfur" (December 2005), online: Human Rights Watch <http://hrw.org/reports/2005/darfur1205/> at 9; Collins, *supra* note 89 at 11.

121 See International Criminal Court, "Situation in Darfur, the Sudan, Prosecutor's Application under Article 58(7)" (27 February 2007), online: International Criminal Court <http://www.icc-cpi.int/library/cases/ICC-02-05-56_English.pdf> at 30 [ICC, "Prosecutor's Application under Article 58(7)"].

122 International Committee of the Red Cross, Press Release, "On his Return from Darfur, ICRC President Deplores Worsening Conditions for the Region's Population" (21 February 2007), online: International Committee of the Red Cross <http://www.icrc.org/web/eng/siteengo.nsf/html/sudan-news-210207>; see also International Criminal Court, "Fifth Report of the Prosecutor of the International Criminal Court, Mr. Luis Moreno Ocampo, to the UN Security Council Pursuant to UNSCR 1593 (2005)" (7 June 2007), online: International Criminal Court <http://www.icc-cpi.int/library/organs/otp/OTP_ReportUNSC5-Darfur_ English.pdf> at 6 [ICC, "Fifth Report of the Prosecutor"]; Office of the United Nations High Commissioner for Human Rights, "Eleventh periodic report of the United Nations for

Because, unfortunately, Arab tribes are often blamed as a whole for the atrocities committed among Africans, it is important to note that the largest and most influential Arab tribes in the region, including the Baggara, the Rizeigat, and the Habbanyia, are not involved in the conflict. They seem to emphasize good neighborly relations over "racial" divides, which are, moreover, not absolute but rather an artificial construct.[123] In addition, it seems that members of the SLA do not consider the Arab tribes as their enemies.[124] Experts have even argued that, "[f]or the people involved, this is a political, not an ethnic or racial conflict."[125] At the same time, while most Arab tribes have remained neutral, a few originally non-Arab but arabized groups joined the side of the government and the *Janjaweed*, largely for strategic reasons.[126] Clashes over land between different Arab tribes, in particular in South Darfur since late 2006, also underline the limits of a model based on an African/Arab dichotomy as sole explanation for the conflict in Darfur.[127]

2.2.3. The delayed response of the international community[128]

Initially, the international community hesitated to take a clear position on and react to the unfolding armed conflict and humanitarian disaster in Darfur. The situation in Darfur deteriorated at the same time as the nego-

Human Rights on the situation of human rights in the Sudan, Killing and injuring of civilians on 25 August 2008 by government security forces: Kalma IDP camp, South Darfur, Sudan" (23 January 2009), online: OHCHR <http://www.ohchr.org/Documents/Countries/11thOHCHR22jan09.pdf>.

123 Flint & de Waal, *supra* note 86 at 124.

124 Res Publica, *supra* note 85 at 17.

125 Khalid Medani, "The Darfur Crisis and the Challenge of Democracy in Sudan" (Paper presented to the Conference *The Challenge of Development in Sub-Saharan Africa: Conflict Resolution, Democratic Governance and Education*, Centre for Developing-Area Studies, McGill University, 29 March 2007) [unpublished].

126 Tubiana, "Le Darfour, un conflit pour la terre?", *supra* note 91 at 112.

127 International Crisis Group, "Darfur: Revitalising the Peace Process" (30 April 2007), online: International Crisis Group <http://www.crisisgroup.org/home/index.cfm?id=4769> at 13 [ICG, "Darfur: Revitalising the Peace Process"].

128 The Security Council resolutions concerning the ICC will be discussed in more detail below.

tiations between the North and the South came to an important point, with all eyes of the international community fixed on the peace talks in Naivasha, Kenya. International negotiators were willing to leave the nascent crisis in Darfur aside or, at least, to postpone open criticism and more active involvement, in order to avoid endangering the promising peace process for the South: "Khartoum effectively held the carrot of peace in front of the noses of the international community while it wielded the stick in Darfur."[129]

Gérard Prunier, an historian and eminent Darfur specialist, argues that the whole year of 2003 and the first half of 2004 were lost time for Darfur, because the government of Sudan knew that "as long as it showed 'good faith' in Naivasha it could do what it wanted in Darfur."[130] Western governments and leaders – in particular U.S. President George W. Bush who tried to boost his election campaign by showing his own Christian electorate that he was acting on behalf of the persecuted Christians in southern Sudan – were praising themselves for solving the civil war, while Darfur had to wait for attention. In fact, the root causes of the North-South conflict and the Darfur conflict are similar and part of the same problem in Sudan. Both conflicts can be correctly understood if considered in the broader context of a center-periphery dichotomy in Sudan, illustrated by important inequalities between the region of the capital and the rest of the country.[131]

The situation had already horribly deteriorated in Darfur when Western politicians finally started to openly condemn the Darfur policy of the Sudanese government. Particularly the United States intensified its discourse: the Congress declared in July 2004 that the first genocide of the

129 John Prendergast, "Resolving the Three Headed War from Hell in Southern Sudan, Northern Uganda, and Darfur" (February 2005) 3 Woodrow Wilson International Center for Scholars, Africa Program Occasional Paper Series at 2.

130 Prunier, *The Ambiguous Genocide*, *supra* note 87 at 122. See also Flint & de Waal, *supra* note 86 at 128.

131 In the words of Prunier, "les inégalités Centre-Périphérie sont absolument massives"; Gérard Prunier, "La paix reste incertaine" (2006) 14 Enjeux Internationaux 28 at 29. Others emphasize the relationship between the elites and their population over a struggle of the periphery against the center; see Roland Marchal, "Le conflit de toutes les ambivalences" (2006) 14 Enjeux Internationaux 34 at 37.

21st century was happening in Darfur.[132] However, the Bush administration, the United Nations, and the European Union showed themselves more reserved. For instance, Jan Egeland, the personal representative of the UN Secretary General, denounced the atrocities as "ethnic cleansing".[133] Overall, the international community could not exercise any coherent pressure on the Sudanese government due to the lack of a unified position. Proposals for economic sanctions through a Security Council resolution were unrealistic from the beginning. China was expected to veto any measures that might endanger its heavy investments in the Sudanese oil industry. Furthermore, both Russia and China had concluded lucrative contracts to sell military equipment to the Sudanese government.[134] The United States has also played a very ambiguous role. While heavily criticizing Khartoum's policy in Darfur, the United States has benefited from increasing Sudanese support to fight international terrorism, which has been suggested as the main reason why the new anti-al-Qaeda ally has not been seriously challenged.[135]

---

132 President Bush waited three more months before declaring that genocide was happening in Darfur; see The White House, Press Release, "President's Statement on Violence in Darfur, Sudan" (9 September 2004), online: The White House <http://www.whitehouse.gov/news/releases/2004/09/20040909-10.html>.

133 UN News Centre, "Sudan: Envoy Warns of Ethnic Cleansing as Security Council Calls for Ceasefire" (2 April 2004), online: UN News Centre <http://www.un.org/apps/news/storyAr.asp?NewsID=10307&Cr=sudan&Cr1=>.

134 Russia and China are the most important suppliers of military equipment for Sudan. According to Amnesty International, precisely these weapons, including helicopters and airplanes, were used to attack civilians in Darfur; see Amnesty International, "Sudan: Arms Continuing to Fuel Serious Human Rights Violations in Darfur" (8 May 2007), online: Amnesty International <http://www.amnesty.org/fr/library/info/AFR54/019/2007/en>.

135 See Res Publica, *supra* note 85 at 28; on the intelligence collaboration of the CIA with Sudanese authorities to spy on the Iraqi insurgency and al-Qaeda, see Greg Miller & Josh Meyer, "U.S. Relies on Sudan Despite Condemning it" *Los Angeles Times* (11 June 2007), online: Los Angeles Times <www.latimes.com>. A 2008 report suggested that the United States considers normalizing its ties with Sudan and removing Sudan from its list of state supporters of terrorism; see "Sudan-US Talks to Resume Next Week after Brief Delay" *Sudan Tribune* (25 May 2008), online: Sudan Tribune <http://

The first international measure deserving mention was the adoption of Security Council resolution 1556 on July 30, 2004, stipulating an arms embargo for the warring parties in Darfur. The embargo excluded, however, the Sudanese army. The resolution stated that

> "all states shall take the necessary measures to prevent the sale or supply, *to all non-governmental entities and individuals*, including the Janjaweed, operating in the states of North Darfur, South Darfur and West Darfur, by their nationals or from their territories or using their flag vessels or aircraft, of arms and related materiel of all types."[136]

This embargo was a first step of the international community to face the conflict in Darfur, but it overlooked the fact that many *Janjaweed* fighters had been incorporated in the army or in proxy forces, such as the PDF. In addition to this deficit, a first assessment of the effects of Resolution 1556 showed that the arms embargo had been constantly violated.[137]

On March 29, 2005, Security Council Resolution 1591 condemned the

> "continued violations of the 8 April 2004 N'djamena Ceasefire Agreement and the 9 November 2004 Abuja Protocols, including air strikes by the Government of Sudan in December 2004 and January 2005 and rebel attacks on Darfur villages in January 2005, and the failure of the Government of Sudan to disarm Janjaweed militiamen and apprehend and bring to justice Janajaweed leaders and their associates who have carried out human rights and international humanitarian law violations and other atrocities…"[138]

Contrary to the United Nations and Western governments, the African Union (AU) has been actively involved in the Darfur since an early stage, most notably by deploying a 7,000 personnel strong mission in Sudan (African Union Mission in Sudan, AMIS). This involvement is praiseworthy but has unfortunately not proved to be very effective. AMIS was only

---

www.sudantribune.com/spip.php?article27273>.

136 S/RES/1556 (2004) [emphasis added].

137 UN Security Council, "Report of the Panel of Experts established pursuant to resolution 1591 (2005) concerning the Sudan prepared in accordance with paragraph 2 of resolution 1665 (2006)", UN Doc. S/2006/795 (3 October 2006).

138 S/RES/1591 (2005).

able to provide very limited protection to civilians and did not have any significant positive effect on the conflict itself.

In sum, although the Sudanese government would obviously have the primary responsibility under international human rights law to protect its citizens, the international community has failed to react and take measures to take the place of the Sudanese government, which is, in fact, the driving force behind the massive violations of international humanitarian and human rights law. In the words of a cynic but accurate commentator, "[t]he sad reality is that Darfur simply does not matter enough, and Sudan matters too much, for the international community to do more to stop the atrocities."[139]

2.2.4. Continued violence despite international efforts

Since the large-scale atrocities orchestrated in 2003 and 2004, the nature of the conflict seems to have shifted towards a chaotic situation. The Darfurian rebel groups have split up into numerous fractions,[140] which are fighting without common goals due to different political, tribal and individual interests.[141] However, attacks on civilians by the Sudanese army and militias have continued. In early 2008, according to a detailed report issued by the UN High Commissioner for Human Rights, several villages in West Darfur were attacked in violation of international humanitarian and human rights law with the objective of driving out the JEM from this region. The pattern of attack was similar to the extensive campaign in 2003 and 2004, with helicopters and Antonov airplanes flying over and bombarding the villages, followed by Arab militia on horses and camels killing people and looting and torching the villages. The attacks killed more than 100 civilians, displaced more than 30,000 people and resulted in extensive destruction of civilian property.[142]

---

139 Nick Grono, "The International Community's Failure to Protect" (2006) 105:421 African Affairs 625.

140 For more information on the splintered groups, see Gérard Prunier, "Darfur, La Chronique d'un « Génocide Ambigu »" *Le Monde Diplomatique* (Mars 2007) 16.

141 Reporters Without Borders, "Darfur: An Investigation into a Tragedy's Forgotten Actors" (April 2007), online: Reporters Without Borders <http://www.rsf.org/IMG/pdf/RSF_Sudan_ENG.pdf> at 6.

142 Office of the United Nations High Commissioner for Human Rights, "Ninth periodic report of the United Nations High Commissioner for Human

The Darfur Peace Agreement (DPA), concluded in Abuja in May 2006, could not end the conflict and, as the Secretary-General noted in July 2008, "continues to be largely ignored by the parties on the ground".[143] Weak on the subject of power sharing,[144] the DPA was only signed by a faction of the SLA led by Minni Minawi; the SLA branch led by Abdel Wahid Mohamed Nur as well as the JEM refused to sign the document. These two groups subsequently formed the National Redemption Front (NRF). To add to the confusion and the level of violence, the different rebel groups have also been fighting each other. As early as in October 2005, for instance, several members of the JEM were killed in an attack of a dissident JEM faction.[145]

On the one hand, since the conclusion of the DPA, Minni Minawi and his "SLA-MM" have been fighting against the NRF on the side of the Sudanese army, whose tactic of dividing the rebel groups seems to be successful.[146] Civilians who are suspected of cooperation with the NRF are now not only exposed to *Janjaweed* and army attacks, which are still ongoing in Darfur and which also occurred in Eastern Chad,[147] but also to attacks carried out by the SLA-MM. Rebel groups have exacerbated the crisis by diverting international aid for their own purposes,[148] often

---

Rights on the situation of human rights in the Sudan, Attacks on civilians in Saraf Jidad, Sirba, Silea and Abu Suruj in January and February 2008" (20 March 2008), online: OHCHR <http://www.ohchr.org/Documents/Press/WestDarfurreport2003.pdf>.

143 UN Security Council, "Report of the Secretary-General on the Deployment of the African Union-United Nations Hybrid Operation in Darfur", UN Doc. S/2008/443 (7 July 2008), online: United Nations <http://daccessdds.un.org/doc/UNDOC/GEN/N08/409/84/PDF/N0840984.pdf?OpenElement> at para. 55 [UN SC, "Report of the Secretary-General on the Deployment"].

144 Since the DPA was not supposed to affect the 2005 power sharing agreement between the North and the South, the DPA gave the Darfurian insurgents only twelve of 450 seats in the national assembly; see ICG, "Darfur: Revitalising the Peace Process", *supra* note 127 at 27.

145 Reporters Without Borders, *supra* note 141 at 6.

146 Suliman Baldo, "La paix, arme de guerre" (2006) 14 Enjeux Internationaux 21 at 22.

147 For a detailed account on attacks on civilians in Chad, see Amnesty International, "Chad, 'Are we citizens of this country?' Civilians in Chad unprotected from Janjaweed attacks" (29 January 2007), online: Amnesty International <http://www.amnesty.org/en/library/info/AFR20/001/2007>.

148 Andrew S. Natsios, "Moving Beyond the Sense of Alarm" in Samuel Totten

through violent attacks on humanitarian workers.[149] On the other hand, some *Janjaweed* fighters appear to have changed sides and now fight the regular army together with rebel groups. One possible reason for this change might by their fear that Khartoum scapegoat them for the atrocities committed among civilians and send them to The Hague.[150]

In July 2007, the international community took the so far most important step to deal with the crisis in Darfur. A joint peace operation by the United Nations and the African Union, baptized UNAMID, was authorized by Security Council resolution 1769 of July 31, 2007, envisaging the deployment of a total personnel of 31,000, including around 20,000 military, in early 2008.[151] Despite this significant commitment, the mission had a difficult start. Numerous hurdles have been encountered, which have slowed down the deployment.[152] In addition to insufficient resources and ill-equipment, the deteriorating security situation has significantly delayed the arrival of the peacekeepers. According to the former Under-Secretary-General for Peacekeeping Operations, Jean-Marie Guéhenno, the force could reach 80 percent of its authorized strength at best by the end of 2008.[153] Moreover, the Sudanese government has repeatedly shown its

---

& Eric Markusen, *Genocide in Darfur, Investigating the Atrocities in the Sudan* (New York: Routledge, 2006) 25 at 31.

149 According to the UN Office for the Coordination of Humanitarian Affairs, in 2007, humanitarian organizations had to relocate on 36 occasions due to insecurity; see OCHA, "Darfur Humanitarian Profile No. 30", *supra* note 116.

150 Alex Perry, "Defections in Darfur?" *Time* (21 March 2007), online: Time Inc. <http://www.time.com/time/world/article/0,8599,1601495,00.html>.

151 S/RES/1769 (2007). See also United Nations, "UNAMID Deployment, Background Fact Sheet", online: United Nations <http://www.un.org/depts/dpko/missions/unamid/UNAMID_Deployment.pdf> [UN, "UNAMID Deployment"].

152 As of April 30, 2008, not even half of the authorized personnel had been deployed; see United Nations, "Darfur – UNAMID – Facts and Figures", online: United Nations <http://www.un.org/depts/dpko/missions/unamid/facts.html>.

153 For more details, see UN Security Council, Press Release, "Darfur Mission Deployment Slowed by Deteriorating Security, Harsh Conditions", UN Doc. SC/9330 (14 May 2008). For the actual figures, see below, note 350.

aversion *vis-à-vis* the mission, *inter alia* by objecting to the deployment of non-African peacekeepers.[154]

Despite the efforts of the international community to calm down the situation in Darfur, the security situation even deteriorated in the first half of 2008. According to a June 2008 report of the Secretary-General on the deployment of the UN-AU operation in Darfur, covering events which took place in May 2008, "significant clashes continued between tribal groups, between rebel movements and between rebel movements and the Government and its affiliated forces."[155] Nearly 200,000 persons were newly displaced in the first half of 2008 in Darfur.[156] Moreover, the peacekeepers do not only seem to be unable to protect the civilians but are also vulnerable themselves: armed groups have repeatedly attacked peacekeepers and have stolen their weapons and equipment.[157] On July 9, 2008, one of the worst attacks on the peacekeepers occurred, with seven members being killed and 22 being injured in a *Janjaweed* ambush.[158]

Another round of peace talks convened by the United Nations and the African Union in Sirte, Libya, in October and November 2007, did not bring any substantial results. Several key rebel figures did not attend the meetings due to internal disputes and a lack of trust *vis-à-vis* the UN and the AU. The choice of the venue was indeed unfortunate, given Colonel Gaddafi's historical role in the conflict, which cannot be described as neu-

---

154 "Sudan 'Blocking' Darfur Mission" *BBC News* (28 November 2007), online: BBC <http://news.bbc.co.uk/2/hi/africa/7116284.stm>.

155 UN SC, "Report of the Secretary-General on the Deployment", *supra* note 143 at para. 7.

156 *Ibid.* at para. 15.

157 See e.g. "In Darfur gibt es keinen Frieden zu sichern" [There is no peace to be kept in Darfur] *Der Standard* (4 July 2008).

158 "UN Fury at Darfur Militia Ambush" *BBC* News (9 July 2008), online: BBC <http://news.bbc.co.uk/2/hi/africa/7498811.stm>. It is pretty obvious that government-sponsored militias are responsible for the attack, since the attack occurred in an area under government control and was intended to inflict casualties rather than to steal vehicles. Moreover, weapons were used which had never been seen in the hands of rebels; see Margaret Besheer, "Concern Grows at UN for Peacekeepers, Stuff in Sudan" *VOA News* (11 July 2008), online: VOA News <http://www.voanews.com/english/2008-07-11-voa65.cfm> and Eric Reeves, "Sudanese Government Responsible of Attack on Darfur Peacekeepers" *Sudan Tribune* (14 July 2008), online: Sudan Tribune <http://sudantribune.com/spip.php?article27838>.

tral.[159] An interesting tendency, however, is the manifest initiative of the SPLA to unify the Darfur rebel movements during and after the peace talks. The objective of the SPLA was not only to facilitate the peace talks but "to create a political and military alliance among all the marginalized groups that oppose the NCP [National Congress Party]."[160]

In May 2008, the JEM drew attention to its political agenda in a particularly visible way by attacking Omdurman, the twin city of Khartoum.[161] The attack surprised both the Sudanese government and the joint African Union – United Nations Hybrid Operation in Darfur (UNAMID) and underlined the fact that the conflict in Darfur is not solely a clash between tribes but a political conflict of concern to the whole country. The Security Council condemned the attack on the capital without denouncing the alleged involvement of Chad, as demanded by the Sudanese government.[162] Although the rebels were defeated rather quickly, and although government positions outside of Darfur, for instance in Kordofan, had been attacked by rebel groups in the past, it is noteworthy that no faction had ever reached the capital before. This sent indeed a powerful message to the Sudanese government.[163] JEM commander Abdel Aziz el-Nur had even

---

159 See Eric Reeves, "Darfur Peace Talks in Libya Produce Only an Emboldened Khartoum" *Sudan Tribune* (13 November 2007), online: Sudan Tribune <http://www.sudantribune.com/spip.php?article24721>.

160 Andrew S. Natsios, "Beyond Darfur, Sudan's Slide Toward Civil War" (2008) 87:3 Foreign Affairs [Natsios, "Beyond Darfur"]. NCP is the ruling National Congress Party.

161 For more information, see UN SC, "Report of the Secretary-General on the Deployment", *supra* note 143. For an account of human rights violations committed by Sudanese officials following the attack, in particular "hundreds of arbitrary arrests and some cases of extra-judicial executions", see Amnesty International, "Darfur Crisis Reaches Sudanese Capital" (23 May 2008), online: Amnesty International <http://www.amnesty.org/en/news-and-updates/darfur-crisis-reaches-sudanese-capital-20080523>.

162 UN News Centre, "Security Council Slates Weekend Attacks by Darfur Rebels near Sudanese Capital" (13 May 2008), online: UN News Centre <http://www.un.org/apps/news/story.asp?NewsID=26661&Cr=darfur&Cr1=>. Besides Chad, the government of Sudan also accused Libya and France for supporting the assault on the capital; see "Sudan Hints at Involvement of Libya & France in Rebel Attack on Capital" *Sudan Tribune* (14 May 2008), online: Sudan Tribune <http://www.sudantribune.com/spip.php?article27137>.

163 "Khartoum under Curfew as 3,000 Darfur Rebels Advance on Capital"

proclaimed the goal of ousting President Bashir.[164] According to the analysis of Amir Idris, a Professor of African Studies, the attack

> "has shattered myths about the unity of the National Congress Party and its military capabilities to confront the rise of regional protests militarily. […] The valuable lesson that can be learned from the recent attack on Omdurman and fighting in Abyei is that the tragedy of the Sudan is a national one that urgently calls for a comprehensive political settlement that addresses effectively the question of citizenship and democratic transformation in the country."[165]

These highly complex issues surrounding the conflicts in Darfur and northern Uganda, including the origins of the conflicts, the role and behavior of the key players and the current situation on the ground that have been presented in this chapter, are closely linked to the referrals of the two situations to the ICC Prosecutor. It is in the light of this context that the referrals and their validity as well as the subsequent selection of cases by the Prosecutor will be analyzed.

The Guardian (11 May 2008), online: The Guardian <http://www.guardian.co.uk/world/2008/may/11/sudan?gusrc=rss&feed=fromtheobserver>.

164 *Ibid.*

165 Amir Idris, "Making Sense of JEM Attack on Sudan's Capital" *Sudan Tribune* (27 May 2008), online: Sudan Tribune <http://www.sudantribune.com/spip.php?article27285>. The perceived unity of the NCP was also questioned by the arrest of one of its leading members, Hassan Bargo, for his alleged involvement in the attack; see "Sudanese Official Arrested in Connection with Rebel Assault on Capital" *Sudan Tribune* (19 May 2008), online: Sudan Tribune <http://sudantribune.com/spip.php?article27203>.

Chapter 3

The referrals of the two situations to the ICC Prosecutor

3.1. Political motivations behind the "self-referral" of the Ugandan government

Northern Uganda constituted the first situation to be referred to the ICC Prosecutor. The government of Uganda triggered the ICC's involvement based on article 14 of the Rome Statute in December 2003,[166] thus trying to raise awareness on the international scene about the long-lasting conflict between the LRA and government troops. For more than 15 years, the government had not been able to defeat the LRA, arrest its leaders or achieve a viable peace agreement. At that point, it tried to increase the international pressure on the LRA and its allies, above all the Sudanese government, by activating the ICC.

Payam Akhavan, former legal advisor to the Prosecutor of the ICTY and ICTR who also advised the government of Uganda in the matter, has argued that the referral was conceived "as a strategy for engaging the international community by committing ICC proponents to the arrest and prosecution of top LRA leaders."[167] Adam Branch, a political scientist and specialist of the armed conflict in Uganda, has also stated that, "indeed, international criminalization is an excellent strategy for states wishing to rally foreign forces to their side and to delegitimize political or military opposition."[168]

166 International Criminal Court, Press Release, "President of Uganda Refers Situation Concerning the Lord's Resistance Army (LRA) to the ICC" (29 January 2004), online: International Criminal Court <http://www.icc-cpi.int/pressrelease_details&id=16&l=en.htm> [ICC, "President of Uganda Refers Situation to the ICC"].

167 Akhavan, "The LRA Case", *supra* note 40 at 410.

168 Branch, "Uganda's Civil War", *supra* note 44 at 183.

These political considerations were the primary motivations of the Ugandan government in referring the situation to the ICC Prosecutor. The referral was one of the measures through which the government tried to weaken the LRA, but bringing the LRA leaders to justice in The Hague has not been the government's ultimate objective. The subsequent policy of the Ugandan government and several statements of the Ugandan President confirm this view. For instance, after referring the situation in northern Uganda to the ICC Prosecutor, Museveni had announced that the Amnesty Act, which, at least in theory, also applies to the LRA leaders, would be amended. As explained by the ICC in a press release in 2004,

> "[i]n a bid to encourage members of the LRA to return to normal life, the Ugandan authorities have enacted an amnesty law. President Museveni has indicated to the Prosecutor his intention to amend this amnesty so as to exclude the leadership of the LRA, ensuring that those bearing the greatest responsibility for the crimes against humanity committed in Northern Uganda are brought to justice."[169]

However, the Amnesty Act has never been amended and continues to formally apply to all Ugandans, which shows that Museveni tries to keep as many doors open as possible. He chose not to seriously put into question the Act, which would have been an essential step to reinvigorate the ICC indictments. It should be noted that a national amnesty granted to the LRA leaders would not bar the ICC from exercising jurisdiction. However, since it is likely that cooperation of Ugandan authorities in a possible arrest of ICC indictees is essential, a national amnesty, if taken seriously by the authorities themselves, would probably impede surrendering indictees to the ICC.

Furthermore, local and traditional justice mechanisms for the leadership of the LRA have clearly continued to be a genuine alternative in the view of the Ugandan government. In 2007, when the LRA leaders had already made a withdrawal of the arrest warrants a precondition for engaging in a peace process, President Museveni stated that "if [the LRA leaders] go through the peace process then we can use alternative justice, traditional justice, which is a bit of a soft landing for them. But if they persist and stay in exile then they will end up in The Hague for their crimes."[170] Even after the signing of the Agreement on Accountability and

---

169 ICC, "President of Uganda Refers Situation to the ICC", *supra* note 166.

170 "Uganda's President Hopes Rebels Choose 'Soft Landing'" *Reuters* (4

Reconciliation in June 2007,[171] which stipulates *inter alia* that the LRA leaders will be tried in national courts, Museveni reportedly reassured the LRA that "instead of using this formal Western type of justice we are going to use the traditional justice, a traditional blood settlement mechanism."[172]

Besides these concerns regarding the government's genuine support for the ICC, it has also been argued that the activation of the ICC reinforced the government's strategy to pursue the military option to the detriment of attempts to achieve a negotiated solution to the conflict.[173] In particular the arrest warrants against five LRA leaders, unsealed by the Pre-Trial Chamber in 2005, seemed to grant the government additional authority to fight the LRA under the pretext of fulfilling its international obligation of trying to enforce the warrants. President Museveni also used the ICC arrest warrants as a pretext to legitimize further incursions of the Ugandan army into the territory of the DRC to get hold of the LRA.[174]

Other arguments have been brought forward to underline that the government of Uganda lacked and still lacks the political will to end the conflict in the north, which also explains why the government is not serious about the ICC involvement. Although the war against the LRA has been costly for the Ugandan government, it also represented certain political benefits for Museveni. As Allen has argued,

> "the horrific violence and weird spirituality of the LRA allowed his government to present himself to people in the south as the guarantee that the oppressions of Amin, Obote and Okello would not return. [...] who else would protect them from the Acholi and other wild northerners?"[175]

Thanks to the war, Museveni has also been able to justify the necessity of maintaining a large army, on which he increasingly bases his own power.[176] The fact that traditional and religious leaders, who tried to negotiate with the rebels, have been accused of collaborating with the LRA also shows

---

June 2007), online: Reuters <http://www.reuters.com/articles/latestCrisis/idUSL04425927>.

171 The Agreement was followed by an annex signed in February 2008.

172 Cited in AI, "Agreement and Annex on Accountability", *supra* note 72 at 8.

173 See e.g. Branch, "Uganda's Civil War", *supra* note 44 at 184.

174 See *ibid.*

175 Allen, *supra* note 37 at 48.

176 Branch, "Uganda's Civil War" *supra* note 44 at 185.

that the government is not particularly keen to achieve a negotiated solution.[177]

These arguments suggest that Museveni's government has not only not been serious about bringing the LRA leaders to justice, but that it has, in fact, not been sincerely interested in ending the war in the north. It has even been argued that "[b]y using the ICC warrants as a red herring, President Museveni has evaded accountability for his own disingenuous role in the peace negotiations."[178]

3.2. Validity of the self-referral

Despite the fact that the decision of the Ugandan government to activate the ICC was driven by political considerations, it has been argued that Kampala's goals are compatible with the objectives put forward in the Rome Statute,[179] in particular due to the gravity of the crimes committed and the international cooperation necessary to arrest and investigate LRA leaders in neighboring countries. It is worth noting that while it is true that the Prosecutor must take into account the gravity of the crimes when determining whether or not to initiate an investigation,[180] a factor that will be further analyzed below, the argument of international cooperation seems to be a novel concept, which is not based on any provision of the Rome Statute. However, as a first basic question, it must be clarified whether a state can, in fact, refer a situation transpiring on its territory to the ICC and whether the ICC is entitled to accept such a referral.

Article 14 of the Rome Statute only stipulates that "[a] State Party may refer to the Prosecutor a situation in which one or more crimes within the jurisdiction of the Court appear to have been committed [...]". The wording itself does not preclude a state from referring a situation within its own territory to the ICC. Yet an examination of the drafting history of the Rome Statute illustrates that article 14 was envisaged as an inter-state complaint rather than as an option for a voluntary transfer of jurisdiction to the ICC. While the 1994 draft statute proposed by the International

177 Refugee Law Project, *supra* note 53 at 9.

178 Golzar Kheiltash, "ICC Arrest Warrants Hang in the Balance as Ugandans Prepare for Second Round of Peace Talks" (2006) 8 International Law Enforcement Reporter 317.

179 Akhavan, "The LRA Case", *supra* note 40 at 411.

180 As stipulated in article 53(1)(c) of the Rome Statute.

Law Commission even labeled such referrals as an article 25 "complaint",[181] this provision was later renamed "Referral of a situation by a State Party" and now constitutes article 14 of the final text. Most notably, article 25(1) of the draft statute stipulated that "[a] State Party may *lodge a complaint* with the Prosecutor alleging that a crime [...] appears to have been committed." [emphasis added]

The crucial question is why the final statute speaks of "referral" instead of "complaint". This change of wording must be perceived as a merely terminological modification, which was not intended to broaden the scope of a state referral. As Bill Schabas has argued,

> "[t]here is no evidence that the change in terminology during the drafting of the *Rome Statute*, from 'complaint' to 'referral' was meant to alter the understanding of the drafters that when a State party triggered the jurisdiction of the Court, it did so against another State party, and not against itself."[182]

This point is not uncontroversial. Akhavan has argued that the *travaux préparatoires* do not suggest that voluntary relinquishment of a state's national criminal jurisdiction to the ICC is impermissible under the Rome Statute.[183] A 1995 report of the Ad Hoc Committee on the Establishment

---

181 International Law Commission, *Draft Statute for an International Criminal Court*, in *Report of the International Law Commission on the work of its forty-sixth session (2 May–22 July 1994)*, UN GAOR, 49th Session, Supp. No. 10, UN Doc. A/49/10 (1994).

182 William A. Schabas, "First Prosecutions at the International Criminal Court" (2006) 27 Human Rights Law Journal 25 at 32 [Schabas, "First Prosecutions"]. For information on the drafting history of the provision "Referral of a situation by a State", see *ibid.* at 27-28. Schabas also questions the utility and necessity of self-referrals; see *ibid.* at 32.

183 Akhavan, "The LRA Case", *supra* note 40 at 414. Akhavan argues that "[i]t is conceivable that a state may be unwilling to prosecute before national courts but nevertheless be willing to do so before the ICC. For instance, the prosecution of an especially powerful accused before national courts could destabilize a government or even result in serious political violence." It could be argued that such a scenario could reasonably be subsumed as (simple) unwillingness in the sense of the Rome Statute in order to allow for the ICC to assume jurisdiction. What is more, arguing with such a scenario seems to be unhelpful to analyze the situation in Uganda, since the Ugandan government would not hesitate to prosecute the LRA leaders at the national level.

of an International Criminal Court indeed contains the proposal of some delegates that "the draft statute should provide for the possibility that a State might voluntarily decide to relinquish its jurisdiction in favor of the international criminal court."[184] The same report suggests that this proposition was met with reservations because of its alleged inconsistency with the principle of complementarity.[185] It is worth noting that article 17 and also a so-called direct admissibility of a case in an inaction scenario, where unwillingness and inability of a national system do not have to be examined to establish the admissibility of a case,[186] are irrelevant for an analysis of the validity of a self-referral. A state referral according to Article 14 can trigger ICC jurisdiction over a *situation* and is therefore fundamentally distinct from the issue of a subsequent decision on the admissibility of a specific *case*.

Regardless of the ultimate interpretation of the complaint/referral issue, the later discussions of the Ad Hoc Committee and the Preparatory Committee on state referrals clearly focused on two other questions. First, it focused on whether states should be able to lodge complaints with respect to a particular individual or a particular crime; second, on whether only "interested states", for instance those whose nationals were victims of crimes committed under the Rome Statute, should be allowed to "complain".[187] As a consequence, the discussions subsequently shifted from

184 UN GAOR, 50th Session, Supp. No. 22, "Report of the Ad Hoc Committee on the Establishment of an International Criminal Court, UN Doc. A/50/22 (1995) at para. 47.

185 Akhavan, nevertheless, comes to the conclusion that "[t]his single reference can hardly be taken as representing an authoritative interpretation of the Statute. See Akhavan, "The LRA Case", *supra* note 40 at 414.

186 See International Criminal Court, Appeals Chamber, "Judgment on the Appeal of Mr. Germain Katanga against the Oral Decision of Trial Chamber II of 12 June 2009 on the Admissibility of the Case", ICC-01/04-01/07-1497 (25 September 2009), online: International Criminal Court <http://www.icc-cpi.int/iccdocs/doc/doc746819.pdf> at para. 78 [ICC Appeals Chamber, "Judgement on the Appeal of Katanga"]. See also Carsten Stahn, "Complementarity: A Tale of Two Notions" (2008) 19 Criminal Law Forum 87 at 91.

187 Philippe Kirsch & Darryl Robinson, "Referral by States Parties" in Antonio Cassese, Paola Gaeta & John R.W.D. Jones, eds., *The Rome Statute of the International Criminal Court: A Commentary* (Oxford: Oxford University Press, 2002) 619 at 621.

the "lodging of complaints in specific cases to the referral of 'situations'",[188] with the reasonable result of leaving the investigation into specific crimes to the ICC Prosecutor.

The terminology of the provision followed this shift: the word "complaint" would have been appropriate for specific cases but was not considered suitable for situations. It must be concluded that this change represented a merely terminological adjustment. Following this line of argument, the government of Uganda would have had to complain against itself by referring the situation in northern Uganda to the ICC, which is clearly not the case. It is therefore altogether unclear how a "self-referral" can reasonably be conceived under the Rome Statute.

As a result of this analysis, it is questionable on which legal basis the ICC Prosecutor accepted the self-referral or why, as some have argued, his office even solicited the referral. In the words of Schabas, "[t]he self-referral cannot have been a spontaneous and unexpected development that emerged as a result of creative thinking by international lawyers in the Ugandan Foreign Ministry. [...] The idea came from The Hague, not Kampala."[189]

One possible explanation is that the Prosecutor felt more confident to start the very first investigations of the ICC with the consent and approval of the territorial state. It can be argued that the Court, which took up its functions only 18 months before the referral by the Ugandan government, would not yet have enjoyed the broad political support necessary to allow for *proprio motu* proceedings by the Prosecutor in a politically controversial situation. It was obvious that the first situations and cases before the ICC would become a test for its strength, effectiveness and perhaps the overall *raison d'être* of the Court. A "failure" right at the nascent stage of the Court would have been considered an enormous setback.

Another factor that can explain the Prosecutor's penchant for a self-referral is that the Prosecutor can act more freely following a state referral then after the initiation of proceedings *proprio motu*, as the judicial control of the Pre-Trial Chamber over the Prosecutor goes further in the latter case. For instance, article 15(3) of the Rome Statute stipulates that in the case of investigations initiated *proprio motu*, the Prosecutor "shall submit to the Pre-Trial Chamber a request for authorization of an investigation". Where a State Party or the Security Council refers a situation to the Prosecutor, such authorization is not required.

---

188 *Ibid.* at 622.

189 Schabas, "First Prosecutions", *supra* note 182 at 31.

These arguments can, however, only explain why it might have been more reasonable and less problematic *in practice* for the Prosecutor to accept Uganda's self-referral, compared to the initiation of *propriu motu* proceedings. From a legal perspective, the validity of self-referrals remains at best obscure. It can be argued that Kampala's referral to the ICC was perceived as coherent and consistent with the Rome Statute primarily because of the truly intolerable circumstances in northern Uganda and the understandable urge to deal with the inability of a recognized government of an ICC State Party to capture or kill the leaders of a particularly atrocious rebel group. However, the Prosecutor could have considered the referral merely as a communication of information on crimes within the jurisdiction of the Court under article 15(1),[190] thus leaving a door open to initiate an investigation.

3.3. Pursuing political goals through the Security Council referral of the situation in Darfur

The referral of the situation in Darfur appears to be less problematic from a legal point of view. Security Council Resolution 1564 established a Commission of Inquiry in September 2004 to examine the violations of international humanitarian law and human rights law committed in Darfur.[191] The commission delivered a report to the Secretary-General in January 2005, recommending a Security Council referral to the ICC Prosecutor. Somewhat surprisingly because of the generally negative attitude of the United States, China and Russia towards the ICC,[192] the Security Council, acting under Chapter VII of the UN Charter, followed this recommendation on March 31, 2005. Resolution 1593 triggered ICC jurisdiction for crimes committed in Darfur since July 1, 2002 and stated that "the Government of Sudan and all other parties to the conflict in Darfur *shall* cooperate fully with and provide any necessary assistance to

---

190 See Héctor Olásolo, *The Triggering Procedure of the International Criminal Court* (Leiden: Martinus Nijhoff Publishers, 2006) at 170.

191 S/RES/1564 (2004).

192 For more information on the political discussion concerning the Security Council referral, in particular in the United States, see Zachary D. Kaufman, "Justice in Jeopardy: Accountability for the Darfur Atrocities" (2006) 16 Criminal Law Forum 343 at 345; see also Matthew Happold, "Darfur, The Security Council, and the International Criminal Court" (2006) 55 I.C.L.Q. 226.

the Court and the Prosecutor".[193] Resolution 1593 also "*urges* all States and concerned regional and other international organizations to cooperate fully."[194]

In other words, the Security Council explicitly obliged the government of Sudan to cooperate with the ICC but failed to establish the same obligation for all UN member states. As will be analyzed later, this is particularly relevant in the case of those states which are not parties to the Rome Statute, are therefore not treaty-bound and have, in the absence of a binding Security Council resolution, no legal obligation to cooperate with the ICC.

The activation of the ICC through the Security Council can be regarded as the first and, apart from the subsequent deployment of a joint UN-AU peacekeeping mission, only major reaction of the international community to the Darfur crisis. Clearly, the international community had to react to the growing crisis in Darfur in some way, but it could not find any stringent means. A military intervention, authorized under chapter VII of the UN Charter or of a "coalition of the willing", was politically not feasible. It should be noted that Darfur is a vast area, nearly the size of France, and that international troops could only have been successful if deployed on a very large scale. No government or international alliance had the political will and/or the resources required to intervene. The emerging principle of a responsibility of states to protect people at risk in another state, possibly involving a "humanitarian intervention",[195] experienced a heavy setback.

The international community found itself in a similar situation as in the beginning of the 1990s, when the conflict in the Balkans seemed to unfold without a realistic solution in sight to stop it. At the time, the Security Council hoped to have some impact by establishing the first international criminal tribunal since Nuremberg and Tokyo. Darfur in 2003 and 2004 represented a similar and probably even worse challenge to the international community than Bosnia in the beginning of the 1990s. As it had been the case for the ICTY, the ICC now offered itself as a relatively inexpensive and, at least for the moment, politically less risky option than a military intervention or other political measures, including sanctions, against the government of Sudan.

---

193 S/RES/1593 (2005) at para. 2 [emphasis added].

194 *Ibid* [emphasis added].

195 As proclaimed in the report of the International Commission on Intervention and State Sovereignty, *The Responsibility to Protect* (Ottawa: International Development Research Centre, 2001).

Through its decision, the Security Council implied that the activation of the ICC is an appropriate measure to contribute to the restoration or maintenance of international peace and security, which, as it has been expressed by eminent commentators, "raises the classical question as to whether international justice can constitute a suitable means to achieve international peace."[196] In principle, the answer must be positive[197] and can be affirmed from a legal perspective. First, the drafters of the Rome Statute recognized that serious crimes "threaten the peace, security, and well-being of the world."[198] Second, by establishing the ICTY and the ICTR, the Security Council had already underlined its conviction that international criminal tribunals contribute to the achievement of international peace and security.

Despite this initial support to the ICC, the Security Council did not persist in fully backing the efforts to achieve justice for the victims in Darfur. Backing the ICC in the situation of Darfur became politically more and more difficult for Western governments as well as for the United Nations as a whole, which explains why support for the ICC progressively decreased to a somewhat half-hearted and unenthusiastic policy.

In sum, it seems that the Security Council regarded the ICC as a political rather than a judicial institution when it referred the situation to the Prosecutor. The subsequent policy of the Security Council makes this more than clear.[199] While the highest political organ of the United Nations had shifted parts of the burden to take action in Darfur to the ICC, it did not sustain its support to the latter. The briefings by the Prosecutor to the Security Council, carried out every six months, did not result in any action supportive of the judicial institution, which would have been necessary to enforce the decisions of the ICC, to ensure cooperation of the Sudanese government and to have therefore a credible impact.

---

196 Luigi Condorelli & Santiago Villalpando, "Referral and Deferral by the Security Council" in Antonio Cassese, Paola Gaeta & John R.W.D. Jones, eds., *The Rome Statute of the International Criminal Court: A Commentary* (Oxford: Oxford University Press, 2002) 627 at 632.

197 See similarly *ibid.* at 632.

198 See para. 3 of the preamble of the Rome Statute.

199 This point will be addressed in more depth below, see c. 4.2.2.1.

3.4. Expectations after the two referrals

3.4.1. Uganda

Following the referral in December 2003, the Prosecutor, in July 2004, formally opened an investigation into the crimes committed during the conflict in northern Uganda.[200] Although the Ugandan government had only touched upon crimes committed by the LRA in its referral, the Prosecutor indicated that crimes committed by all parties to the conflict would be investigated. Luis Moreno Ocampo stated that "the scope of the referral encompasses all crimes committed in Northern Uganda in the context of the ongoing conflict involving the LRA."[201] This determination is clearly in compliance with the overall purpose of the Rome Statute of providing non-selective justice; a referral limited to certain parties to a conflict is not acceptable.[202] However, and as expected, the Prosecutor's first and so far only target became the LRA leadership. This approach is linked to both the gravity requirement put forward by the Prosecutor and the fact that the Office of the Prosecutor (OTP) had to rely on the support of the Ugandan government to carry out its investigations. Targeting members of the Ugandan army or even of the government itself would not have been a strategically sensible step for the Prosecutor.

At the beginning of the proceedings, northern Uganda seemed to be an easy first case for the ICC. First, there was ample evidence that atrocious crimes had been committed by the LRA after July 1, 2002. Second, there was no doubt that the crimes for which the LRA leaders are manifestly responsible amount to war crimes and crimes against humanity and fall, therefore, under the jurisdiction of the ICC. Third, full cooperation of the Ugandan authorities with the ICC was widely expected after the referral, since Kampala was obviously interested in expeditious proceed-

200 International Criminal Court, Press Release, "Prosecutor of the International Criminal Court Opens an Investigation into Northern Uganda" (29 July 2004), online: International Criminal Court <http://www.icc-cpi.int/press-release_details&id=33&l=en.html>.

201 International Criminal Court, "Decision to Convene a Status Conference on the Investigation in the Situation in Uganda in Relation to the Application of Article 53" (2 December 2005), ICC-02/04-01/05-68, online: International Criminal Court <http://www2.icc-cpi.int/iccdocs/doc/doc97225.PDF> at paras. 3 and 4.

202 See also Kirsch & Robinson, *supra* note 187 at 625.

ings in order to increase the pressure on the LRA leaders. Yet this expectation only partly materialized. Despite the so-called self-referral, we will see later that cooperation by the Ugandan government could not be assured, and the voluntary referral turned out to be a rather ambiguous and not necessarily helpful mechanism for the ICC.

At the same time, the ICC was promptly criticized for being the main obstacle to the peace process, a fear that has been voiced by both international and local non-governmental organizations since the activation of the Court. Especially those activists and negotiators who were directly involved in the peace efforts condemned the "intervention" of the Court and predicted that "[t]his kind of approach is going to destroy all efforts for peace", as members of the Acholi Religious Leaders' Peace Initiative stated.[203] Similar concerns were also raised by the Ugandan Amnesty Commission,[204] which has a pertinent expertise in the field of reintegrating former LRA fighters into society, but which also saw its *raison d'être* being put in danger by the activation of the ICC. It is important to note that the opponents of the ICC involvement did usually not base their criticism on a total rejection of prosecutions in general or on the ICC as an institution, but emphasized that the timing for initiating the investigations was ill-considered.

3.4.2. Darfur

The involvement of the ICC has been given much weight in the case of Darfur, in particular due to the lack of any other concerted measure of the international community, the humanitarian dimension of the conflict and its substantial mediatization. Similarly to the situation in northern Uganda, however, the expectations following the Security Council referral were mixed; the referral has been criticized for focusing too much on the future and only potential punishment of perpetrators rather than on immediate relief and the prevention of mass atrocities. The possibility of deterring violence in Darfur thanks to the ICC has even been dismissed as a "specious hope".[205]

203 UN Office for the Coordination of Humanitarian Affairs, "UGANDA: Peace Groups and Government Officials Worried about ICC Probe into LRA" (30 January 2004), online: IRIN <http://www.irinnews.org/Report.aspx?ReportId=48356>.

204 *Ibid.*

205 Eric Reeves, "Darfur: Genocide Before Our Eyes" in Joyce Apsel, ed.,

A more optimistic view of the referral suggests that the ICC involvement represents a significant threat for key players of the conflict and may, above all, pressure the Sudanese government to cut support for the *Janjaweed*. Members of the SLA expressed their hope that the ICC would quickly indict those who they consider responsible for the worst atrocities committed in Darfur, in other words senior figures of the regime in Khartoum, including President Omar al-Bashir and Vice-President Ali Osman Taha. It has also been argued that it would be sufficient to make public the names of the 51 individuals which are on the still secret list of the Commission of Inquiry to stigmatize and de-legitimize the Sudanese leadership.[206]

3.5. The selection of cases and their admissibility under article 17 of the Rome Statute

3.5.1. The general system of the principle of complementarity

Article 17 is the linchpin to analyze the extent to which cases can and should be declared admissible before the ICC. In the following, the general system of the principle of complementarity will be briefly addressed, before this principle will be applied to the cases arising in the situations of northern Uganda and Darfur.

The ICC complements national criminal systems and does not remove the primary obligation of states to investigate and prosecute alleged perpetrators of international crimes. As the preamble of the Rome Statute recalls, "it is the duty of every State to exercise its criminal jurisdiction over those responsible for international crimes." The ICC can therefore not deal with situations where genuine investigations and prosecutions are being or have been carried out in domestic courts. Unwillingness and inability of a national system to carry out investigations and/or prosecutions are the two concepts which outline the principle of complementarity in more detail. According to article 17(1)(a) of the Rome Statute, a case is inadmissible when "[t]he case is being investigated or prosecuted by a State which has jurisdiction over it, unless the State is unwilling or genuinely unable to carry out the investigation or prosecution."

Darfur: Genocide Before Our Eyes (New York: Institute for Study of Genocide, 2005) 26 at 30.

206 See Res Publica, *supra* note 85 at 30.

"Unwillingness" means, according to article 17(2), "shielding the person concerned from criminal responsibility for crimes within the jurisdiction of the Court", an "unjustified delay in the proceedings which in the circumstances is inconsistent with an intent to bring the person concerned to justice", or the absence of independence and impartial proceedings which are "inconsistent with an intent to bring the person concerned to justice." In general, it should be noted that it is clear from the wording of article 17 and its drafting history that the threshold for admissibility is very high.[207]

Regarding inability, a State can only be considered unable if, according to article 17(3), "due to a total or substantial collapse or unavailability of its national judicial system, the State is unable to obtain the accused or the necessary evidence and testimony or otherwise unable to carry out its proceedings." The wording of this provision, in particular the term "collapse", also underlines that the threshold to allow the ICC to assume jurisdiction because of inability of a national system is very high. Moreover, article 17(3) establishes a combined requirement, meaning that the judicial system must have totally or substantially collapsed and at least one of the three factual considerations must be met.[208] Therefore, it is for instance not sufficient that the authorities cannot get hold of alleged perpetrators or key witnesses; the national judicial system must have at least "substantially" collapsed in order to render a case admissible under the inability clause.

3.5.2. The case against the LRA leaders

Since the self-referral by the Ugandan government has been accepted, this analysis will move to the next crucial step, namely the selection of cases by the Prosecutor. After a brief overview over the indictments and warrants of arrests, the choice of cases and their admissibility will be analyzed in more depth, including a discussion (a) on the issue of complementarity and (b) on the gravity requirement.

---

207 For more information, see John T. Holmes, "Complementarity: National Courts versus the ICC" in Antonio Cassese, Paola Gaeta & John R.W.D. Jones, eds., *The Rome Statute of the International Criminal Court: A Commentary* (Oxford: Oxford University Press, 2002) 667 at 675 [Holmes, "National Courts versus the ICC"].

208 See also *ibid.* at 678.

3.5.2.1. The indictments

The Prosecutor's investigation into the situation in northern Uganda involved over fifty missions to Uganda and focused on attacks committed between July 2002 and July 2004.[209] On July 8, 2005, arrest warrants against five LRA leaders were issued by the Pre-Trial Chamber, namely against Chief Commander Joseph Kony, Deputy Commander Vincent Otti, Army Commander Raska Lukwiya, and senior Brigade Commanders Okot Odhiambo and Dominic Ongwen. These arrest warrants were unsealed three months later, on October 14, 2005,[210] and remain outstanding at the time of writing. Since Army Commander Lukwiya was killed in a fight between the LRA and the Ugandan army in August 2006, the arrest warrant against him was officially withdrawn in 2007.[211] The officially unconfirmed but likely death of Deputy Commander Otti in late 2007 brought the number of outstanding arrest warrants down to three, although the warrant against Otti has not been formally withdrawn by the ICC.

It seems appropriate to focus the analysis on the arrest warrant against the leader of the LRA, since it is the most extensive document and since the other four warrants contain similar charges. The warrant of arrest against Joseph Kony, issued on July 8, 2005, cites 33 counts of crimes against humanity and war crimes according to articles 7(1)(a), (c), (g) and (k) and 8(2)(c) and (e) of the Rome Statute, most of which combined with individual criminal responsibility according to 25(3)(b) of the Statute.[212] These charges assert Kony's responsibility for ordering and/or inducing sexual

---

209 International Criminal Court, "Statement by the Chief Prosecutor on the Uganda Arrest Warrants" (14 October 2005), online: International Criminal court <http://www2.icc-cpi.int/NR/rdonlyres/3255817D-FD00-4072-9F58-FDB869F9B7CF/143834/LMO_20051014_English1.pdf> at 3.

210 See International Criminal Court, "The Investigation in Northern Uganda" (14 October 2005), online: International Criminal Court <http://www2.icc-cpi.int/NR/rdonlyres/2919856F-03E0-403F-A1A8-D61D4F350A20/277306/Uganda_PPpresentation6.pdf>.

211 International Criminal Court, Pre-Trial Chamber II, "Decision to Terminate the Proceedings Against Raska Lukwiya" (11 July 2007), ICC-02/04-01/05-348, online: International Criminal Court <http://www2.icc-cpi.int/iccdocs/doc/doc297945.pdf>.

212 International Criminal Court, Pre-Trial Chamber II, "Warrant of Arrest for Joseph Kony Issued on 8 July 2005 as Amended on 27 September 2005" (27 September 2005), ICC-02/04-01/05-53.

enslavement, rape, attacks against civilians, murder, pillaging, and forced conscription of children, committed "as part of a widespread or systematic attack" against civilians.[213] Due to the limits on the temporal jurisdiction of the ICC, the warrant only refers to crimes committed after July 2002. The crimes committed by the leader of the LRA since the 1980s and up to July 2002 do not fall under the jurisdiction of the Court, although they may be relevant in a trial as evidence of a pattern of conduct.[214]

3.5.2.2. Admissibility of the case

a) Complementarity according to article 17

The analysis whether the case against the LRA leaders is admissible must start with article 17 of the Rome Statute and the principle of complementarity. None of the three "unwillingness" options of article 17(2) outlined in section 3.5.1. speaks of the possibility that the State which has primary jurisdiction over the case can simply prefer that the ICC take up the case. Unwillingness, in the sense of the Rome Statute, is the general reluctance of bringing an alleged perpetrator of core crimes to justice. It is not the preference for trials in The Hague over domestic proceedings. As a result, a State cannot be unwilling, in the meaning of the Rome Statute, when it has the genuine intent of bringing the person concerned to justice, be it before domestic courts or before an international court.

Regarding inability, the national judicial system of Uganda clearly does not fulfill the requirements established by the Rome Statute. The "inability" of the Ugandan authorities to apprehend the LRA leaders would fulfill one of the requirements of article 17(3), namely that the "State is unable to obtain the accused". However, once apprehended, the ICC indictees could have been brought before Ugandan courts: "Uganda has a sophisticated criminal justice system with a proudly independent judiciary."[215] Clearly, the system cannot be considered to have *collapsed*, neither totally nor substantially. There is no reason to interpret article 17(3) more broadly in order to consider the Ugandan authorities "unable" in the sense of the Rome Statute.[216] The problem with the LRA is therefore not a problem of

213 As stipulated in article 7 of the Rome Statute.

214 Akhavan, "The LRA Case", *supra* note 40 at 412.

215 Schabas, "First Prosecutions", *supra* note 182 at 31.

216 As it has been argued by Akhavan in "The LRA Case", *supra* note 40 at 415, stating that the Ugandan system is "'unavailable' because the presence of the accused in a neighboring state prevents Uganda from taking them into custody."

impunity;[217] the only "problem" with respect to the LRA leaders lies in the fact that the Ugandan authorities have been unable to apprehend them.

Other factors, such as the prospect of unfair proceedings against the LRA leaders in Uganda, are unlikely to render the case admissible. Although it should not be taken for granted that the LRA leaders would enjoy fair trial guarantees in Uganda, the risk of unsatisfactory trials according to international human rights standards does not make the case admissible before the ICC. The ICC is not a human rights court. The "quality" of justice or degree of fairness should not, *per se*, determine the choice between domestic proceedings and the ICC. The deliberations during the drafting process of the Rome Statute underline this view: "It was extremely important to many States that proceedings cannot be found "non-genuine" [...] because of a lack of full compliance with all human rights standards."[218]

Following the above-made analysis, the case against the LRA leaders is not admissible. Yet it has been argued that the provisions of article 17(a)-(c) only apply if a state has already investigated or prosecuted the case; if no investigations have been commenced, the case would therefore be somehow "directly" admissible. As a matter of fact, in 2003, the government of Uganda seemed to prefer that investigations be carried out by the ICC Prosecutor instead of national proceedings. Since no investigations had been commenced at the domestic level, the case against the five LRA leaders appeared not to be inadmissible under article 17; according to this line of reasoning, inability and unwillingness of the domestic system did not even have to be examined at this stage. Moreover, it has been argued that "a positive interpretation of complementarity would maintain that Article 17 limits ICC jurisdiction through the criterion of unwillingness or inability only when there is a conflict between the ICC and a national criminal jurisdiction."[219] This view was confirmed in a decision in the case against Germain Katanga in the situation of the DRC in September 2009, in which the Appeals Chamber stated that "[i]naction on the part of a State having jurisdiction (that is, the fact that a State is not investigating

217 See similarly Schabas, "First Prosecutions", *supra* note 182 at 31.

218 International Criminal Court, "Informal Expert Paper: The Principle of Complementarity in Practice" (2003), online: International Criminal Court <http://www.icc-cpi.int/iccdocs/doc/doc656350.PDF> at 8 [ICC, "Informal Expert Paper"].

219 Akhavan, "The LRA Case", *supra* note 40 at 413.

or prosecuting, or has not done so) renders a case admissible before the Court, subject to article 17 (1) (d) of the Statute".[220]

This argument of "direct admissibility" without a proper test of article 17 is not convincing. It does not appear consistent with the objectives of the Rome Statute to declare a case admissible simply because no domestic proceedings have been carried out. The preamble of the Rome Statute clearly states in its paragraph six that "it is the duty of every State to exercise its criminal jurisdiction over those responsible for international crimes." According to article 1 of the Statute, the Court is "complementary to national criminal jurisdictions". In other words, "[t]he Statute recognizes that States have the first responsibility and right to prosecute international crimes."[221] Therefore, it must be concluded that the ICC has not been set up as a substitute to states which are not unwilling nor unable (in the sense of the Rome Statute) – or simply "inactive" – to carry out national proceedings. As the President of the ICC, Philippe Kirsch, has noted, "[i]t is the essence of the principle [of complementarity] that if a national judicial system functions properly, there is no reason for the ICC to assume jurisdiction."[222] A coherent analysis of the principle of complementarity does not leave room for another conclusion.

Moreover, this question of admissibility is indirectly linked to the issue of self-referrals. As explained above, the wording from the draft statute ("complaint") was changed in the final version ("referral of a situation") to make the language fitting for situations but not for specific cases. According to the interpretation of the Appeals Chamber, however, by remaining simply "inactive" in a certain case, a state can indirectly refer a specific case against an individual to the Court,[223] a scenario that the negotiators of the Statute had clearly wanted to avoid.

Several comments to the Rome Statute underline this view. Bergsmo, Cissé and Staker, for instance, include the "admissibility test" of the complementarity principle, as stipulated in article 17, as a requirement for the

220 ICC Appeals Chamber, "Judgement on the Appeal of Katanga", *supra* note 186 at para. 2.

221 ICC, "Informal Expert Paper", *supra* note 218 at 3.

222 Philipp Kirsch, "Keynote Address by Ambassador Philippe Kirsch" (1999) 32 Cornell International Law Journal 438.

223 For a similar opinion, see William Schabas, "A Major Complementary Ruling by the Appeals Chamber of the International Criminal Court" (27 September 2009), online: PhD studies in human rights <http://humanrightsdoctorate.blogspot.com/2009_09_01_archive.html>.

Prosecutor to proceed in a case, without distinguishing whether the state which has primary jurisdiction over the case has already carried out an investigation.[224] John T. Holmes was guided by a similar approach in his commentary to the principle of complementarity, focusing on the argument that "the Prosecutor will have to establish facts supporting the contention that the State is not genuine in its investigatory of prosecutory efforts – i.e. that it is actively blocking the pursuit of justice."[225] It appears that when the Rome Statute was adopted, the possibility of considering a case admissible because a state, which is *a priori* able and willing to proceed, simply opts for proceedings before the ICC had not been foreseen.

Since an "unwilling" State – in the sense of the Rome Statute – is unlikely to refer a situation to the ICC, admissible cases in the context of self-referred situations are, therefore, only conceivable if a state is unable "genuinely to carry out the investigation or prosecution" (article 17(1)(a), due to an at least "substantial collapse or unavailability of its national judicial system" (article 17(3)). Plausible examples include the situation in Rwanda after the genocide in 1994, where only a handful of magistrates and lawyers were available, or the situation in Somalia since 1991, where the official authorities have not been able to carry out any credible criminal proceedings.[226]

b) The gravity requirement[227]

If one follows the argument of "positive complementarity", namely that a case would only have to undergo a strict admissibility test if there is a conflict between the ICC jurisdiction and a national jurisdiction, the Prosecutor, at first sight, seems to have made a logical step in targeting the leaders of the LRA. Arguing that they bear the greatest responsibility for the worst crimes committed in northern Uganda, the Prosecutor made

224 See Bergsmo, Cissé & Staker, *supra* note 30 at 143. The focus clearly lies on challenges to the admissibility of a case, which can be made by states which have jurisdiction over the case, by the suspect or by the territorial state or state of nationality.

225 Holmes, "National Courts versus the ICC", supra note 207 at 684.

226 This impunity has been described as the root cause of the country's humanitarian and political crisis, see UN Office for the Coordination of Humanitarian Affairs, "Somalia: Impunity 'the Root Cause of Crisis" (27 February 2007), online: IRIN <http://www.irinnews.org/report.aspx?ReportId=76993>.

227 For an in-depth analysis of the "gravity criterion", see Schabas, "Prosecutorial Discretion", *supra* note 34 at 736-748.

the gravity of the crimes committed one of his central arguments of his strategy:

> "The criteria for selection of the first case was gravity. We analyzed the gravity of all crimes in northern Uganda committed by the LRA and Ugandan forces. Crimes committed by the LRA were much more numerous and of much higher gravity than alleged crimes committed by the UPDF. We therefore started with an investigation of the LRA."[228]

By explaining his decisions whether or not to initiate an investigation in other situations, the Prosecutor has also repeatedly argued with article 53(1)(c),[229] which stipulates that the gravity of the crime and the interests of the victims must be taken into consideration.

This "gravity requirement" seems to be met in the case of the LRA; one could hardly imagine more atrocious crimes than those for which the LRA is allegedly responsible. However, despite the fact that in comparable situations of impunity strategic choices must undoubtedly be made given the limited human and financial resources of the ICC, gravity should not be the principal test for the selection of cases. When this policy is assessed under the overall purpose of the ICC, the test fails. As has been underlined by Schabas, the importance of meeting this gravity criterion seems to be a novel concept, developed by the Office of the Prosecutor in 2005 in order to defend the selection of the first cases.[230] Interestingly, in his response to the communications received concerning the situation in Iraq, the Prosecutor even seemed to apply a quantity test, comparing a handful of willful killings in Iraq to the thousands of willful killings in northern Uganda, the DRC and Darfur.[231]

---

228 International Criminal Court, "Statement by the Chief Prosecutor on the Uganda Arrest Warrants" (14 October 2005), online: International Criminal Court <http://www2.icc-cpi.int/NR/rdonlyres/3255817D-FD00-4072-9F58-FDB869F9B7CF/143834/LMO_20051014_English1.pdf> at 2-3.

229 See e.g. International Criminal Court, "Update on Communications Received by the Office of the Prosecutor of the ICC" (10 February 2006), online: International Criminal Court <http://www2.icc-cpi.int/NR/rdonlyres/F596D08D-D810-43A2-99BB-B899B9C5BCD2/277421/OTP_Update_on_Communications_10_February_2006.pdf>.

230 Schabas, "Prosecutorial Discretion", *supra* note 34 at 737.

231 International Criminal Court, "Iraq Response", annex to "Update on Communications Received by the Office of the Prosecutor of the ICC" (10

It is worth noting that the question of gravity was largely ignored during the negotiations of the Rome Statute[232] and that the scope of the Rome Statute is already limited to the "most serious crimes of concern to the international community as a whole", as stipulated in the preamble of the Statute, thus rendering every crime under the Statute grave *per se*. Moreover, it is evident that gravity cannot stand alone but must be read in conjunction with the overall purpose of the Statute, namely to end impunity. The latter objective, which becomes diminished via the emphasis on gravity as a criterion for selecting which crimes to prosecute, is not compatible with the narrow objective of bringing before the ICC those who are most responsible for the worst crimes. The number of victims, for instance, should only be an auxiliary criterion for the selection of situations and cases by the Prosecutor and should only be considered subsequently to the fundamental principle of ending impunity for core crimes. In other words, it is insufficient to simply select the "gravest cases".

Moreover, according to the principle of complementarity, the Prosecutor's scope of action inherently depends on the possible exercise of jurisdiction by national systems. This means, *in concreto*, that indicting those who are allegedly responsible for the gravest crimes committed in northern Uganda falls short of a reasoning that is faithful to the requirements of the Rome Statute. It also fails those victims who have not only suffered from crimes committed by the LRA, but also from crimes committed by government forces. Even if considered overall "less grave" according to a standard as yet undefined in the Rome Statute, these crimes are, without an initiative from The Hague, less likely to be investigated and prosecuted at the national level than crimes committed by the LRA.[233] As a result, similar to the complementarity argument analyzed above, the gravity test, which was developed by the OTP following the Ugandan referral, is not persuasive.

February 2006), online: International Criminal Court <http://www.icc-cpi.int/library/organs/otp/OTP_letter_to_senders_re_Iraq_9_February_2006.pdf> at 9.

232 See Schabas, "Prosecutorial Discretion", *supra* note 34 at 736.

233 In the words of Schabas, "we are confronted with the classic impunity paradigm: individuals acting on behalf of the state that shelters them from its own courts." Schabas, "Prosecutorial Discretion", *supra* note 34 at 748.

3.5.2.3. Admissibility revisited?

In the case of Uganda, the question of unwillingness might, however, turn out to be of significant importance if the Ugandan government fulfills its promises *vis-à-vis* the LRA leaders to offer a national procedure of justice, as agreed to in the February 2008 accord mentioned above. If a trial was actually initiated in The Hague, the Ugandan government can be expected to challenge the admissibility of the case before the ICC according to article 19(2)(b), arguing that it is now both willing and able to carry out proceedings against the LRA leaders. Although it would be a rather striking evidence of the political game played by the Ugandan government, this would be a weighty argument for the ICC, since one of the general principles of the Rome Statute is to favor national trials.

One possibility might be proceedings before a special court in Uganda, which was proposed in an annex to the peace agreement.[234] Several problems arise even if the LRA leaders were brought before such a court. First, war crimes and crimes against humanity are not specifically recognized as crimes under Ugandan law, which means that, due to the principle of non-retroactivity in criminal law, perpetrators of such crimes cannot be tried in Uganda. The LRA leaders could probably also be tried for murder and other "normal" crimes codified in the Penal Law of Uganda. This would, however, not adequately address the characteristics of the crimes committed by the LRA and would probably not correspond to the demands of the international community as well of those who have suffered from LRA atrocities. Furthermore, the Special Court could only try non-state actors, thus barring it from proceeding against members of the Ugandan army and perpetuating a delivery of one-sided justice in Uganda.[235] Proceedings carried out before the Special Court are nevertheless more likely to correspond to the principle of complementarity than other local mechanisms. It can be expected that at least some proceedings at the national level might be carried out in the form of an alternative or traditional justice mechanism, which would probably not fulfill the requirements of "genuine proceedings" in the sense of article 17. Undoubtedly, the ICC would then have the competence to re-assume jurisdiction over the case.

234 See Katy Glassborow & Joe Wacha, "ICC Judges to Review LRA Cases" *Institute for War & Peace Reporting* (19 November 2008), online: Institute for War&Peace Reporting <http://www.iwpr.net/?p=acr&s=f&o=347885&apc_state=henh>.

235 *Ibid.*

In conclusion, in the situation of Uganda, the Prosecutor focused on the leaders of the LRA, arguing that they bear the greatest responsibility for the worst crimes committed in northern Uganda. This may be true, but, to put it bluntly, the objective of the Rome Statute is not to help national governments chase individuals who cannot be arrested. The ICC was set up to substitute national proceedings in case of (true) unwillingness or inability in order to fight impunity for genocide, crimes against humanity and war crimes.

A thorough analysis of alternatives open to the Prosecutor would go beyond this book. By way of example, instead of carrying out investigations and prosecutions, the Prosecutor could, in situations like northern Uganda where the domestic system is neither genuinely unwilling nor unable to proceed, try to find incentives to further domestic proceedings or provide technical assistance to the national criminal justice system concerned. An external expert paper, prepared in 2003 for the OTP, suggests that

> "[t]he Prosecutor can, acting within the mandate provided by the Statute, encourage the State concerned to initiate national proceedings, help develop cooperative anti-impunity strategies, and possibly provide advice and certain forms of assistance to facilitate national efforts."[236]

A legal basis for such cooperation can be found in article 93(10) of the Rome Statute, which stipulates that the ICC may "cooperate and provide assistance to a State Party conducting an investigation into or trial in respect of conduct which constitutes a crime within the jurisdiction of the Court or which constitutes a serious crime under the national law of the requesting State."

3.5.3. The case against Ahmad Harun and Ali Kushayb

Compared to the case against the LRA leadership, the first case selected in the situation of Darfur is less complex and controversial from a legal point of view, but at least as problematic from a political perspective.

As a result of the Security Council referral, the ICC has jurisdiction over crimes committed in Darfur, although Sudan has not ratified the Rome Statute. In addition to this initial step triggering ICC jurisdiction, specific cases must also be admissible according to the principle of complementarity. This criterion applies in the case of a Security Council referral,

---

236 ICC, "Informal Expert Paper", *supra* note 218 at 4.

since article 17 does not make a distinction between the different trigger mechanisms.[237] Moreover, in the words of commentators to the Rome Statute, "the criteria of admissibility are to be considered intrinsic characteristics of the Court."[238] This means that Sudan must either be unable or unwilling to carry out the investigation and/or prosecution in the cases selected by the Prosecutor.

The Sudanese judicial system can be considered functional from a general point of view. Even though crimes have been committed on a large scale, it should, nonetheless, not be unable to carry out investigations and prosecutions in the sense of the Rome Statute.[239] However, the numerous crimes committed in Darfur have been dealt with very insufficiently by the national court system. The little efforts of the Sudanese government to tackle the crimes committed in Darfur, such as through its National Commission of Inquiry, established in May 2004, and the Special Court for Darfur, established in June 2005, have had very limited effects. Only a few low-level officers were indicted, and only for crimes that would probably not even fall under the jurisdiction of the ICC.[240] According to the Prosecutor, only seven trials "with no connection to the campaign of crimes coordinated by Ahmed Harun, perpetrated by Ali Kushayb and others, and as the Prosecution alleges, ordered by Mr Al Bashir," had been concluded by November 2008.[241]

237 See the general analysis above and Giuliano Turone, "Powers and Duties of the Prosecutor" in Antonio Cassese, Paola Gaeta & John R.W.D. Jones, eds., *The Rome Statute of the International Criminal Court: A Commentary* (Oxford: Oxford University Press, 2002) 1137 at 1142.

238 Condorelli & Villalpando, *supra* note 196 at 637.

239 The argument that the national system could be considered "unavailable" following a Security Council referral, thus legally disabling the state to carry out the proceedings (see *ibid.* at 640), seems ultimately not convincing in the light of the overarching principle of complementarity.

240 For instance for stealing property; see UN Human Rights Council, "Report of the High-Level Mission on the Situation of Human Rights in Darfur pursuant to Human Rights Council Decision S-4/101", UN Doc. A/HRC/4/80 (7 March 2007) at 16. For a thorough analysis of the deficiencies of the Special Court, see Human Rights Watch, "The Lack of Conviction, The Special Criminal Court on the Events in Darfur" (June 2006), online: Human Rights Watch <http://hrw.org/backgrounder/ij/sudan0606/sudan0606.pdf>.

241 ICC, "Address to the ASP", *supra* note 36 at 9.

Human rights organizations, such as Amnesty International, have dismissed the establishment of the Special Court as a tactic by the Sudanese government to avoid ICC prosecutions.[242] The timing of the establishment of the Special Court, shortly after the Prosecutor had announced the opening of investigations into the situation in Darfur, certainly gives rise to allegations that it was only set up to try to thwart ICC jurisdiction. Since the end of 2006, however, the Sudanese Ministry of Justice has been committed to showing more concrete actions. It arrested, for instance, Ali Kushayb, an important militia leader who is also denounced by the ICC Prosecutor as one of the persons who is most responsible for the crimes that have been committed in Darfur.[243] Nevertheless, it is obvious that the judicial system has been unwilling to truly investigate most of the militia leaders and those members of the government who bear individual responsibility for the crimes committed in Darfur. Even if investigations are carried out, it is, furthermore, unlikely that they will fulfill the requirements of article 17(2)(c) of the Rome Statute that such investigations be conducted independently and impartially, as well as with the "intent to bring the person concerned to justice."

Generally speaking, it is, therefore, not difficult for the Prosecutor to prove the admissibility of cases in the situation of Darfur. Here, an involvement of the ICC perfectly corresponds to the objectives of the Rome Statute due to the role of the government of Sudan, its influence on the judicial system and its unwillingness to end impunity for the crimes committed in Darfur.

In his application to the Pre-Trial Chamber to issue summonses to appear against Ahmad Harun, a member of the Sudanese government, and Ali Kushayb, the Prosecutor argued that this case was admissible,

---

242 Amnesty International, "Sudan: National court for Darfur crimes lacks credibility, and is no replacement for ICC investigations" (14 June 2005), online: Amnesty International <http://www.amnesty.org.uk/news_details.asp?NewsID=16169>; see also Global Policy Forum, "Sudan: Judiciary Challenges ICC over Darfur Case" (24 June 2005) online: Global Policy Forum <http://www.globalpolicy.org/intljustice/icc/2005/0624collaborate.htm> and Dawn Yamene Hewett, "Sudan's Court and Complementarity in the Face of Darfur" (2006) 31 Yale J. Int'l L. 276 at 279.

243 ICC, "Prosecutor's Application under Article 58(7)", *supra* note 121 at 89. Regarding the admissibility of the case against Ali Kushayb, the OTP affirmed that its own investigations and those made by the Sudanese did not relate to the same conduct; see ICC, "Fifth Report of the Prosecutor", *supra* note 122 at 8.

since the "Sudanese authorities have not investigated or prosecuted the case which is the subject of the Application."[244] Two months later, on April 27, 2007, the Pre-Trial Chamber confirmed this view and issued arrest warrants for Ahmed Harun and Ali Kushayb, stating that

> "without prejudice to any challenge to the admissibility if the case under article 19(2)(a) and (b) of the Statute and without prejudice to any subsequent determination, the Chamber finds that the case against Ahmed Harun and Ali Kushayb falls within the jurisdiction of the Court and appears to be admissible."[245]

The arrest warrants include counts of war crimes and crimes against humanity according to articles 7(1) and 8(2)(c) and (e) of the Rome Statute, in particular with respect to attacks on civilians, murder, rape, persecution, pillaging and destruction of property.[246] The individual criminal responsibility of Ahmed Harun is based on articles 25(3)(b) and (d) of the Statute,[247] which means that he suspected to have ordered or to have contributed to the commission of the crimes in Darfur as Sudanese Minister for Humanitarian Affairs. Ali Kushayb's individual criminal responsibility is based on articles 25(3)(a) and (d) of the Statute, indicating the Prosecutor's view that the militia leader personally participated in attacks on civilians and contributed to the commission of other war crimes and crimes against humanity.

---

244 International Criminal Court, "Fact Sheet, The Situation in Darfur, the Sudan" (27 February 2007), online: International Criminal Court <http://www2.icc-cpi.int/NR/rdonlyres/08D1428F-62DA-4C0F-AF47-17FABFFAF995/143641/ICCOTP_FactSheetDarfur20070227_en.pdf>.

245 International Criminal Court, Pre-Trial Chamber I, "Decision on the Prosecution Application under Article 58(7) of the Statute" (27 April 2007), ICC-02/05-01/07, online: International Criminal Court <http://www.icc-cpi.int/library/cases/ICC-02-05-01-07-1_English.pdf> at para. 25.

246 International Criminal Court, Pre-Trial Chamber I, "Warrant of Arrest for Ahmad Harun" and "Warrant of Arrest for Ali Kushayb" (27 April 2007), ICC-02/05-01/07-2 and ICC-02/05-01/07-3, online: International Criminal Court <http://www.icc-cpi.int/iccdocs/doc/doc279813.PDF> and <http://www.icc-cpi.int/iccdocs/doc/doc279858.PDF>.

247 *Ibid.*

3.5.4. *"Going up the ladder" – the case against the Sudanese President*

On July 14, 2008, the Prosecutor filed an application to the Pre-Trial Chamber to issue an arrest warrant against the Sudanese President Omar al-Bashir.[248] In the view of the Prosecutor, Bashir, as the President of Sudan and *de jure* and *de facto* commander of the armed forces, is the main instigator of the crimes committed in Darfur.[249] With this application, the Prosecutor seemed to respond to strong concerns raised by human rights NGOs and commentators *vis-à-vis* his previous strategy of targeting the mid-level perpetrators Ahmed Harun and Ali Kushayb. Critics had consistently voiced that although indicting and even trying a minister and a militia leader might send a strong signal to the international community, it would not change anything for the victims on the ground; in reality, those truly responsible for ordering and backing the crimes committed in Darfur, namely top government officials, would have to be targeted.

By including charges for genocide according to article 6(a), (b) and (c) of the Rome Statute in his application, the Prosecutor made a second strong statement and confronted the view of the 2005 Commission of Inquiry, which had found no evidence for the commission of genocide in Darfur.[250] According to the Prosecutor,

> "AL BASHIR intends to destroy in substantial part the Fur, Masalit and Zaghawa ethnic groups as such. Forces and agents controlled by AL BASHIR attacked civilians in towns and villages inhabited by the target groups, committing killings, rapes, torture and destroying means of livelihood. AL BASHIR has thus forced the displacement of a substantial part of the target groups and attacked them in the camps for internally displaced persons ("IDPs"), causing serious and bodily harm – through rapes, tortures and forced displacement in traumatizing con-

---

248 International Criminal Court, "Prosecutor's Application for Warrant of Arrest under Article 58 Against Omar Hassan Ahmad Al Bashir, Summary of the Case" (14 July 2008), online: International Criminal Court <http://www2.icc-cpi.int/NR/rdonlyres/64FA6B33-05C3-4E9C-A672-3FA2B58CB2C9/277758/ICCOTPSummary20081704ENG.pdf> [ICC, "Prosecutor's Application for Warrant of Arrest Against Al Bashir"].

249 *Ibid.* at 1.

250 For further information on this discussion, see below, c. 5.2.2. and also note 115.

> ditions – and deliberately inflicting on a substantial part of those groups conditions of life calculated to bring about their physical destruction. AL BASHIR's conduct simultaneously constitutes genocide against the Fur, Masalit and Zaghawa ethnic groups, crimes against humanity and war crimes against any civilian population in the area, including members of the target groups."[251]

Following the Prosecutor's application, the Pre-Trial Chamber issued an arrest warrant against Bashir eight months later, on March 4, 2009.[252] The majority of the judges did, however, only confirm the charges of war crimes and crimes against humanity but did not follow the Prosecutor's view that there were reasonable grounds to believe that Bashir had acted with genocidal intent. The Pre-Trial Chamber, somewhat surprisingly, used in its decision a high threshold similar to the one necessary for a conviction. The judges argued that the evidence presented by the Prosecutor did not exclusively lead to the "only reasonable conclusion" that the Sudanese government has pursued a genocidal policy in Darfur.[253] This decision was appealed by the Prosecutor and reversed by the Appeals Chamber, which remanded the decision to the Pre-Trial Chamber. In July 2010, the judges used the correct standard of proof, namely "reasonable grounds to believe" that Bashir is criminally responsible for genocide under article 6 of the Rome Statute, and issued a second warrant of arrest.[254] The decisions of

251 International Criminal Court, "Prosecutor's Application for Warrant of Arrest Against Al Bashir", *supra* note 248 at 1-2.

252 International Criminal Court, Pre-Trial Chamber I, "Warrant of Arrest for Omar Hassan Ahmad Al Bashir", ICC-02/05-01/09-1 (4 March 2009), online: International Criminal Court <http://www.icc-cpi.int/iccdocs/doc/doc639078.pdf>.

253 International Criminal Court, Pre-Trial Chamber I, "Decision on the Prosecution's Application for a Warrant of Arrest against Omar Hassan Ahmad Al Bashir", ICC-02/05-01/09-3 (4 March 2009), online: International Criminal Court <http://www.icc-cpi.int/iccdocs/doc/doc639096.pdf> at para. 201. The Prosecutor appealed this decision on March 13, 2009; see Pre-Trial Chamber I, "Prosecutor's Application for Leave to Appeal the 'Decision on the Prosecution's Application for a Warrant of Arrest against Omar Hassan Ahmad Al Bashir'", ICC-02/05-01/09-12 (13 March 2009), online: International Criminal Court <http://www.icc-cpi.int/iccdocs/doc/doc644001.pdf>.

254 International Criminal Court, Pre-Trial Chamber I, "Second Warrant of Arrest for Omar Hassan Ahmad Al Bashir", ICC-02/05-01/09-95 (12

the Pre-Trial Chamber and the Appeals Chamber as well as the different opinions of expert organizations[255] on the charges of genocide underlines the delicateness, both from a legal and political perspective, of the specific question of genocidal intent.[256]

The analysis of the admissibility of the case against Bashir is similar to the one of the cases against Ahmed Harun and Ali Kushayb; the ICC has jurisdiction over the case as a consequence of the referral made by the Security Council. Furthermore, Sudan has made no attempts of investigating the role and alleged criminal responsibility of its President for the crimes committed in Darfur. The case therefore appears *a priori* admissible.

The intense discussions following the press conference on July 14, 2008 on whether the Prosecutor should have made his application public or whether it would have been wiser to apply – in secret – for a sealed warrant and the expulsion from Darfur of more than a dozen international humanitarian organizations by the Sudanese government as an immediate reaction to the issuance of the arrest warrant[257] evidence the significant political repercussions that the decisions of the ICC have. The Prosecutor's application and the decision of the Pre-Trial Chamber underscore the fact that the ICC, as an institution, can have significant impact on key political players and that the institution should not and cannot be perceived as an exclusively judicial body. Indicting a sitting head of state will also always be perceived as a political statement.

Besides criticism regarding the potentially highly negative consequences for peace negotiations and the safety of international personnel,

---

July 2010), online: International Criminal Court <http://www.icc-cpi.int/iccdocs/doc/doc907140.pdf>.

255 See, for instance, the decision of Human Rights Watch's International Justice Program not to take a position on the question of genocide due to insufficient information on the specific question of genocidal intent. Human Rights Watch, "Sudan: ICC Warrant for Al-Bashir on Genocide" (13 July 2010), online: Human Rights Watch <http://www.hrw.org/en/news/2010/07/13/sudan-icc-warrant-al-bashir-genocide>.

256 See also above, *supra* note 115.

257 This decision left more than one million people without access to food, water and healthcare services; see UN Office for the Coordination of Humanitarian Affairs, "Sudan, Situation Report #2" (13 March 2009), online: ReliefWeb <http://www.reliefweb.int/rw/rwb.nsf/db900SID/MUMA-7Q52WN?OpenDocument>; UN News Centre, "Darfur: UN-African peacekeeper shot, as concern grows over humanitarian aid" (10 March 2009), online: UN News Centre <http://www.un.org/apps/news/story.asp?NewsID=30142&Cr=darfur&Cr1>.

which will be further analyzed below, it has also been argued that an application for a sealed warrant would have been more efficient, considering the fact that the Sudan government cannot be expected to cooperate with the ICC in this case. In Antonio Cassese's view, for instance, the warrant of arrest could have been made public once Bashir traveled to a foreign country. Now, Bashir can "simply refrain from traveling abroad and thus avoid arrest."[258] In comparison, Jean-Pierre Bemba, former Vice-President of the DRC, who was wanted for his involvement in the armed conflict in the Central African Republic, was successfully arrested by Belgian authorities in Brussels in May 2008 following the issuance of a confidential warrant.[259]

An interesting and not uncontroversial point is the immunity of Bashir as a sitting head of state. Although article 27 of the Rome Statute clearly states that nobody enjoys immunity before the court, article (98)1 provides that

> "[t]he Court may not proceed with a request for surrender or assistance which would require the requested State to act inconsistently with its obligations under international law with respect to the State or diplomatic immunity of a person or property of a third State, unless the Court can first obtain the cooperation of that third State for the waiver of the immunity."

Since the Security Council, in resolution 1593 (2005), obliged Sudan to cooperate with the Court but only *urged* all other states to do so, there are no compelling legal obligations for states – besides Sudan – to disregard Bashir's immunity. Clearly, Bashir's *procedural* immunity cannot be considered to have been implicitly removed by the Security Council through the

---

258 Antonio Cassese, "The Decision on Darfur has been Tactically Mishandled" *The Daily Star* (18 July 2008). See also Antonio Cassese, "Il colpo di scena del procuratore" *La Repubblica* (15 July 2008) [an English translation, "Flawed International Justice for Sudan", is available at <www.mediafire.com/?zyzjnofumlz>].

259 See International Criminal Court, Press Release, "ICC Arrest Jean-Pierre Bemba – massive sexual crimes in Central African Republic will not go unpunished" (24 May 2008), online: International Criminal Court <http://www2.icc-cpi.int/menus/icc/situations%20and%20cases/situations/situation%20icc%200105/related%20cases/icc%200105%200108/press%20releases/icc%20arrest%20jean_pierre%20bemba%20%E2%80%93%20massive%20sexual%20crimes%20in%20central%20african%20republic%20will%20not%20go%20unpunis>.

deferral to the ICC, as it has been suggested by some commentators.[260] The argument that one of the founding principles of international law governing inter-state relations can be implicitly removed by the Security Council cannot convince. States would therefore – from a legal perspective – have to act according to international law and respect Bashir's immunity *ratione personae*, as long as the Security Council does not make another, more explicit determination regarding Bashir's immunity.

In conclusion, the referrals of the situations of northern Uganda and Darfur to the ICC Prosecutor and their acceptance as well as, at least to some extent, the selection of cases by the Prosecutor have been guided rather by political deliberations than an interpretation faithful to the principles of international criminal justice as proclaimed in the Rome Statute. Due to the strategy of the government of Uganda and the Security Council, the ICC has been transformed into an institution that is not merely legal but also political in character. This politicization has had complex and often problematical effects on the conflicts in northern Uganda and Darfur.

260 See e.g. Dapo Akande, "The Bashir Indictment: Are Serving Heads of State Immune from ICC Prosecution?" Oxford Transitional Justice Research Working Paper Series (30 July 2008), online: University of Oxford <http://www.csls.ox.ac.uk/documents/Akande.pdf> and the discussions on the blog Opinio Juris, online: Opinion Juris <http://opiniojuris.org/2008/07/11/icc-prosecutor-to-charge-sudans-president-with-genocide/>. See also Dapo Akande, "International Law Immunities and the International Criminal Court" (2004) 98:3 A.J.I.L. 407.

Chapter 4

The effects of the ICC involvement on the conflicts – no justice without peace?

4.1. Uganda

4.1.1. Weakening the LRA leaders

A major factor in the conflict, as mentioned above, is that the LRA had become an important ally of the Sudanese government in its fight against the SPLA. In times of military offenses by the Ugandan army, the LRA could retreat to southern Sudan, where it reassembled its forces and train new "recruits" and from where it launched its incursions into Ugandan territory. Reportedly, Sudanese authorities also provided the LRA with weapons, food and medicine.[261] Cutting this strong link between the LRA and the Sudanese government had therefore become one of the key measures, arguably even a precondition, in fighting the LRA itself.

Over the years, several agreements were concluded between the governments of Uganda and Sudan. In the Nairobi Agreement of December 1999, for instance, the two governments agreed, *inter alia*, "not to harbour, sponsor or give military support or logistical support to any rebel groups".[262] In a follow-up agreement, signed in November 2000, the Sudanese government explicitly committed itself to the "relocation, disarming and disbanding of the LRA".[263] Overall, these agreements did not lead to a significant improvement of the situation. A 2001 report issued by the UN High Commissioner for Human Rights noted an "apparent cut-off of food support and reduction in military support to the LRA in the Sudan."[264] The

261 See Akhavan, "The LRA Case", *supra* note 40 at 416.

262 Cited in Commission on Human Rights, "Report of the UNHCHR", *supra* note 43 at para. 32(d).

263 *Ibid.* at para. 33(a).

264 *Ibid.* at para. 34.

report, however, also noted that compliance with the agreements "appears to be meeting some resistance from the military and security services in and around Juba."[265]

One of the major problems in pressuring the governments of Uganda and Sudan to end support for proxy rebel groups, respectively the SPLA and the LRA, was that, for decades, the conflict in northern Uganda went on largely unnoticed in the world. Powerful states did not and still do not have any political or economic interest in the region and did not condemn Khartoum for supporting the LRA.[266] The referral of the situation in northern Uganda to the ICC Prosecutor in December 2003 and the subsequent indictments mobilized the international community to a certain extent and stigmatized the LRA and its leadership. As a consequence, the government of Sudan faced increased pressure to stop sponsoring this group. The International Crisis Group noted in a report in April 2005 that "the ICC has already had a positive impact on the peace process by sobering the LRA and influencing Khartoum to reduce support."[267] Most importantly, the governments of Sudan and Uganda concluded a protocol in March 2004 – only four months after the referral to the Prosecutor – allowing the Ugandan army to penetrate Sudanese territory in order to pursue the LRA into southern Sudanese territory.[268] According to Akhavan, "[t]his unhindered access has measurably weakened the LRA's military capability [and] encouraged significant defections among LRA commanders.[269]

It seems therefore reasonable to maintain that the involvement of the ICC increased the pressure on Khartoum to end support for the LRA, which significantly weakened both the military and political strength of the rebel group.

---

265 *Ibid.* at para. 34.

266 Akhavan, "The LRA Case", *supra* note 40 at 404.

267 International Crisis Group, "Shock Therapy for Northern Uganda's Peace Process" (11 April 2005), online: International Crisis Group <http://www.crisisgroup.org/home/index.cfm?id=3366&l=1>.

268 Tim Allen, "War and Justice in Northern Uganda: An Assessment of the International Criminal Court's Intervention" (February 2005), online: Crisis States Research Centre, London School of Economics <http://www.crisisstates.com/download/others/AllenICCReport.pdf> at 23. The operation was named "Operation Iron Fist II".

269 Akhavan, "The LRA Case", *supra* note 40 at 404.

4.1.2. The ICC – between encouraging and hampering peace negotiations in northern Uganda

4.1.2.1. Bringing the rebel leaders to the negotiating table

The involvement of the ICC, together with military pressure, arguably isolated the LRA and pressured Joseph Kony and other LRA leaders to come back to the negotiating table.[270] "As the first real consequence for 20 years of LRA brutality, the ICC has already had an impact on the ground in Northern Uganda by driving the LRA into a more formal peace process."[271] It has also been argued that "[t]he threat of apprehension and prosecution presents the LRA with clear negative consequences if the peace process fails."[272]

It is clear that the ICC does not want to become a bargaining chip in any peace negotiation but must aim at remaining politically independent and faithful to its vocation as an international criminal justice institution. Yet the involvement of the Court can be valuable for peace negotiations. This reasoning is particularly clear in the case of northern Uganda and has been used by advocates as a strategic argument to induce peace negotiations. The International Crisis Group, for instance, has pressured the international community to "continue to provide strong support for prosecution and only consider asking the court to suspend its activity when and if the LRA leaders begin to implement a fair settlement."[273]

The strategic question whether the Ugandan government, and in fact the international community more generally, should try to bring the LRA leaders to the negotiating table or whether their isolation would be a more useful tactic is not new. As early as in 2001, two years before the activation of the ICC in this situation, the UN High Commissioner for Human Rights, Mary Robinson, recommended in a report on a mission of her office to northern Uganda that "[t]he international community should

---

270 Akhavan, "The LRA case", *supra* note 40 at 404. At the same time, Akhavan has also argued that "[t]he view that dialogue with fanatical murderous leaders would somehow lead to a peaceful settlement is a chimera;" *ibid.* at 419.

271 John Prendergast, "The Answer to the Lord's Resistance Army" (June 2007), online: Center for American Progress <http://www.enoughproject.org/files/publications/answer_lra.pdf> at 9.

272 ICG, "Northern Uganda: Seizing the Opportunity for Peace", *supra* note 37 at 15.

273 *Ibid.* at 15.

take the necessary steps to isolate further the top leadership of the LRA and to hold it accountable for the gross human rights violations for which it is responsible."[274] At the same time, the High Commissioner also advocated for the "amnesty and reconciliation process for persons abducted by the LRA",[275] underlining a twofold approach towards accountability for the crimes committed in the conflict: strong measures in the form of individual criminal accountability for the core LRA members; soft ones in the form of amnesty for abducted, lower-level members.

Although the ICC is not the only factor that is influential for the peace process, it is indeed striking that the most promising negotiations were held after the referral of the situation to the ICC Prosecutor and after the issuance of arrest warrants against the LRA leadership. It seems that exercising pressure on Kony and his deputies by threatening them with international trials has been a successful measure. Furthermore, due to the involvement of the ICC, the question of justice has become one of the major issues in the peace negotiations, illustrated by the conclusion in 2008 of an agreement on "accountability and reconciliation".[276] This agreement significantly contributed to the prospect that the thousands of victims of grave crimes in Uganda will see some form of justice delivered.

Despite this encouraging development, it is, however, not entirely comprehensible why the leaders of the LRA have been influenced to such an important extent by the ICC indictments. In fact, several factors seem to make LRA trials in The Hague more appealing than domestic ones. First, since the system of international criminal justice offers fair trials, which are held under the supervision of international judges, the rights of the indictees are respected according to international criteria. The Ugandan judicial system would undoubtedly also be able to hold trials in the case of the LRA leaders, but the safeguards regarding the protection of the rights of the accused as well as other factors, such as the probably higher threshold to establish command responsibility under international criminal law, are likely to be disadvantageous for the LRA leaders if exclusively domestic trials were being held. Second, the heaviest penalty under the Rome Statute is life punishment, while the Ugandan criminal code contains the death penalty.

274 Commission on Human Rights, "Report of the UNHCHR", *supra* note 43 at para. 80.

275 *Ibid.* at para. 79.

276 See *supra* note 72.

A good reason for the LRA leaders to strongly oppose the ICC might be their reduced possibility of obtaining a negotiated solution if they surrender and stand trial in The Hague. One might think that the LRA leaders see the ICC as an unmovable institution that wants to put them on trial, no matter if and when a peace deal is concluded. In this regard, the ICC cannot be a favorable option for them. Compared to the somewhat rigid forum of international criminal justice that the ICC represents, the Ugandan system presents itself as much more flexible, with alternative, traditional justice mechanisms being negotiable.

4.1.2.2. Endangering the peace process and prolonging the suffering of the victims

> "[T]he compatibility of trials against LRA leaders with efforts to end the conflict in northern Uganda remains controversial."[277]

At the same time of *stimulating* peace negotiations, the ICC involvement has subsequently also *delayed* the peace process. In short, the ICC has helped to set off promising peace negotiations to solve the conflict in northern Uganda, but it has since been a major obstacle to conclude these negotiations. Several problems can be identified.

First, negotiating peace with individuals who are facing trial is generally a problematical matter. Possible prosecutions are likely to represent an obstacle to the conclusion of a peace agreement. Moreover, it has often been argued that amnesty offers can be an indispensable element in peace negotiations. Governments have used this tool in order to raise the probability of stopping an ongoing conflict or to secure the transition from a dictatorial regime to a democratic form of rule of law. Furthermore, in certain situations the prospect of prosecution arguably creates a "nothing-to-lose"-attitude among the leaders of belligerent groups, with the result that conflicts last longer than they would have to.

The Ugandan situation reflects these political concerns very well. In 2006, rather promising peace negotiations started in Juba, South Sudan. Analysts noted that at that point both the Ugandan government and the leadership of the LRA were "devoted and ready to reach a nonviolent conclusion of the 21-year old insurgency".[278] The lengthy negotiations, however,

---

277 Akhavan, "The LRA Case", *supra* note 40 at 405.

278 Yusuf Kiranda, "Juba Peace Talks Collapse, A Golden Opportunity for

revealed that the question of the ICC indictments has been a very controversial issue, not so say the most controversial issue. In the end, disagreement over the question of providing justice, whether in The Hague or before a domestic forum, blocked the signing of the final document.

Spokespersons of peace initiatives in northern Uganda, such as the Acholi Religious Leaders Peace Initiative (ARLPI), have broadly condemned the "interference" of the ICC and have argued that peace will be even more difficult to achieve because of the ICC involvement: "Obviously, nobody can convince the leaders of a rebel movement to come to the negotiating table and at the same time tell them that they will appear in courts to be prosecuted."[279] The ARLPI has suggested that it would be wiser to have "peace first and the justice later on" and that the ICC involvement would prevent the rebels from accepting the amnesty offer.[280] Since the referral of the situation to the ICC Prosecutor, the Ugandan government has also become more and more reluctant to support the ICC. As explored above, the government initially aimed to raise awareness about the conflict on the international scene by activating the ICC, thus increasing the political pressure on the LRA leaders. Since then, it has been trying to convince the Prosecutor to drop or at least suspend the indictments to enable the conclusion of a peace agreement and traditional forms of justice and reconciliation in northern Uganda.[281]

Second, the ICC has been criticized for having a negative impact on the peace process, which goes further than this rather simple and now almost classic "peace versus justice" debate. Because of its one-sided

Peace is Slipping through our Hands", Konrad-Adenauer-Stiftung (12 June 2008), online: Konrad-Adenauer-Stiftung <http://www.kas.de/proj/home/pub/36/1/dokument_id-13956/index.html>.

279 Father Carlos Rodriguez of the Acholi Religious Leaders Peace Initiative, cited in: Adam Branch, "International Justice, Local Injustice" *Dissent Magazine* (Summer 2004), online: Dissent Magazine <http://www.dissent-magazine.org/article/?article=336> [Branch, "International Justice, Local Injustice"].

280 See Will Ross, "Ugandans Ask ICC to Spare Rebels" *BBC News* (16 March 2005), online: BBC <http://news.bbc.co.uk/2/hi/africa/4352901.stm>.

281 See UN Office for the Coordination of Humanitarian Affairs, "UGANDA: Locals want rebel leader forgiven" (7 December 2006), online: IRIN <http://www.irinnews.org/report.aspx?reportid=59805> [OCHA, "UGANDA"]; see also "Peace or Justice?" *Guardian Weekly* (10 January 2007), online: Guardian Unlimited <http://www.guardian.co.uk/guardianweekly/story/0,,1987173,00.html>.

approach in targeting exclusively the LRA leaders, which will be analyzed in more depth below, the ICC has arguably closed many doors to achieve a negotiated agreement. According to Branch,

> "by criminalizing the LRA leadership, the ICC denies the rebels the possibility of political relevance or of becoming a political force. Their leaders are to be hunted down and captured, and the rest of the LRA is to disintegrate. [...] It denies that the existence of the LRA is a symptom of deeper national problems that would require a political solution involving the LRA, the Ugandan government, and the various political and social factions among the Acholi."[282]

This argument, which goes beyond the simpler notion of "interference", underlines once again that the "peace versus justice" debate is oversimplifying and cannot grasp the complexities and dynamics of a conflict. Although the LRA cannot be considered as a political force legitimately representing the Acholi people and other marginalized groups in northern Uganda, it is certainly true that the ICC has contributed to reducing the armed conflict in the north to a fight between a "criminal" group and the armed forces of a government. Despite the fact that no trial has been held and no judgment has been delivered against the LRA leaders, the indictments have somehow legitimized military efforts of the Ugandan government against the LRA. As a by-product, the crimes committed by the Ugandan army have largely been neglected. Another unfortunate consequence of the ICC involvement is that political demands of the people living in the marginalized regions in the north have been sidelined and overshadowed by international justice concerns.

Third, the ICC indictments definitely led to some confusion in northern Uganda about whether members of the LRA could still trust the government when accepting the amnesty program or whether they would be sent to The Hague after surrendering. Some statements from ICC officials and the ICC outreach program have contributed to clarifying the situation. Traditional leaders from northern Uganda, for instance, asked the Prosecutor in a joint press release that "whoever has already benefited from amnesty will not be investigated or prosecuted by the ICC."[283] The

282 Branch, "Uganda's Civil War", *supra* note 44 at 191.

283 International Criminal Court, Press Release, "Statements by ICC Chief Prosecutor and the Visiting Delegation of Acholi Leaders from northern Uganda" (18 March 2005), online: International Criminal Court <http://

Prosecutor, who could naturally not provide blanket promises not to proceed in certain cases, replied that he was "mindful of traditional justice and reconciliation processes."[284] Moreover, empirical research has shown hat the ICC has neither significantly furthered nor hindered the acceptance of amnesty. Allen has argued that he "found no evidence that the ICC intervention has actually undermined the process".[285] Rather, the ICC might have convinced a number of people to come out of the bush and accept the amnesty offer in order to avoid prosecution.[286]

Fourth, in addition to the confusion about its respect of the national amnesty law, the ICC has also been criticized for its stance on the amnesty process itself. Although the Ugandan Amnesty Act is inconsistent with the requirements of the Rome Statute, since it only requires a former combatant to report to an official and to surrender his weapons,[287] thus granting a quasi-unconditional amnesty, the ICC has been accused for not dealing with the amnesty law in a very sensitive manner.

> "The ICC irresponsibly frames the Amnesty Act not as the product of mobilization by the Acholi trying to find peace and duly promulgated by the Ugandan Parliament, but as a gift from the Ugandan executive, to be withdrawn by President Museveni at his convenience."[288]

Following this line of argument, the ICC could have, at least, recognized the Amnesty Act as a negotiated and potentially constructive means to achieve peace in Uganda, which should not be revoked in a unilateral move by the Ugandan government but only in cooperation with the legislative branch and civil society. The ICC's standpoint has unduly strengthened the position of the Ugandan government both *vis-à-vis* the LRA and those traditional and religious leaders who still believe in and advocate for the amnesty program as a non-violent way to end the war and peacefully reintegrate former members of the LRA into society.

---

www2.icc-cpi.int/NR/exeres/2B9064A4-9944-4A55-8123-1B62B0634239.htm>.

284 *Ibid.*

285 Allen, *supra* note 37 at 124.

286 *Ibid.*

287 For more information on the Amnesty Act, see Refugee Law Project, *supra* note 53.

288 Branch, "Uganda's Civil War", *supra* note 44 at 184.

Fifth, another important question besides the one on the ICC's impact on the peace negotiations is whether the ICC has increased and prolonged the risks for civilians to suffer from LRA violence. After the referral to the ICC Prosecutor, it was widely feared that the LRA, well-known for committing revenge massacres among the civilian population for alleged cooperation with the Ugandan government,[289] would start a brutal campaign against civilians. It was also for this reason that the referral to the ICC was heavily criticized, with peace activists arguing that an unconditional amnesty for the LRA leadership would be an indispensable requirement to maintain the truce and protect civilians in northern Uganda.[290]

4.1.3. Delivering one-sided "justice"

One of the basic principles of criminal justice goes back to the very meaning of the word "justice", which implies fairness and impartiality. The objective of any forum involved in the delivery of justice should therefore be to provide equitable justice, without taking sides. The ICC must also endeavor to appear as independent as possible in order to remain a credible and respected institution, perhaps even more so because of its inherent link to political organs.

The acceptance of voluntary referrals by States Parties which want to deal with international crimes committed by rebel groups inevitably gives room for perceptions of one-sided justice. As a result, the image of an independent and impartial prosecutor in this situation might be affected.[291] In the situation of Uganda, the Prosecutor clearly did not combat such perceptions from the beginning. Most notably, the press conference to announce the referral of the situation in northern Uganda was held together with President Museveni, which made the ICC look like a political instrument of the Ugandan government. Subsequently, only rebel leaders were targeted by the Prosecutor, although efforts have been made to underline that crimes committed by the Ugandan army have also been under examination by the Prosecutor's office.[292] It has even been speculated

289 See Allen, *supra* note 37 at 103.

290 See e.g. Branch, "International Justice, Local Injustice", *supra* note 279.

291 See also Human Rights Watch, "Courting History, The Landmark International Criminal Court's First Five Years" (July 2008), online: Human Rights Watch <http://hrw.org/reports/2008/icc0708/icc0708web.pdf> at 41 [HRW, "Courting History"].

292 ICC, "Address to the ASP", *supra* note 36 at 4.

that the OTP actively planned to indict members of the UPDF;[293] so far, these speculations have not materialized in any document issued by the ICC.

The fact that only the crimes committed by one side of the conflict seem to have been seriously investigated by the OTP is certainly difficult to accept for many victims. As Human Rights Watch has noted,

> "Representatives of civil society and community-based organizations that we [Human Rights Watch] interviewed in Kampala and northern Uganda in March 2007 consistently criticized the ICC's failure to either investigate and prosecute UPDF [Uganda People's Defence Force] abuses or to explain why this was not being done."[294]

Moreover, ICC investigators have relied on logistical support form the Ugandan government and have used government vehicles and officials to carry out parts of the investigations.[295] As a State Party, Uganda is certainly duty-bound to cooperate with the ICC and provide such support. In the case of northern Uganda, however, this support seems to have benefited only the investigatory work into crimes committed by the LRA. The fact that ICC investigators openly relied on logistical support from the government did not add to the perception of the ICC as a neutral institution in the eyes of the people in northern Uganda.

The sequencing strategy of the Prosecutor has also fuelled the suspicion that only the crimes of one side have been thoroughly investigated. Although, according to the OTP, investigating one group at a time is more cost-efficient and less risky for the investigatory teams on the ground, this strategy further delays the whole investigatory process and may create wrong perceptions of selective justice.[296] In another situation before the ICC, namely the DRC, the problem of sequencing and the subsequent delays in investigating the crimes committed by certain groups created significant damage to the credibility of the ICC, as noted by Human Rights Watch.[297] The sequencing strategy is also directly opposite to the politically

293 According to Allen, at least one warrant of arrest had already been prepared in 2005; Allen, *supra* note 37 at 100.

294 HRW, "Courting History", *supra* note 291 at 42. For similar arguments, see Allen, *supra* note 37 at 98-99.

295 Allen, *supra* note 37 at 97.

296 For more information, see HRW, "Courting History" *supra* note 291 at 51.

297 *Ibid.* at 64.

more sensitive "initial proportion strategy"[298], a more pragmatic approach that will be further analyzed below.

4.2. Darfur

4.2.1. Increasing the pressure on key players

A prelude to future ICC indictments occurred in April 2006. Security Council Resolution 1672 named four individuals allegedly responsible for crimes committed in Darfur and imposed travel sanctions on them, as stipulated in Security Council Resolution 1591.[299] The four individuals were Major General Gaffar Mohamed Elhassan, a commander of the Sudanese army, the well-known leader of the Jalul Tribe Musa Hilal, the SLA-commander Adam Yacub Shant, and Gabril Abdul Kareem Badri, a commander of the National Movement for Reform and Development. By choosing individuals from the different warring parties, the Security Council tried not to openly take sides in the conflict. This was a noteworthy step, but the Security Council did not target the root of the problems by stigmatizing political leaders, in particular members of the Sudanese government. Although some feared that the sanctions would have negative effects on the peace talks, others, such as the United States argued that it would, in fact, strengthen the political and diplomatic process.[300] In any case, the adoption of Resolution 1672 did not change Khartoum's attitude towards Darfur and did not have any significant impact.

With the activation of the ICC, a new, potentially compelling player had become involved in Darfur with the possibility of targeting the key players. The following section will analyze the possible effects of the ICC involvement on those players who have shaped the ongoing conflict in Darfur. Some of the effects of the activity of the ICC are or might turn out to be similar to the ones in the situation of northern Uganda, in particular with respect to influencing the peace process. Other effects are utterly different due to the openly hostile attitude of the Sudanese government towards the ICC.

---

298 See below, c. 4.2.3.

299 S/RES/1672 (2006) at para. 3.

300 See Moghalu, *supra* note 26 at 154.

4.2.1.1. Weakening the government of Sudan

The Sudanese government[301] seems to be a perfect target for the ICC. Since the political leaders exercise effective control over the army, the violations of international humanitarian law and human rights law committed by the regular Sudanese army are directly attributable to government officials.[302] As individual criminal responsibility according to article 25 of the Rome Statute is difficult to establish for senior government officials,[303] the focus here will be on the responsibility of superiors according to article 28. The President of Sudan, for instance, exercises *de jure* authority over the army; according to the 1998 Sudanese constitution, which was in force until July 2005, the President is "responsible for the command of the armed forces and other organized forces."[304] He is "Commander in Chief of the Armed Forces" according to the 2005 Interim National Constitution.[305] Due to the extremely hierarchical political and military organization in Sudan, *de facto* control of senior government officials over the army can also be assumed. This reasoning corresponds to the one made in the *Celebici* case, in which the ICTY judges ruled that *de jure* or *de facto* possession of powers or control over subordinates was sufficient to qualify a civilian as a superior.[306]

---

301 It should be mentioned that parts of the coalition forming the national government since 2005 are supportive of the ICC, namely members of the SPLA. Most notably, in 2008, foreign minister Deng Alor advocated for the government's compliance with its international obligations and cooperation with the ICC; see Wasil Ali, "Feature: Justice a Threat to Peace in Darfur?" *Sudan Tribune* (30 June 2008), online: Sudan Tribune <http://sudantribune.com/spip.php?article27689>.

302 This assumption can, however, not be made without the remark that it is one thing to know pretty well what has been going on, but another one to establish responsibility of superiors and prove beyond reasonable doubt effective control of superiors over their subordinates.

303 However, contribution to the commission of crimes according to article 25(3)(d) might be conceivable.

304 *Constitution of the Republic of Sudan 1998*, trans. by Curtis Francis Doebbler, online: International Committee of the Red Cross <http://www.icrc.org/ihl-nat.nsf/162d151af4 44ded44125673e00508141/d728f18be88d9482c1256dc60 0507f33/$FILE/Constitution%20Sudan%20-%20EN.pdf> at article 42.

305 *Constitution of the Republic of Sudan 2005*, online: Sudantribune.com <http://www.sudantribune.com/IMG/pdf/20050316_SUDAN_DRAFT_CONSTITUTIONAL_TEXT.pdf> at article 65(a).

306 *Prosecutor v. Zejnil Delalic et al. (Celebici)*, IT-96-21-T (Judgment, 16

Regarding the mental element, according to article 28(b)(i) of the Rome Statute, a non-military superior is criminally responsible for crimes committed by subordinates if he "either knew, or consciously disregarded information which clearly indicated, that the subordinates were committing or about to commit such crimes." Although the threshold is higher than for military commanders, it would be enough to prove that members of the government knew about or were willfully blind regarding the atrocities committed by the Sudanese troops in Darfur.[307]

Members of the government can also be considered responsible for crimes committed by the *Janjaweed*, which is consistent with the concept of control established by the ICTY Appeals Chamber in *Tadic*:

> "In order to attribute the acts of a military or paramilitary group to a State, it must be proved that the State wields overall control over the group, not only by equipping and financing the group, but also by coordinating or helping in the general planning of its military activity."[308]

When attacks are carried out jointly by the Sudanese army and the militia, the latter are under the effective control of government officials, thus acting as *de facto* agents of the Sudanese state.[309]

Moreover, political considerations of the government of Sudan are an obstacle to a peaceful resolution of the conflict. Peace in Western Sudan might further the creation of a common political front in Darfur, which could have threatened the central government's reelection in the elections

---

November 1998) (International Criminal Tribunal for the former Yugoslavia, Trial Chamber) at para. 370.

307 For a more profound analysis of the "willfully blind" standard for non-military superiors of the Rome Statute, see Kai Ambos, "Superior Responsibility" in Antonio Cassese, Paola Gaeta & John R.W.D. Jones, eds., *The Rome Statute of the International Criminal Court: A Commentary* (Oxford: Oxford University Press, 2002) 823 at 870. The ICC civilian standard is higher than the standard of the *ad hoc* tribunals; see Greg R. Vetter, "Command Responsibility of Non-Military Superiors in the International Criminal Court (ICC)" (2000) 25 Yale J. Int'l L. 89 at 123.

308 *Prosecutor v. Dusko Tadic*, IT-94-1-A (Judgment, 15 July 1999) (International Criminal Tribunal for the former Yugoslavia, Appeals Chamber) at para. 131.

309 See also UNCOI, *supra* note 96 at para. 123.

scheduled for late 2009.[310] An insecure situation in the West is therefore important for the political survival of Bashir's National Congress Party. Weakening, if not overthrowing, the regime in Khartoum seems to be a prerequisite to lasting peace in Darfur.

The political history of numerous countries has shown that regime change was a necessary precondition to start prosecutions or other accountability mechanisms to deal with the crimes of the past.[311] This was the case with the TRC in South Africa, the ICTR in Rwanda and the hybrid tribunal in Cambodia to try the Khmer Rouge.[312] The situation in Sudan is radically different. At the moment, nothing indicates a possible regime change or overthrow of the Islamist government,[313] which is in power since the 1989 coup. Its position can even be considered to have been strengthened by the international community's negotiation strategy to achieve peace for the South, while holding government officials individually account-

---

310 ICG, "Darfur: Revitalising the Peace Process", *supra* note 127 at 6. As the 2005 Interim Constitution states, "[g]eneral elections at all levels of government shall be held no later than the end of the fourth year of the Interim Period", in other words at the latest in 2009; see article 216, *Constitution of the Republic of Sudan 2005*, *supra* note 305. The elections, which were boycotted by Bashir's two main challengers, were finally held in April 2010. See "President Omar al-Bashir declared winner of Sudan poll" *BBC News* (26 April 2010), online: BBC <http://news.bbc.co.uk/2/hi/africa/8643602.stm>.

311 See Rosanna Lipscomb, "Restructuring the ICC Framework to Advance Transitional Justice: A Search for a Permanent Solution in Sudan" (2006) 106 Colum. L. Rev. 182 at 191.

312 Although established while the conflict was still going on in Bosnia, the ICTY also delivered mainly *ex post facto* justice; see above, c. 1.2.

313 One must be careful in labeling the current regime as "Islamist", in particular since the removal of the leader of the Sudanese Islamist movement, Hassan al Turabi, from official powers in 1999/2000. Despite this transformation, it is clear that the Sudanese state remains devoted to an Islamist neo-fundamentalism; see Alex de Waal & A.H. Abdel Salam, "Islamism, State Power and *Jihad* in Sudan" in Alex de Waal, ed., *Islamism and Its Enemies in the Horn of Africa* (Bloomington: Indiana University Press, 2004) 71 at 113. Therefore, the term "Islamist" seems appropriate, although the Islamist model of the current government is radically different from the model of political Islam conceived by Turabi. For more information on the important influence of Turabi on Sudanese politics in the 1980s and 1990s, see *ibid.* at 75.

able seemed to be a less important concern for a long time.[314] Despite this political unwillingness of the international community to exercise genuine pressure on the government of Sudan for its Darfur policy, the ICC has the potential to stigmatize the top leaders. The effects should not be underestimated, since, as it has been argued, "stigmatization eventually contributes to the loss of power and influence on the part of leaders, especially those who can no longer act as representatives on the international stage."[315] Ultimately, successful prosecutions could provoke a regime change in Khartoum.

There is evidence that the government of Sudan and its politics are susceptible to international action. In the case of Darfur, the reactions to offers of humanitarian aid, to the Security Council intervention and to the ICC involvement show that Khartoum is far from being indifferent to possible negative consequences of an international condemnation of the regime. The government's discourse has rather been marked by important efforts to avoid such a condemnation.[316] Precedents to the reactions in the Darfur case underline the effectiveness of international pressure on the present government. In 1996, a Chapter VII resolution by the Security Council imposed travel sanctions on members of the government and the armed forces and obliged all countries to "significantly reduce the level and number of staff at Sudanese diplomatic missions and consular posts and restrict or control the movement within their territory of such who remain,"[317] in order to pressure the government to surrender the three men suspected of having attempted to assassinate Egyptian president Hosni Mubarak.[318] Although the suspects were never extradited, these diplomatic sanctions had an immediate impact on Khartoum's policy, in particular with respect to its support for terrorists. Numerous foreign extremists, including Osama bin Laden and dozens of Egyptian Islamists, were asked to leave the country shortly after Resolution 1054 had been adopt-

314 See also Lipscomb, *supra* note 311 at 192. In early 2009, the situation had not changed significantly due to the possible indictment of President Bashir.

315 Akhavan, "The Yugoslav Tribunal", *supra* note 12 at 272.

316 For more details, see Castillo, *supra* note 108 at 175.

317 S/RES/1054 (1996). It is interesting to note that, probably due to their lightness, the sanctions did not strengthen the regime in Khartoum, thus standing in sharp contrast to the situations in Iraq and Libya; see Tim Niblock, *"Pariah States" & Sanctions in the Middle East, Iraq, Libya, Sudan* (Boulder, Colo.: Lynne Rienner Publishers, 2001) at 213.

318 For more information on these sanctions, see *ibid.* at 204.

ed.[319] According to Tim Niblock, a specialist of the politics of the Arab and Islamic worlds, the regime's tendency for ideological expansionism has also been curtailed as a result of the sanctions.[320]

One can therefore conclude with an Egyptian expert of Sudanese politics that proactive steps taken by the international community, even if only in the form of light diplomatic sanctions, should not be dismissed as an illusionary hope in the case of Darfur:

> "La pression n'est pas inutile car, sur un autre terrain, les sanctions internationales en matière de terrorisme ont effectivement provoqué au Soudan l'arrêt du projet de l'Internationale islamiste du Dr Turabi et le départ de dirigeants islamistes qui financent les actions terroristes dans le monde, tel Oussama Ben Laden, en mai 1996."[321]

Since Khartoum has shown in the past that its policies have been influenced by concerted international action, such as sanctions, threats to indict senior members of the government should certainly be influential. Even though the ICC's potential impact is therefore extremely valuable, the inability to apprehend the indicted persons might be the most important obstacle for the ICC to have any direct effects on both the political and the militia leaders, since the ICC cannot count on the cooperation of the present regime. Nevertheless, there is evidence that the indictment of Ahmad Harun, who remains the current Minister of State for Humanitarian Affairs, provoked certain effects. If Harun presently enjoys a peaceful life in Sudan, it seems possible that he will be sacrificed by the top of the government. In the words of an Arab tribal leader, "he knows

---

319 *Ibid.* at 212.

320 *Ibid.* at 217.

321 ["The pressure is not useless because, in another field, international sanctions with respect to terrorism actually made Sudan stop the international Islamist project of Dr Turabi and led to the departure of Islamist leaders like Osama bin Laden, who finance global terrorism, in May 1996."] Didar Fawzy-Rossano, *Le Soudan en question* (Paris: Éditions de la Table Ronde, 2002) at 262. For a different and more nuanced view of the failure of Hassan al Turabi's political Islam in Sudan, see de Waal & Abdel Salam, *supra* note 313 at 106, who argue that divisions between Turabi and Bashir were insinuated throughout the 1990s. In short, de Waal and Abdel Salam describe the 1999/2000 split between Turabi and Bashir as "entirely self-inflicted" and the dispute as "simply over power;" see *ibid.* at 108.

that he may have little time."[322] Moreover, Harun lives under the imminent threat of being handed over to the ICC if he travels abroad. In 2008 he reportedly cancelled a trip to Mecca fearing that he would end up in The Hague.[323]

Furthermore, even without any cooperation of the Sudanese government and without the option that a multinational force be clearly mandated to arrest indictees in Sudan, more subtle effects than mere incapacitation are conceivable. The activity of the ICC can have an important influence on diminishing support for the government among the Sudanese population. Since the beginning of the ICC involvement in the situation of Sudan, critical voices towards the National Congress Party have become louder, as various newspaper articles and editorials show. A March 18, 2007 editorial in the daily newspaper *The Citizen*, for instance, condemned the support for the *Janjaweed* and called the Sudanese government "a racist regime that is in many respects worse than the apartheid regime in South Africa, which at least had the dignity not to employ rape as a tactic of suppression."[324] This is an important development, since the government had initially felt powerful enough to suspend independent newspapers, such as the Arabic-language *Al-Ayam* and the English-language *Khartoum Monitor*, or to close *Al-Jazeera* in Sudan after it had reported the atrocities in Darfur.[325] By showing the criminal face of the Sudanese government, the ICC can, therefore, significantly contribute to weakening the regime in Khartoum in the long run. According to experts of the Sudanese political system, it is also because of the ICC indictments that the NCP took the 2010 elections very seriously and mounted a genuine election campaign.

322 Cited in Maggie Farley, "Darfur War Crimes Suspect Has Free Rein Despite ICC Warrants" *Los Angeles Times* (5 August 2007).

323 The ICC had apparently convinced one of Sudan's neighboring countries to divert Harun's airplane and arrest him on its territory. "Sudan rejects calls to hand over 2 wanted by ICC for their role in Darfur crisis" *Associated Press* (7 June 2008), available online at: Sudan.Net <http://www.sudan.net/news/posted/16044.html>.

324 Cited in Reporters Without Borders, *supra* note 141 at 8.

325 Flint & de Waal, *supra* note 86 at 115. Unfortunately, arrests of Sudanese editors and column writers increased in spring 2007; in May 2007, all media coverage related to the Darfurian rebel movements was temporarily banned by the Sudanese government; see International Crisis Group, "A Strategy for Comprehensive Peace in Sudan" (26 July 2007), online: International Crisis Group <http://www.crisisgroup.org/home/index.cfm?id=4961&l=1> at 7.

The government of Sudan also seemed to acknowledge that an overly rigid policy would only win the voices of some of Khartoum's hardliners but not the elections.[326]

Despite this pressure that is being exercised by the ICC, weakening the Sudanese government seems a difficult task as a matter of fact. In addition to the long-lasting negotiation strategy of the United Nations to give more emphasis to the peace process in southern Sudan and the indecisiveness of the international community to tackle the Darfur crisis, the strong position of the government is due to three mostly internal factors. Oil revenues secure a permanent income that serves to build up the army, which is today one of the strongest in the region; there is no viable internal opposition to the regime; and the central government is protected by the geographical vastness of the country.[327] A military intervention into Darfur by an international force would require enormous resources.

In short, Security Council Resolution 1593 obliged Sudan to cooperate with the ICC, but, so far, the government has not had to face any stringent consequences for its non-compliance. Its powerful allies in the world are apparently still determined to prevent the Security Council from taking more decisive action. Severe economic sanctions (according to article 41 of the UN Charter) or a military operation (according to article 42 of the UN Charter) against the will of the Sudanese government are, at least under the current circumstances, not realistic. China and Russia are likely to block any invasive measure to be taken by the Security Council due to economic considerations, while the Islamic Conference, the Arab League and other traditionally anti-US and anti-Israel organizations and states support Sudan for ideological reasons.[328] Furthermore, the Sudanese government is aware that the United States does not have the political and material resources to launch another major war as long as the military engagements in Iraq and Afghanistan persist and that Europeans are "not ready to die for Darfur".[329]

---

326 Interview of Annette Weber, researcher at the German Institute for International and Security Affairs (3 July 2007).

327 Collins, *supra* note 89 at 22.

328 In addition to China, Malaysia and India have also heavily invested in the Sudanese oil sector; see e.g. Jean-Paul Marthoz, "Le Soudan, pays de tous les enjeux" (2006) 14 Enjeux Internationaux 13 at 14.

329 "[L]les Européens ne sont pas prêts à mourir pour le Darfur," *ibid.* at 15 [trans. by author].

From a realistic point of view, the ICC cannot be expected to have a major immediate impact on the position of the Sudanese government in the current circumstances, but it is more than just a "symbolic act that can bring Khartoum in need to explain."[330] Members of the government have clearly become more anxious since the Security Council referral and in particular since the Prosecutor's application for an arrest warrant against President Bashir. The possibility that someone will be surrendered to the ICC is a reality. A Sudan Tribune commentator noted in June 2008 that "[a]ccording to a senior official, the leadership 'is getting very nervous' and considers surrendering Ahmad Harun and Ali Kushayb to shield itself from further indictments."[331] In sum, in addition to contributing significantly to a gradual shift from a climate of complete impunity to accountability for grave crimes in Sudan, the ICC involvement has the potential to significantly weaken the position of the Sudanese government, thus being an important factor in bringing about change to Khartoum's policy toward Darfur.

4.2.1.2. Pressuring the Sudanese government to cut support for the Janjaweed

If the Sudanese government cannot be easily targeted in a direct manner through the ICC involvement, it can, however, be incited to change its policy in Darfur. Thanks to the ICC and the preliminary work of the Commission of Inquiry, crimes committed by the Sudanese army and the *Janjaweed* against the Fur, the Masalit and the Zaghawa have been documented and made known to the international society. Khartoum's method of arming and supporting the militias, allowing them to murder, rape, and pillage with guaranteed impunity, has been particularly criticized. The government knows that its Darfur policy is now closely followed by foreign governments and international human rights organizations and that it must show some good will to maintain or regain certain credibility. To save the situation, or at least to appear in a better light, the government is likely to cut its support for the *Janjaweed*. As shown above, there is evidence that the government is susceptible to pressure exercised through the channel of the ICC. In the case of northern Uganda, the activation of the

330 Jochen Stahnke, "Erste Kriegsverbrecher benannt" [First War Criminals Named] *Die Zeit* (28 February 2007), online: Die Zeit <http://www.zeit.de/online/2007/09/ICC-Darfur> (trans. by author).

331 Ali, *supra* note 301.

ICC increased the pressure on Khartoum to end support for the LRA, which had found a safe harbor in southern Sudan. If the government had to change its policy in the case of the LRA, it is also conceivable that continuing to support militias within its own boundaries will become unbearable as a consequence of the ICC involvement.

Leaders of the *Janjaweed* themselves have also acted in response to the ICC involvement. They apparently began to fear being used as scapegoats and being blamed by the Sudanese government as the ones responsible for the crimes committed in Darfur since 2003. At the present time, it does not seem realistic that Khartoum seriously considers cooperating with the ICC; but should the government give in to the international pressure and take one step in this direction, it is likely that militia leaders will be "sacrificed". Under these circumstances, it is not surprising that some militia groups are no longer loyal to the government and have started to fight side by side with the rebels against the Sudanese army.[332]

Even though it is encouraging for advocates of international criminal justice that the involvement of the ICC seems to have had its first measurable positive effect on the conflict in Darfur, the *Janjaweed* issue is, however, extremely complex. Several other factors are at least as important as the ICC threat. Generally, there is no clear frontline in Darfur. The rebel groups have split, with some of them developing from organized armed groups which fight the central government into armed bandits whose fighting patterns and attacks on civilians are now similar to those of the *Janjaweed*.[333] It is also doubtful that Khartoum can still exercise control over the militia leaders and somehow manage the situation. Disarming the *Janjaweed* would be a highly difficult task.[334] Moreover, the decreasing loyalty of some militia leaders is not very surprising and is not necessarily linked to possible trials of militia leaders in The Hague. According to Alex de Waal, the economic relationships between Arabs and non-Arabs have been so close in Western Sudan that, "given enough time they are likely

332 Perry, *supra* note 150.

333 Adam Wolfe, "China Claims Success on Darfur", Power and Interest News Report (24 April 2007), online: PINR <http://www.pinr.com/report.php?ac=view_report&report_id=643&language_id=1>.

334 See e.g. Flint & de Waal, *supra* note 86 at 122. "Forcible disarmament of the *Janjaweed* is almost certainly impossible," *ibid.* at 127; see also Jérôme Tubiana, "Le Darfur: un conflit identitaire?" (2005) 214 Afrique Contemporaine 165 at 175.

to make common cause against the government."[335] Presumptions that the ICC is the cause for certain actions of the warring parties should, therefore, be made with awareness of the multifaceted dynamics of the conflict.

4.2.1.3. Bringing the rebel leaders to the negotiating table

Even though it is unquestionable that most crimes in Darfur have been committed by the Sudanese army and the *Janjaweed*, the conflict is not only black-and-white. Rebels have reportedly also targeted the civilian population and looted civilian property[336] as well as attacked and raped aid workers,[337] acts that amount to war crimes and crimes against humanity as defined in the Rome Statute. Civilians reportedly call Minni Minawi's troops "Janjaweed 2".[338] For a long time, the international community barely acknowledged this fact. Yet it should be noted that one SLA-commander was among the four individuals against whom travel sanctions were imposed by Security Council Resolution 1672, and that there are also speculations that some of the SLA and JEM leaders are on the sealed list of the Commission of Inquiry.[339]

More recently, some methods of war employed by rebel groups have also been criticized and condemned by the international community. Examples include the rebel attack in May 2008 on Khartoum's twin city Omdurman, in which the JEM allegedly used child soldiers,[340] and the attack on AMIS peacekeepers in North Darfur in September 2007. In November 2008, the Prosecutor requested the issuance of arrest warrants against three rebel leaders allegedly responsible for this attack, without publicizing their names.[341] Five of the major rebel groups made an important statement after this announcement, affirming their intention to coop-

335 Cited in Lydia Polgreen, "Militia Talks Could Reshape Conflict in Darfur" *New York Times* (15 April 2007).

336 In early 2005, hundreds of rebels had already shown "abusive behavior"; see Flint & de Waal, *supra* note 86 at 88.

337 "Sudan 'Backs UN-led Darfur Force'" *BBC News* (18 June 2007), online: BBC <http://news.bbc.co.uk/2/hi/africa/6760781.stm>.

338 ICG, "Darfur: Revitalising the Peace Process", *supra* note 127 at 8, note 45.

339 According to Flint and de Waal, seven of the 51 individuals named are rebel leaders; see Flint & de Waal, *supra* note 86 at 132.

340 UN SC, "Report of the Secretary-General on the Deployment", *supra* note 143 at para. 51.

341 ICC, "Eighth Report of the Prosecutor", *supra* note 116 at paras. 52-55.

erate with the ICC even if the Court might indict members of their own groups.[342] Moreover, members of the rebel groups seem to acknowledge the fact that some of their leaders are probably on the list of the Commission of Inquiry and risk to be indicted by the ICC, as evidenced by Abu Garda, who is indicted for his role in the 2007 attack on AMIS peacekeepers and who appeared before the Court in May 2009.[343]

Looking at the personal background and the strategies of the rebel leaders helps to understand the possible impact of the ICC threat on them and how it affects the dynamics of the conflict. The leaders of the SLA and the JEM mostly have a different background than the people they represent. Having lived in cities far away from their traditional homeland, leaders like Minni Minawi and Abdelwahed Mohamed Nur were educated in Arabic or English[344] or, such as in the case of SLA's most prominent Masalit commander Khamis Abakir, have lived abroad for many years.[345] Moreover, JEM's leaders are politically and diplomatically experienced, since several of them, like Dr Khalil Ibrahim, had been part of the National Islamic Front government or were educated in Europe.[346] They are susceptible to international pressure to negotiate as well as to pressure from the ICC. Indicting rebel leaders could therefore lead to similar – or even more positive – effects as in the case of the LRA.[347]

Contrary to the indictments against members of the Sudanese government and the *Janjaweed*, targeting rebel leaders has not been perceived as an obstacle to peace negotiations. The rebels know that they are not immune from indictments, but they are certain that the crimes committed by government troops and the *Janjaweed* are much more serious than those rebel leaders could be held responsible for. Overall, some rebel factions are, at least for the time being, a supporting force for the ICC that are, at the same time, also susceptible to pressure exercised through the ICC.

---

342 See *ibid.* at para. 57.

343 International Criminal Court, "Case Information Sheet, The Prosecutor v. Bahr Idriss Abu Garda", ICC-02/05-02/09 (16 October 2009), online: International Criminal Court <http://www.icc-cpi.int/NR/rdonlyres/BF7BC998-49F6-4588-A9ED-16413A750D14/280960/CISAbu_GardaEn2.pdf>.

344 Tubiana, "Le Darfour, un conflit pour la terre?", *supra* note 91 at 114.

345 Flint & de Waal, *supra* note 86 at 66.

346 *Ibid.* at 91.

347 See above, c. 4.1.2.1.

4.2.1.4. Pressuring the international community to act

The involvement of the ICC also has the potential to make the international community exercise more coherent pressure on key players in the conflict to stop violence and negotiate an agreement. The ICC is a meaningful institution for two reasons. First, since the entry into force of the Rome Statute and the start of the ICC's practical functioning, the Court has attracted significant media attention. Its decisions and involvement are now closely observed. This interest increased with the first referrals and the Prosecutor's announcement of the first investigations. The world was therefore well informed thanks to the broad coverage of the events when arrest warrants were issued against Ahmad Harun and Ali Kushayb, and even more so when the arrest warrant against President Bashir was issued. Second, courts *per se* can be considered authoritative institutions to shape public opinion as long as their independence and impartiality are assured. An international court is, moreover, responsible to the international society as a whole,[348] which is, in the case of the ICC, represented by the Assembly of States Parties. The Rome Statute provides different mechanisms to guarantee the independence of the Court *vis-à-vis* national governments as well as the Security Council.[349] For these reasons, findings of the ICC are likely to have the same or even greater authority than statements made by governments or international human rights organizations. It is a meaningful step if some Western governments, the International Crisis Group or the UN Office of the High Commissioner for Human Rights declare that the Sudanese government is responsible for committing genocide, crimes against humanity and war crimes in Darfur; it is another one if individuals are singled out and charged for these crimes by an independent international prosecutor, who is ready to put these individuals on trial and whose applications have been confirmed by independent judges in The Hague. Charges by the ICC cannot easily be dismissed as politicized actions out of ideological reasons towards some individuals or governments.

---

348 Here, the ICC's backing by currently 110 states and its goal to reach universal ratification are emphasized over the fact that several states, including three permanent members of the Security Council, have been rejecting ICC jurisdiction so far. As a matter of fact, the ICC is responsible to a large international society and clearly represents internationalized interests.

349 For instance, independence of the judges and of the Prosecutor, as stipulated in articles 40 and 42 of the Rome Statute.

Thanks to this position, the ICC can play an important supportive role in raising awareness on the responsibility of some individuals for international crimes and, more generally, in urging the international community to prevent further crimes. The stigmatization of those who are allegedly most responsible for the international crimes committed in Darfur, namely the top of the Sudanese government, through the ICC channel has made it more difficult for the international community not to take stringent measures against the regime. This indirect impact on an ongoing conflict can be an extremely valuable contribution to the prevention of further crimes, and it can be expected that the an ICC can make this contribution also in other contexts. In addition, an ICC involvement is not exclusive to the detriment of more rigorous diplomatic pressure or even a military intervention.[350] In fact, such measures could be a consequence of the awareness-raising work of the ICC.

Unfortunately, recent developments have shown that the authoritative position of the ICC still has to be built up in order to generate a meaningful response from the international community to core crimes. In the situation of the DRC, for instance, four individuals have been indicted by the ICC and three arrested, but even since then the violent development in the country can only be considered to have been "monitored" by the international community. A new outbreak of violence in North Kivu in the fall 2008, during which war crimes and crimes against humanity were committed,[351] was not prevented nor has it triggered any meaningful immediate reaction by the international community.

350 The debate whether or not a military intervention would be helpful has split in particular French NGOs trying to find solutions to end the conflict; while organizations like Urgence Darfour fight vigorously for a military option, spokespersons of Médecins Sans Frontières, for instance, affirm that a military intervention would aggravate the conflict; see Agnès Gruda, "Le Darfour n'est pas le Rwanda" *La Presse* (13 April 2007).

351 "In towns like Kibumba, Kiberisi, Kanyabayonga, Kirumba, Kayna and Kiwanja murder, rape, looting and pillage are being committed every day, by all sides, with impunity;" Lisa Clifford, "ICC Risks Losing the Plot in Congo" *Institute for War and Peace Reporting* (21 November 2008), online: Institute for War & Peace Reporting <http://www.iwpr.net/?p=acr&s=f&o=347941&apc_state=henh>.

4.2.2. Concrete dangers of the ICC involvement in the situation of Darfur

Many international criminal lawyers and human rights groups have been arguing that genocide, crimes against humanity and war crimes must and can be prevented. Insisting on prosecuting those responsible for these crimes has been an important approach, that has, however, also been severely criticized:

> "[A] strategy that many such groups favor for achieving this goal—the prosecution of perpetrators of atrocities according to universal standards—risks causing more atrocities than it would prevent, because it pays insufficient attention to political realities."[352]

This section addresses those facets of the ICC involvement that may prolong the conflict in Darfur and aggravate the humanitarian situation of the victims.

4.2.2.1. Fewer prospects of achieving a peace agreement – the ICC prolonging the conflict

> "The pursuit of criminals is one thing. Making peace is another."[353]

One of the major problems in Darfur is that the conflict has dramatically aggravated the humanitarian situation. An estimated 2.5 million Darfurians live in refugee camps in Western Sudan and Eastern Chad, and approximately six million people depend on food aid. Fortunately, mass atrocities, as they were committed in 2003 and 2004 by the *Janjaweed* and the Sudanese army, are not the main characteristic of the conflict any more, but the effects of the lasting crisis on the civilian population are still as invasive.

It is obvious that an inclusive peace agreement is urgently needed to increase the probability of stopping violence lastingly; the mere fact that the level of violence has decreased does not save Darfurians from starving to death. Security cannot be reestablished in the region without dis-

---

352 Snyder & Vinjamuri, *supra* note 17 at 5.

353 Anonymous, "Human Rights in Peace Negotiations" (1996) 18:2 Hum. Rts. Q. 249 at 258.

armament of both the militias and the rebel groups, which would ideally be accompanied by the retreat of the Sudanese army and the deployment of a multi-national force. An agreement between the warring parties is an essential prerequisite for peace and also for some form of power sharing similar to the Comprehensive Peace Agreement concluded between Khartoum and the government of southern Sudan in 2005.[354] However, promising any form of political influence to Darfur's rebels is likely to be rejected by Khartoum's hardliners.

To settle the conflict in Darfur, precisely those individuals that are most influential and needed have been and are likely to be targeted by the Prosecutor in the future: government officials, most notably President Bashir, members of the *Janjaweed* militia and also leaders of the different rebel groups. One major problem is that it does not seem realistic to assume that those who are or will be indicted by the ICC could play an important role in peace negotiations or be part of a new, viable government. It is difficult for the international community to negotiate with individuals who are allegedly responsible for war crimes and who continue to hold important political positions. The situation is particularly problematic if these individuals are key national players without whom a political vacuum would emerge. The Sudanese government has of course realized this aspect; by portraying the ICC as an obstacle to peace, Khartoum has already been trying to make the ICC a bargaining chip in the peace negotiations.[355]

The involvement of the ICC in Darfur and its possible threat to the peace process has also been recognized as highly problematic by several Security Council members. The fact that the Security Council has not taken action after the Prosecutor's regular briefings, at least by calling on Sudan to cooperate with the ICC, is partly due to political concerns that such statements might "spoil the peace efforts in Darfur", as argued by China, Russia, South Africa, Burkina Faso, Libya and Indonesia in June 2008 after the seventh report of the Prosecutor to the Security Council.[356] At best, a consensus on a presidential statement could be reached, as illus-

---

354 Fore more information on the CPA, see below, c. 5.1.2.

355 Nick Grono & David Mozersky, "Sudan and the ICC: A Question of Accountability" (31 January 2007), online: International Crisis Group <http://www.crisisgroup.org/home/index.cfm?id=4640&l=1>.

356 "Sudan Vows 'Strong' Response to ICC Arrest Attempts of Darfur Suspect" *Sudan Tribune* (9 June 2008), online: Sudan Tribune <http://www.sudantribune.com/spip.php?article27457>.

trated by a June 2008 statement, in which the Security Council "urge[d] the Government of Sudan and all other parties to the conflict in Darfur to cooperate fully with the Court, consistent with resolution 1593 (2005), in order to put an end to impunity for the crimes committed in Darfur."[357] In the subsequent resolution on Darfur, the Security Council made one of the only references to the issue of impunity in a resolution on Darfur, however without mentioning the ICC:

> "*Emphasizing* the need to bring to justice the perpetrators of such crimes and *urging* the Government of Sudan to comply with its obligations in this respect, and *reiterating* its condemnation of all violations of human rights and international humanitarian law in Darfur [...]"[358]

At the same time, the Security Council also reaffirmed, in the wording of previous resolutions, "its strong commitment to the sovereignty, unity, independence and territorial integrity of Sudan and its determination to work with the Government of Sudan, in full respect of its sovereignty, to assist in tackling the various challenges in Sudan".[359]

Achieving peace in Darfur will not be possible through the same means as in northern Uganda, which also means that the role of the ICC is likely to be different in the course of a peace process. The frontline in northern Uganda is clear: the LRA *versus* President Museveni's government. Negotiations are marked by clear bargaining chips, such as amnesty for members of the LRA. Compared to this long-lasting duel, the situation in Darfur is chaotic. The Abuja peace agreement has failed. A completely new process, which brings together the Sudanese government, militia leaders, the numerous, splintered rebel groups, as well as the governments of neighboring states that have been involved in the conflict, such as Chad, would be necessary. Clearly, there is still a long way to go before sincere peace negotiations can be initiated, with the role of the ICC being even less clear than in the situation of northern Uganda.

---

357 UN Security Council, "Statement by the President of the Security Council", UN Doc. S/PRST/2008/21 (16 June 2008), online: United Nations <http://daccessdds.un.org/doc/UNDOC/GEN/N08/384/05/PDF/N0838405.pdf?OpenElement>. This statement represented the first reaction of the Security Council to the briefings of the ICC Prosecutor.

358 S/RES/1828 (2008).

359 *Ibid.*

4.2.2.2. Endangering the (full) deployment of a peace operation

The humanitarian situation in Darfur has been deteriorating drastically since the outbreak of protracted armed violence in 2003. Continuous humanitarian aid has been an urgent need, but numerous NGOs operating in the area had to pull out or limit their activities due to security concerns.[360] While a peacekeeping operation alone cannot solve the crisis,[361] a strong international force certainly has the capacity to increase the level of security significantly through its presence in buffer zones and internally displaced persons camps. Although the international community did not react to the unfolding disaster as quickly as it should have, there was broad international consensus that the 7,000 AMIS troops, which could not cope with the situation,[362] had to be supplemented by a stronger peace operation. As a result, the Security Council decided in August 2006 that the United Nations Mission in Sudan (UNMIS) shall be strengthened by up to 20,000 troops and its mandate be extended from southern Sudan to Darfur.[363] The Sudanese government, however, successfully blocked the

360 Médecins Sans Frontières, "A cause de l'insécurité, des zones inaccessibles, des personnes sans assistance" (25 October 2006), online: Médecins Sans Frontières <http://www.msf.fr/site/actu.nsf/actus/darfouritvjs251006>. Oxfam announced in June 2007 that it would withdraw permanently from Gereida due to security concerns; see "Sudan 'Backs UN-led Darfur Force'", *supra* note 325.

361 Well before the deployment of a UN peacekeeping mission in Darfur, Médecins Sans Frontières, one of the major NGOs operating in Darfur, warned that a military intervention would face many difficulties, because any foreign troops would have to fight against the Sudanese army; due to the policy of the Sudanese government, the situation would be hardly different for a UN mission. See Médecins Sans Frontières, "De mauvaises réponses à de bonnes questions" (23 March 2007), online: Médecins Sans Frontières <http://www.msf.fr/site/actu.nsf/actus/darfouritwgab230307>.

362 For more information, see Center of International Cooperation, *Annual Review of Global Peace Operations 2006* (Boulder, Colo.: Lynne Rienner Publishers, 2006) at 37. For the role of the African Union in Darfur, see Jeremy I. Levitt, "The Peace and Security Council of the African Union and the United Nations Security Council: The Case of Darfur, Sudan" in Niels Blokker & Nico Schrijver, *The Security Council and the Use of Force, Theory and Reality – A Need for Change?* (Leiden: Martinus Nijhoff Publishers, 2005) 213 at 240.

363 S/RES/1706 (2006).

deployment of a UN mission and even of a joint mission of the United Nations and the African Union. In June 2007, Khartoum finally showed some willingness to allow the deployment of a hybrid UN-AU peacekeeping force in Darfur, which was authorized by the Security Council on July 31, 2007.[364] While this was an important step, diplomats correctly remained skeptic as the government of Sudan has rarely acted according to such promises in the past. As a result of these political constraints and a significant lack of resources, the mission was only partly deployed in late 2008, reaching not even half of the military strength authorized by Security Council resolution 1769.[365]

Given the fact that there had already been a UN mission operative in southern Sudan, it appears obscure why the government of Sudan was so reluctant to admit a UN force into Darfur. Khartoum's fear that a UN mission in Darfur would cooperate with the ICC and ultimately arrest members of its armed forces and transfer them to The Hague was certainly a factor.[366] Strongly opposed to the ICC, the government objected to any means which might potentially support the activity of the ICC. In the words of Andrew Natsios, the former special envoy of the United States to Sudan,

> "They [the Sudanese government] are especially fearful that it [the hybrid UN-African Union peacekeeping force] will collect evidence of the 2003-4 slaughters in preparation for war crimes trials before the International Criminal Court in The Hague. [...] In fact, the more aggressively the international community pursues war crimes trials and Western advocacy groups demand justice in Darfur, the more aggressively the NCP is likely to resist the UN-AU peacekeeping force there, even after it is fully deployed."[367]

364 S/RES/1769 (2007).

365 As of 31 October 2008, only 8,935 troops were deployed in Darfur; resolution 1769 had authorized up to 19,555 military personnel. In early 2010, nearly 17,000 military personnel were deployed in Darfur; see United Nations, "Darfur - UNAMID - Facts and Figures", online: United Nations <http://www.un.org/Depts/dpko/missions/unamid/facts.html>.

366 "Le Soudan rejette la légitimité de la CPI sur le Darfour" *Le Monde* (27 February 2007).

367 Natsios, "Beyond Darfur", *supra* note 160.

Although there is no evidence that a UN mission would actually arrest and surrender persons indicted by the ICC, it is evident that investigators of the Office of the Prosecutor take advantage from a UN operation deployed on the ground. To pursue investigations in the Democratic Republic of Congo, for instance, the Prosecutor affirmed that his office relied heavily on cooperation with the UN mission in the DRC (MONUC), in particular due to the security situation. Logistical assistance, such as flight transportation, has also been essential. "And while we are striving to become as autonomous as possible in the circumstances, in some areas we will simply not be able to operate without such support."[368]

Moreover, attempts have been made by the Ugandan government in mid-2006 to carry out a joint operation between the Congolese authorities and MONUC in order to execute the arrest warrants against the leaders of the LRA,[369] who have been hiding in the northeast of the DRC.[370] In mid-2008, MONUC, mandated to support the Congolese army in dealing with foreign armed groups that threaten Congolese civilians,[371] even delivered a very clear message with respect to the possible arrest of ICC indictees:

> "MONUC is aware of its mandate to detain the LRA leaders who have been indicted by the International Criminal Court, and would seek to do so if it came across them while carrying out its mandated duties. The captured LRA leaders would have to be immediately handed over to the Congolese authorities who, since the Democratic Republic of the Congo is a State party to the Rome Statute and has other agreements with the Court, would then be expected to hand over the suspects for arraignment in The Hague. … [J]oint FARDC [Forces armées de la République démocratique du Congo]-MONUC operations against

368 International Criminal Court, "Statement by Luis Moreno-Ocampo, Prosecutor of the International Criminal Court, Informal meeting of Legal Advisors of Ministries of Foreign Affairs" (24 October 2005), online: International Criminal Court <http://www.icc-cpi.int/library/organs/otp/speeches/LMO_ 20051024_English.pdf> at 2.

369 ICG, "Northern Uganda: Seizing the Opportunity for Peace", *supra* note 37 at 7.

370 *Ibid.* at 8.

371 MONUC was originally established by S/RES/1279 (1999). Several references to the necessary withdrawal of foreign troops were made in subsequent Security Council resolutions; see, for instance, S/RES/1291 (2000) at para. 7(c).

> foreign armed groups, including LRA, will continue insofar as the MONUC capacity and mandate allow."[372]

Even though the capacity and resources of MONUC might not allow for an operation to arrest Joseph Kony in Garamba National Park in the near future, this statement speaks a very clear language with respect to the political willingness of enforcing ICC arrest warrants.

The operations in Liberia and Bosnia are also good examples to show that peacekeeping forces can be important players in delivering indictees to international criminal tribunals. With the unanimously adopted Resolution 1638, the Security Council took an important step to reform UN practice by expanding the mandate of the UN mission in Liberia (UNMIL) to "apprehend and detain former President Charles Taylor in the event of a return to Liberia and to transfer him or facilitate his transfer to Sierra Leone for prosecution before the Special Court for Sierra Leone."[373] Charles Taylor was later arrested by Nigerian officials, when he tried to flee Nigeria in March 2006; after Taylor had been repatriated to Liberia, UN peacekeepers transferred him to Freetown.[374] With this new policy, the Security Council underlined the importance of fighting impunity and extended the means of the UN to achieve this objective in Liberia and Sierra Leone. After the establishment of the *ad hoc* tribunals for ex-Yugoslavia and Rwanda and the support for other tribunals, such as the SCSL, resolution 1638 is an illustration of the Security Council's further efforts to sponsor international criminal justice, in this case on the level of enforcement. The non-coercive nature of a peace operation is not an obstacle, in particular if the host government approves the extension of the mission's mandate: resolution 1638 did not shift UNMIL towards a peace-enforcement mission.[375] However, if the Liberian government had not given its consent, the task, which arguably amounted to a duty,[376] to

372 UN SC, "Report of the Secretary-General pursuant to resolutions 1653 and 1663", *supra* note 67 at para. 31.

373 S/RES/1638 (2005). The mission in Somalia, UNOSOM II, was given a similar mandate. For more information, see Micaela Frulli, "A Turning Point in International Efforts to Apprehend War Criminals, The UN Mandates Taylor's Arrest in Liberia" (2006) 4 Journal of International Criminal Justice 351 at 352.

374 *Ibid.* at 351.

375 *Ibid.* at 359.

376 In the wording of Security Council Resolution 1638, the mandate "shall include"; see S/RES/1638 (2005).

apprehend Taylor could hardly have been reconciled with the initial mandate of the peacekeeping force.

The NATO-led force in Bosnia and Herzegovina (IFOR/SFOR) did not receive an explicit authorization from the Security Council to apprehend war crimes suspects but was mandated to ensure the implementation of the Dayton Peace Accord, including its provision that all parties must cooperate with the ICTY. One can therefore conclude that, by arresting indictees, the international force only enforced compliance with the Peace Accord.[377] Using non-mandatory language, the North Atlantic Council specified that "IFOR should detain any persons indicted by the International Criminal Tribunal who come into contact with IFOR in its execution of assigned tasks, in order to assure the transfer of these persons to the International Criminal Tribunal,"[378] thus expressly mandating the multinational force to execute arrest warrants issued by the ICTY. Indeed, several indictees were subsequently arrested and transferred to The Hague by SFOR. Similarly, KFOR also arrested several indictees in Kosovo at the request of the ICTY Prosecutor.

The situation in Darfur could develop in a similar manner. The Prosecutor has already shown that peacekeeping troops on the ground are considered an important source of information for the investigations of his office. In his early reports to the Security Council, the Prosecutor revealed that contacts with AMIS had been made and underlined the importance of expeditious assistance of the AU to the work of the OTP.[379] Cooperation of

377 For a further discussion on this controversial point and the question whether the multinational force is obliged to execute arrest warrants, see Paula Gaeta, "Is NATO Authorized or Obliged to Arrest Persons Indicted by the International Criminal Tribunal for the Former Yugoslavia?" (1998) 9 E.J.I.L. 174. On the difficult relationship between the ICTY and IFOR, see Gary Jonathan Bass, *Stay the Hand of Vengeance: the Politics of War Crimes Tribunals* (Princeton: Princeton University Press, 2000) at 251.

378 Cited in Gaeta, *supra* note 377 at 3. To facilitate the arrest of indictees by the peacekeeping force, the ICTY amended its Rules of Procedure and Evidence in 1996 by adopting Rule 59*bis*, allowing the ICTY to transmit a warrant of arrest to an "appropriate authority or international body"; see ICTY, *Rules of Procedure and Evidence* (adopted 11 February 1994, as amended on 25 June and 5 July 1996), UN Doc. IT/32/Rev.9 (1996).

379 See e.g. International Criminal Court, "Second Report of the Prosecutor of the International Criminal Court, Mr. Luis Moreno Ocampo, to the UN Security Council Pursuant to UNSCR 1593 (2005)" (13 December 2005), online: International Criminal Court <http://www.icc-cpi.int/library/

the joint UN-AU mission with the ICC also became an issue. Prominent NGOs, such as Human Rights Watch and the International Crisis Group, openly pressured the Security Council in a telling manner to explicitly mandate the peace mission to support the work of the ICC in Darfur: "The mission should also be specifically empowered to provide appropriate assistance to the International Criminal Court's investigations in Darfur including the arrest of individuals indicted for crimes against humanity and war crimes."[380]

In sum, the fact that international forces played a substantial role in Liberia and Bosnia in arresting war criminals is an important development towards the enforcement of international criminal law, which might also be relevant in the case of Darfur. Nevertheless, it has been persuasively argued that the Sudanese government had been opposed to a peacekeeping force in Darfur long before the referral to the ICC, since it is "determined to wipe out the rebel groups in Darfur, at almost any cost".[381] It was also evident that, as with UNMIS, the mandate of a peacekeeping mission would be limited to a clearly defined region and would, therefore, most likely not lead to the arrest of government officials.[382] Mandates can, however, be extended once a force is on the ground, as the case of Liberia has shown. Furthermore, a general tendency towards implementing international law, including international criminal law, seems to be emerging. Even if executing ICC arrest warrants is not one of the tasks for which the joint UN-AU mission in Darfur has received a clear mandate, international forces, as shown in Liberia, Bosnia and the DRC, are increasingly sought to cooperate with international criminal tribunals.

Whether or not Khartoum's fear that a UN or joint UN-AU mission in Darfur might arrest members of the Sudanese army and the militias is justified, it is evident that the deployment of international peacekeepers at least facilitates to a certain extent the work of the OTP on the ground, as it has been the case in the DRC. Because of this, the ICC has definitely not been a supporting factor in persuading the Sudanese government to

organs/otp/ LMO_UNSC_ReportB_En.pdf> at 7.

380 Human Rights Watch & International Crisis Group, "Security Council Must Take Action to Protect Civilians in Darfur, Joint Human Rights Watch and International Crisis Group Letter to the Members of the U.N. Security Council Regarding Darfur" (31 January 2006), online: Human Rights Watch <http://hrw.org/english/docs/2006/01/31/sudan12577.htm>.

381 Grono & Mozersky, *supra* note 355.

382 *Ibid.*

approve and cooperate with the UN-AU mission for Darfur. Arguably, the involvement of the ICC was also one of the reasons why Khartoum insisted on such a strong African component in the operation, including a Force Commander from Nigeria, who reports to a Joint Special Representative from the Republic of the Congo.[383] This compromise definitely reduced the *marge de manœuvre* of the operation and, due to the fact that Khartoum repeatedly rejected contingents from non-African states, delayed the deployment.[384]

After the announcement of the Prosecutor in June 2008 that senior Sudanese officials might be indicted, the discussion over the potential impact of the ICC involvement on the deployment of the UN-AU peace operation resumed. Some Western diplomats linked the July 2008 *Janjaweed* attack on peacekeepers, which left seven soldiers dead, to the imminent indictments.[385] Out of fear that indicting senior officials might restrict the humanitarian work and hinder the efforts of the peacekeeping force, analysts have argued that UNAMID deployment and the 2005 peace agreement between the North and the South should be the priority of the international community, and not criminal prosecutions.[386] Andrew Natsios even predicted that if the ICC Prosecutor continued with his plans, "it will drive the country closer to dissolution."[387]

In this context, it is worth noting that the reaction of the Sudanese government to the indictment of President Bashir was obviously particularly sharp. Already after the Prosecutor's application for an arrest warrant, Khartoum threatened that it could no longer assure the safety of UN-AU peacekeepers in Darfur if an arrest warrant was issued.[388] Finally,

383 UN, "UNAMID Deployment", *supra* note 151.

384 As of late 2008, the following countries had deployed troops in Darfur: Bangladesh, China, Egypt, Ethiopia, Gambia, Kenya, Nigeria, Rwanda, Senegal and South Africa. The composition "respects concerns expressed by the Government of Sudan, maintaining a predominantly African character"; see United Nations, "Darfur - UNAMID - Background", online: United Nations <http://www.un.org/Depts/dpko/missions/unamid/background.html>.

385 "UN Fury at Darfur Militia Ambush", *supra* note 158.

386 See Ali, *supra* note 301.

387 *Ibid.*

388 See e.g. Human Rights Watch, "Sudan, justice and peace" (16 July 2008), online: Human Rights Watch <http://www.hrw.org/en/news/2008/07/15/sudan-justice-and-peace>.

by expelling international aid organizations from Darfur, the Sudanese government followed a strategy of presenting the arrest warrant as a cause for further suffering of Darfurians, under the pretext that humanitarian organizations had provided the ICC Prosecutor with information.[389] This strategy proved to be successful to a certain extent: Western governments decided to balance support for the ICC against humanitarian concerns, while the Security Council ignored the arrest warrant and Sudan's obligation to cooperate with the ICC under resolution 1593 and only urged the Sudanese government in a non-binding statement to reverse the expulsion.[390]

Again, the direct impact of the activity of the Prosecutor on the political situation in Darfur cannot be denied. The possibility and potential benefits of applying for and issuing a sealed arrest warrant have already been discussed.[391]

4.2.3. Evaluation and suggested further proceedings

The two important dangers of the ICC involvement in the Darfur conflict must be considered seriously, but they should not fuel doubts neither on the involvement itself nor the ICC as an institution. Since the ICC cannot be perceived as an exclusively legal institution, the potentially negative impact of indictments and arrest warrants must not be ignored but rather clearly addressed. Being an obstacle to a peace agreement, to the (full) deployment of a peacekeeping mission or to the work of humanitarian organizations are serious challenges. Establishing such a link does not suggest that the ICC should give in to pressure from any side, be it the Sudanese government or certain powerful voices among the international community. Yet the key political players, including the ICC Prosecutor, should not only be aware of these links but should also anticipate for instance increased

389 This allegation has been refuted by the Prosecutor; see "ICC Prosecutor says he received 'zero' information from NGO's in Sudan" *Sudan Tribune* (21 March 2009), online: Sudan Tribune <http://www.sudantribune.com/spip.php?article30580>. Reportedly the Sudanese government only waited for a chance to expel the organizations; see "Aid Group's Expulsion, Fears of More Misery" *New York Times* (22 March 2009).

390 See "Darfur mediator says Bashir warrant imperils talks" *Reuters* (26 March 2009), online: Reuters <http://www.reuters.com/article/NewsMaps/idUSTRE52P7FO20090326>.

391 See above, c. 3.5.4.

violence or the suspension of peace negotiations as a response to decisions and announcements coming from The Hague.

This argument does not only make sense from a pragmatic and politically conscious point of view. It also has a legal basis. First, article 53 of the Rome Statute obliges the Prosecutor to take into account the interests of justice, which include the interests of victims, in his prosecutorial strategy. As will be analyzed further below,[392] the Prosecutor must be aware of possible negative effects of indictments and must act accordingly if such announcements are likely to put a greater risk on the victims. Assaults on peacekeepers, for example, can be expected to further weaken the peace operation and additionally delay the full deployment, which would, given the higher security risks, definitely not be in the interests of the victims. Second, in the situation of Darfur, the ICC has a clear mandate to contribute to international peace and security, as evidenced by the Security Council through resolution 1593. A proactive prosecutorial strategy, which increases the pressure on senior members of the Sudanese government, but which might at the same time contribute to a deterioration of the security situation on the ground, must be perceived has being part of the efforts of the international community to deal with the crisis in Darfur. However, the decision on the timing of issuing indictments must take into account the impact on other measures, such as the full deployment of a peacekeeping operation or possibly the progress made in negotiating a peace agreement.

One of the essential principles of international criminal justice remains valid without doubt in the situation of Darfur: long-lasting peace cannot be achieved through impunity for grave crimes. The assumption that removing criminal leaders is a necessary prerequisite to achieve durable peace, as evidenced by the examples of Foday Sankoh and Slobodan Milosevic, will be addressed in more detail below.[393] In the words of the ICC Prosecutor, "threats against victims, peacekeepers and aid workers should be seen for what they are – criminal intent – and not rewarded with promises of impunity."[394] In addition to general arguments favoring long-term peace over a short-term ceasefire, the situation in Darfur underlines the validity of the premise that peace and justice do not have to contradict each other and are not mutually exclusive goals or concepts. Moreover, since the ICC entered the scene when a reliable peace process was still out of sight, its

392 See c. 5.3.

393 See c. 5.1.2.

394 ICC, "Eighth Report of the Prosecutor", *supra* note 116 at para. 85.

potential impact on pressuring key actors to change their policy and attitude has more political weight than the risk that peace negotiations might, in the end, be prolonged because the question of individual accountability must be addressed. In other words, the involvement of the ICC can – at least potentially – help to bring about peace through profounder means than what short answers to a somewhat simplifying "peace versus justice" debate can offer.

For these reasons, the above-mentioned prospects of the ICC involvement in the Darfur conflict, in particular the potential to make the Sudanese government change its Darfur policy, clearly outweigh the political dangers that come with international indictments. Even if indicting government officials is always a delicate matter, as their cooperation is essential to deal with the humanitarian situation and the peaceful resolution of a conflict, government officials must not be shielded against prosecutions. Proceeding cautiously is, however, essential. Since the negative impact on the victims of a conflict can be more serious when the actors still in power are targeted, evidence must be carefully collected. The more risky a case is from a political point of view, the stronger the Prosecutor's file should be. Since the judges confirmed the view that there are "reasonable grounds to believe"[395] that the top of the Sudanese government is responsible for crimes committed within the jurisdiction of the ICC, which means *in concreto* that superior responsibility can be established by the Prosecutor according to article 28(b) of the Rome Statute, then the Prosecutor was right not to restrain himself from taking similar steps as in the case of the Harun and Kushayb indictments. In other words, the prospect of weakening the top of the Sudanese government ultimately outweighs the risk that the subsequent lack of cooperation of the government with international players might aggravate the situation of Darfurians.

In any case, it is essential that the ICC remains an impartial institution and, equally important, that it also appears impartial in the eyes of the warring parties. Otherwise, the ICC will be considered a biased instrument, only activated to abet one side's victory, if not in the battlefield, then in the courtroom. The danger of becoming a political instrument is real; in the case of northern Uganda, the ICC has been harshly criticized and branded as a tool of President Museveni to exercise political pressure through judicial action. The activation of the ICC by the Ugandan government itself, which has a strong interest in putting as much pressure as possible on its military opponents, stands of course in sharp contrast

395 In the wording of article 58(1)(a) of the Rome Statute.

to the situation in Darfur, where the ICC was activated by an external body. Nonetheless, the ICC also risks being criticized as a political instrument regarding its involvement in the Darfur conflict. It has been argued that, through the Darfur referral, the Security Council confused the legal sphere with political strategy.[396] The question is how the ICC can show its willingness and capability to act independently and impartially in Darfur and emphasize that it is not an instrument of Western governments or the Security Council, which has given in to the pressure of some powerful Western states, to exercise political pressure on the widely unloved Islamist government of Sudan.

One possible way of facing this challenge is to adopt the "initial proportion strategy",[397] a pragmatic approach first proposed in the context of the ICTY that takes into account the direct political effects of indictments and aims to diminish them as much as possible. In a few words, according to this strategy, a prosecutor should start by selecting a similar amount of individuals of the various warring parties to avoid appearing partial. Cooperation with the tribunal can be expected to be amplified if each party to the conflict has not only something to "lose" but also something to "win", i.e. through the arrest of opponents. Once a settlement of the conflict is reached and another outbreak of violence is unlikely, the prosecutor would be able to proceed more freely at lower political risks.

Applied to the Darfur conflict, the Prosecutor should not only target members of the government and the militia but also rebel leaders. A first notable step was the indictment of Abu Garda for his alleged involvement in an attack on peacekeepers. Generally, thanks to the large prosecutorial discretion and due to the substantial violations of international humanitarian law committed by various rebel groups, the question of sufficient gravity is not an obstacle. If the Prosecutor pursues a consistent procedure, further leaders of rebel groups should be targeted next. This strategy would also facilitate a rectification of the perception of the conflict which is largely still reduced to an oversimplifying black-and-white offenders-victims scheme in the world opinion. The Prosecutor would have to maintain this equilibrium as long as necessary in order to avoid appearing as a biased instrument. Subsequently, the Prosecutor could return to a policy that follows article 17(1)(d) and the preamble of the Rome Statute more

396 Marchal, *supra* note 131 at 36.

397 This prosecutorial strategy was proposed by Aleksandar Fatić in the context of the ICTY; see Aleksandar Fatić, *Reconciliation via the War Crimes Tribunal?* (Aldershot: Ashgate, 2000) at 84.

closely; in other words he could then set up a simple list of those who are allegedly most responsible for the worst crimes committed in the region, regardless of their affiliation with a certain group.

Chapter 5

A possibly proactive role of the ICC Prosecutor through his prosecutorial discretion

The last chapters have shown that the newly set up permanent international criminal court has assumed a partly political role in the situations of northern Uganda and Darfur. This development, although largely denied by Court officials and in particular by the OTP, must not be ignored. The reasons for this development have been addressed in the chapter analyzing the referrals to the ICC Prosecutor. In a nutshell, the decision made by the Prosecutor to accept, or even solicit, voluntary referrals by states has been unhelpful to strengthen the position and independence of the Court. With respect to Darfur, the outcome of the process can be described as similar, although it is obvious that the political and legal *marge de manœuvre* of the Prosecutor is much more limited in this situation; first, because of the significant authoritativeness of a referral made by the Security Council by invoking chapter VII of the UN Charter; second, because of the simple fact that, since Sudan has not ratified the Rome Statute, the Prosecutor could not have initiated proceedings *proprio motu* in this situation. Nevertheless, as it will be argued, the ICC, and in particular the Prosecutor, is not doomed to be dependent on the political will of the Security Council or States Parties.

The following chapter explores the possible scope of action of the Prosecutor and analyzes the general legal obligation to prosecute under international law, its specific impact on the discretion of the ICC Prosecutor as well as its significance for the conflicts in northern Uganda and Darfur. It also looks at the relevance of article 53 of the Rome Statute and its provision regarding "the interests of justice" and the Prosecutor's policy and perception of its own prosecutorial discretion. This political discretion of the ICC Prosecutor will be assessed in the context of the powers of the Security Council, in particular with respect to article 16 of the Rome Statute. It will also be studied whether self-referrals by States Parties and referrals by the Security Council lead to better results of the investigatory and prosecutorial work, compared to investigations initiated *proprio motu*, or whether they make the ICC unnecessarily dependent on the referring authority.

5.1. The legal obligation to prosecute under international law

To address the issue of prosecutorial discretion, it is important, regardless of any practical and strategic considerations, to analyze whether international law has created a legal obligation to prosecute.[398] In the context of the situations of northern Uganda and Darfur, it is particularly interesting to address this fundamental question in order to determine whether the discretion of the ICC Prosecutor may be limited by a general obligation to prosecute, for instance to the detriment of nationally granted amnesties or a (temporary) situation of complete impunity, in other words whether the Prosecutor would act in breach of international law if he did not indict certain individuals in a given situation. Such an obligation would clearly reduce the *marge de manœuvre* of the Prosecutor and would not give room for anything else but strictly legal deliberations; political consequences could hardly be taken into account. To pursue the analysis, relevant international instruments and state practice will be explored before the legal consequences affecting the discretion of the ICC Prosecutor and their concrete application to the situations of Uganda and Darfur will be addressed.

398 The term "prosecute" is to be read in accordance with the principle *aut dedere aut judicare*, which encompasses prosecution and extradition as possibilities. On the duty to prosecute, see generally Diane Orentlicher, "Settling Accounts: the Duty to Prosecute Human Rights Violations of a Prior Regime" (1990) 100 Yale L. J. 2537; Michael P. Scharf, "The Letter of the Law: The Scope of the International Obligation to Prosecute Human Rights Crimes" (1996) 59 Law & Contemp. Probs. 41. For on overview on the question of amnesties as a violation of a duty to prosecute, see Olivia Le Fort, "The Politics of Amnesty" (LL.M. Thesis, McGill University Faculty of Law, 2005) [unpublished]. For a more general analysis of the relevance of amnesties for international criminal tribunals, see Dov Jacobs, "Puzzling Over Amnesties: Defragmenting the Debate for International Criminal Tribunals", online: SSRN <http://papers.ssrn.com/sol3/papers.cfm?abstract_id=1562088>.

5.1.1. The legal framework

It seems obvious that from a strict legal point of view, the ICC Prosecutor, unlike states, is not obliged to prosecute in any case. A possible obligation for states is "*relevant* but it is not *determinative* of the stance of the ICC in carrying out its mandate".[399] However, justifying an exercise of discretion which would lead to staying away from prosecutions would be significantly more difficult for the ICC Prosecutor in situations where states are obligated to prosecute. It appears redundant to stress that when states are under an international obligation to prosecute but do not fulfill their obligation, the ICC should be at the forefront. Since the ICC was set up as an institution to end impunity, it cannot easily refuse to act according to those provisions of international law that form the material basis of its jurisdiction. With respect to amnesties, it has been convincingly argued that "[i]t would be inappropriate for an international criminal court to defer to a national amnesty where the amnesty violates obligations contained in the very international conventions that make up the court's subject matter jurisdiction."[400]

The Rome Statute indeed contributes to the tendency towards an obligation to prosecute by stipulating in its preamble the "duty of every State to exercise its criminal jurisdiction over those responsible for international crimes" and by "affirming that the most serious crimes of concern to the international community as a whole must not go unpunished." Yet this duty could only find its place in the preamble, as states were not able to agree on its inclusion into the body of the Rome Statute at the Diplomatic Conference.[401] Therefore, there is no explicit obligation codified in the Rome Statute, since the preamble is not legally binding but can only be relevant to the interpretation of the treaty.[402] This problem is aggravated by the fact that the substantial part of the Rome Statute is silent about any obligation to prosecute and does not clarify the issue of how the ICC will deal with

---

399 Darryl Robinson, "Serving the Interests of Justice: Amnesties, Truth Commissions and the International Criminal Court" (2003) 14 E.J.I.L. 481 at 490.

400 Michael P. Scharf, "The Amnesty Exception to the Jurisdiction of the International Criminal Court" (1999) 32 Cornell Int'l L.J. 507 at 515 [Scharf, "The Amnesty Exception"].

401 *Ibid.* at 492.

402 As indicated in article 31(2) of the *Vienna Convention on the Law of the Treaties*, 23 May 1969, 1155 U.N.T.S. 331 (entered into force 27 January 1980).

nationally granted amnesties or pardons, regardless of whether or not they violate or are relevant for an international obligation to prosecute.

Several international instruments as well as customary international law have created a clear legal obligation for states to prosecute. According to article 4 of the Genocide Convention, anyone who commits genocide "shall be punished".[403] It would, therefore, be very difficult for the ICC Prosecutor not to proceed in cases where genocide has allegedly been committed or to justify the respect of domestically granted amnesties or a situation of impunity, even if temporary, concerning crimes falling under article 6 of the Rome Statute. In addition, the Genocide Convention is also recognized as customary international law and is therefore binding on states which are not parties to the convention.[404] This is relevant in the case of Darfur, since Sudan has only signed but not ratified the Convention. Although a certain degree of discretion can still be recognized due to the fact that the convention is "unclear as to the precise modalities of such punishment",[405] the discretion is minimal and the purpose of the Genocide Convention to compel States Parties to punish perpetrators clear.

Similarly, states must punish perpetrators of grave breaches under the 1949 Geneva Conventions. States Parties must "provide effective penal sanctions for persons committing, or ordering to be committed, any of the grave breaches of the present convention."[406] The obligation is absolute: there is no room for immunities or amnesties. However, there is no international obligation to prosecute "other serious violations of the laws and

---

403 *Convention on the Prevention and Punishment of the Crime of Genocide*, 9 December 1948, 78 U.N.T.S. 277 (entered into force 12 January 1951). The obligation is not based on the principle of universal jurisdiction, but of territorial jurisdiction, which means that *genocidaires* must be tried by the state where the genocide was committed or by an international criminal tribunal; see article 6 of the convention. Similar obligations arise under the Torture Convention and the Apartheid Convention.

404 *Prosecutor v. Kayishema and Ruzindana* (1999), ICTR-95-1-T (Judgment, 21 May 1999) (International Criminal Tribunal for Rwanda, Trial Chamber) at 88.

405 Leila Nadya Sadat, "Exile, Amnesty and International Law" (2006) 81 Notre Dame L. Rev. 955 at 1020 [Sadat, "Exile, Amnesty"].

406 Article 129 of the *Geneva Convention Relative to the Treatment of Prisoners of War (Geneva III)*, 12 August 1949, 75 U.N.T.S. 135 (entered into force 21 October 1950) and Article 146 of the *Geneva Convention Relative to the Protection of Civilian Persons in Time of War (Geneva IV)*, 12 August 1949, 75 U.N.T.S. 287 (entered into force 21 October 1950).

customs applicable in international armed conflict" (article 8(2)(b) of the Rome Statute). Furthermore, the duty to prosecute is limited to international armed conflicts and does not extend to internal armed conflicts, as the grave breaches provision only applies to those conflicts which involve two or more states.

In addition to genocide and war crimes, the third type of crime in the Rome Statute is crimes against humanity.[407] As no specific treaty exists for crimes against humanity, states are not required to prosecute these violations under treaty law, although many human rights lawyers and activists argue that customary international law has not only created permissive jurisdiction, but, in fact, obliges states to prosecute perpetrators of crimes against humanity. Indeed, a trend towards the recognition of a duty to prosecute international crimes is observable; national and regional jurisprudence ground this obligation in the respect of human rights law. In *Velasquez-Rodriguez*, for instance, the Inter-American Court ruled that a situation of impunity violated the American Convention on Human Rights;[408] it affirmed that states must investigate and prosecute those responsible for human rights violations. Both the European Court of Human Rights and the UN Human Rights Committee have reiterated this obligation.[409] The jurisprudence of these bodies, the establishment of

407 A fourth crime, namely the crime of aggression, is listed in the Rome Statute. However, the ICC cannot exercise jurisdiction over this crime, since a consensus on its definition was not found at the Rome Conference. A definition was finally included at the Review Conference in June 2010, but the ICC will only be able to exercise jurisdiction over the crime of aggression after a decision of two thirds of the States Parties after January 1, 2017. See International Criminal Court, Assembly of States Parties, "Resolution RC/Res.6" (adopted at the 13th plenary meeting, on 11 June 2010), online: International Criminal Court <http://www.icc-cpi.int/iccdocs/asp_docs/Resolutions/RC-Res.6-ENG.pdf>. The proceedings of the Special Working Group on the Crime of Aggression, established by the ICC Assembly of States Parties, provide an interesting insight into the highly political debates surrounding this crime.

408 *Velasquez-Rodriguez Case (Honduras)* (1988), Inter-Am. Ct. H.R. (Ser. C) No. 4, Annual Report of the Inter-American Court of Human Rights: OAS/ser. L/V/III, doc.13, app. IV (1988).

409 *Kurt v. Turkey* (1998), 74 E.C.H.R. (Ser. A) 1152, 27 E.H.R.R. 373; *Bleier v. Uruguay*, U.N. Human Rights Committee, UN Doc. A/37/40 (1982); *Mojica v. Dominican Republic*, U.N.Human Rights Committee, UN Doc. CCPR/C/51/D/449/1991 (1994).

international criminal tribunals,[410] as well as the important change in attitude of states concerning the exercise of universal jurisdiction since the Pinochet case are part of the tendency towards an undisputed prosecution of crimes against humanity.

This *tendency* towards prosecuting core crimes does, however, not necessarily go along with a generalized *obligation* to prosecute. Although the issue remains controversial, Michael P. Scharf, a law professor and specialist in the field of international criminal law, concludes that "there is scant evidence that customary international law requires the prosecution of crimes against humanity."[411] Since some states still use amnesties as a policy instrument without any objections of the international community, it has been argued that "any conclusion that a generalized duty to prosecute exists would thus fly in the face of current state practice."[412] In contrast, Darryl Robinson, former legal advisor to the ICC Prosecutor, affirms that there is a general duty, or at least an emerging duty to prosecute those who committed crimes under the Rome Statute, as "it would seem incongruous and convoluted to recognize a duty for some ICC Statute crimes [...], but not for equally serious or more serious ICC Statute crimes."[413] These arguments seem coherent and convincing from a practical point of view, but the issue of a legal obligation to prosecute the various crimes is more complex; international law does – unfortunately – not always follow common sense logic.

Robinson concedes, however, two limitations to the asserted duty. First, it can be enough for a transitional government to prosecute those individual most responsible for the crimes committed. Second, a necessity exception to a general duty to prosecute is conceivable in situations of

410 Both the ICTY and the ICTR stipulate an obligation to hold individuals accountable for war crimes, genocide and crimes against humanity; see article 7(1) of the ICTY statute and article 6(1) of the ICTR statute.

411 Scharf, "The Amnesty Exception", *supra* note 400 at 519. Sadat comes to a similar conclusion; see Leila Nadya Sadat, *The International Criminal Court and the Transformation of International Law, Justice for the New Millennium* (Ardsley, N.Y.: Transnational Publishers, 2002) at 66 [Sadat, "Transformation"].

412 Dwight G. Newman, "The Rome Statute, Some Reservations Concerning Amnesties, and a Distributive Problem" (2005) 20 Am. U. Int'l L. Rev. 293 at 313.

413 Robinson, *supra* note 399 at 492.

"grave and imminent threat."[414] These limitations largely correspond to the position and role of the ICC Prosecutor, who is generally committed to prosecute those individuals most responsible for the worst crimes, but who must also make strategic choices because of limited resources and take into account the interests of the victims.[415]

Another important differentiation is made by Law Professor Leila Nadya Sadat who argues that blanket amnesties have become less and less acceptable in recent years. Although amnesties are, in general, still permissible under international law, decisions of regional courts suggest that "a prohibition against the grant of blanket amnesties for the commission of *jus cogens* crimes may now have crystallized has a matter of general customary international law."[416]

In addition to state practice, the question of *opinio juris*, which is the second necessary element to constitute customary international law, must also be addressed. There is little evidence that states have ever prosecuted crimes against humanity with the sense of a legal obligation. Only the statements of a few states' representatives, such as Uruguay, El Salvador and Chile, can be interpreted as recognizing their amnesty laws as an exception to a general duty to prosecute.[417] However, most states that avoided criminal trials and granted amnesties instead did not make any declarations concerning a legal obligation to prosecute. It can therefore be concluded that most states do not recognize a legal obligation to prosecute crimes against humanity despite increasing evidence of *opinio juris*.[418]

In summary, a legal obligation to prosecute crimes against humanity or war crimes other than grave breaches of the Geneva Conventions is currently developing thanks to customary law, but state practice is far from being pervasive at the moment. The following case studies are intended to underline this argument, showing that states have often avoided individual

---

414 *Ibid.* at 493.

415 See below, c. 5.3.

416 Sadat, "Exile, Amnesty", *supra* note 405 at 1022.

417 Karen Gallagher, "No Justice, no Peace: The Legalities and Realities of Amnesty in Sierra Leone" (2000) 23 Thomas Jefferson L. Rev. 149 at 183; however, Gallagher underlines that these states were under the additional regime of the American Convention on Human Rights. Their declarations might, therefore, not originate from the *opinio juris* of a general customary international law duty.

418 See similarly *ibid.* at 186.

accountability mechanisms when international crimes had been committed.

5.1.2. State practice

The following examples, including formal amnesty programs and blanket amnesties for perpetrators of international crimes[419], is far from exhaustive. Many states, in particular in Latin America, have relied on various forms of amnesties, sometimes in combination with truth and reconciliation commissions (TRCs), over the last decades. The examples chosen illustrate both positive and negative effects of avoiding individual accountability and also reflect the approval of large-scale amnesties by the international community.

5.1.2.1. South Africa - the success of a TRC

The South African transition from an apartheid regime to a representative democracy following the 1994 elections was relatively smooth and non-violent. An important aspect of this successful transition was that the new government, dominated by the African National Congress, avoided a climate of retributive justice and emphasized the need for long-term reconciliation within the country. The government had realized that by facing, but at the same time accepting, what had happened during the former regime, the basis for future cooperation could be built. It was clear that "[s]uccess in the constitutional negotiations depended to a large degree on making a deal with the previous regime, and Nuremberg-type trials were not an option if the country was to reach democratic elections without a coup or chaos."[420]

As part of the negotiated transfer of power, a TRC was established in 1995, mandated to grant full amnesty to those who confessed entirely their crimes, as long as these crimes had been politically motivated. Although

419 Generally, an obligation to prosecute prohibits the granting of amnesties. Sadat observes that the two questions are often related, but still distinct. Even if an obligation to prosecute is answered in the negative, international law does not necessarily recognize the legality of amnesties in the case of mass atrocities; see Sadat, "Exile, Amnesty", *supra* note 405 at 1019.

420 Peter Storey, "A Different Kind of Justice: Truth and Reconciliation in South Africa" *Christian Century* (10 September 1997), online: FindArticles <http://www.findarticles.com/p/articles/mi_m1058/is_n25_v114/ai_19844884>.

South Africa's TRC was not directly linked to the regular legal system, its decisions were binding on national courts.[421] To decide on amnesties in particular cases, the TRC had to take several criteria into account, such as the motive and the objective of the perpetrator, the context of the crime, its gravity, the proportionality of the act to the objective pursued,[422] and other aspects which are also typically taken into account when sentences are to be determined in ordinary criminal trials.

Although the TRC has also been criticized for various reasons,[423] its achievements are considerable, some of them being similar to the benefits of criminal trails: both TRCs and prosecutions help to bring about truth. The crimes of the past will not be forgotten. The model of South Africa stands therefore in sharp contrast to the blanket amnesties that were typically granted after the transition from military regimes to democracy, such as the amnesties granted for crimes committed during the Argentinean "dirty war" in the 1970s.[424] Furthermore, in the case of the South African TRC, individuals were also publicly identified, which produced individual responsibility, enabled societal instead of legal sanctions and created some form of reparation for the victims. It is worth noting that the South African way of dealing with the crimes of its past was largely supported by the international community.[425] Although, during the apartheid regime,

421 Paul Lansing, & Julie C. King, "South Africa's Truth and Reconciliation Commission: The Conflict Between Individual Justice and the National Healing in the Post-Apartheid Age" (1998) 15 Ariz. J. Int'l & Comp. L. 753 at 767.

422 Kevin A. O'Brien, "Truth and Reconciliation in South Africa: Confronting the Past, Building the Future?" (2000) 15:2 International Relations 1 at 9.

423 See e.g. Lansing & King, *supra* note 421 at 771. According to studies, 50 to 60 per cent of the victims regret having testified before the amnesty commission; see Yves Beigbeder, *Judging War Criminals* (New York: St. Martin's Press, 1999) at 121.

424 Lansing & King, *supra* note 421 at 784. The South African example also shows that TRCs work best when a reformist political coalition wants to bring about democratic changes. Referring to Chad's President Idriss Déby's false efforts to reveal the atrocities of the former regime by installing a truth commission, Snyder and Vinjamuri come to the conclusion that "[i]n the absence of an effective reformist coalition, truth commissions are at best an empty gesture and at worst a fig leaf covering up continued abuses." Snyder & Vinjamuri, *supra* note 17 at 33.

425 Another good example of an amnesty program backed by the international community is Haiti. In 1993, at about the same time when the ICTY

UN General Assembly resolutions repeatedly called for an implementation of the Apartheid Convention and for prosecutions of offenders, the General Assembly finally appreciated the transition to democracy without reiterating its demands for prosecutions.[426]

The example of South Africa has shown that a transition relying on amnesties does not always promote a climate of impunity that must be rejected as violating victims' rights or the interests of the international community. Furthermore, as Sadat underlines, TRCs *per se* do not threaten individual accountability and do not automatically preclude criminal prosecutions.[427]

5.1.2.2. Mozambique – constructive impunity?

Mozambique chose another way to cope with the crimes of its civil war. The General Peace Agreement of October 1992 not only ended a brutal civil war, that had cost nearly one million lives since its outbreak after Mozambique's independence in 1975, but also granted blanket amnesties to former combatants of both sides, even though atrocious crimes had been committed against civilians.[428] The ruling party, the Front for Liberation of Mozambique (FRELIMO), and the opposition party, the Mozambican National Resistance (RENAMO), had concluded that no truth-telling in exchange for amnesty would take place; they simply wanted to "move on".[429] Therefore, Mozambique did not install a war crimes tribunal or a truth commission, thus disregarding the two most common mechanisms to deal with crimes in a post-conflict period. Former combatants were successfully reintegrated into society through traditional healing and cleansing

---

was established, the Security Council and the Organization of American States pressured the re-instated President Aristide to accept the negotiated broad amnesty for the military; see Jessica Gavron, "Amnesties in the Light of Developments in International Law and the Establishment of the International Criminal Court" (2002) 51 I.C.L.Q. 91 at 106.

426 *Ibid.* at 115.

427 Sadat, "Transformation", *supra* note 411 at 53.

428 See Ruth Wedgwood, Harold K. Jacobson & Allan Gerson, "Peace Building, The Private Sector's Role" (2001) 95 A.J.I.L. 102 at 108; Gallagher, *supra* note 417 at 188; Cobban, *Amnesty after Atrocity?*, *supra* note 16 at 142.

429 Cobban, *Amnesty after Atrocity?*, *supra* note 16 at 141.

rituals.[430] The peace agreement also allowed rebel leaders to become part of the political scene.[431]

It is important to note that the peace process was heavily supported by the international community, which carried most of the costs for disarmament, demobilization and reintegration.[432] Concentrating on material poverty and underdevelopment was considered more imperative to achieve a peaceful transition and long-lasting peace than addressing reconciliation *per se*; a South African model of reconciliation was not considered necessary.[433] Moreover, the implementation of the peace agreement was facilitated by the UN peacekeeping mission ONUMOZ, deployed in December 1992. Thanks to the lasting stability, Mozambique has since then experienced a modest, but noteworthy economic recovery.[434]

5.1.2.3. Lomé, Dayton and Naivasha – ambiguous ways to achieve peace

Generally, international negotiators encounter greater difficulties when mass atrocities are still going on and when, at the same time, a peace agreement is urgently needed to end fighting, than when violence has already stopped and reconciliation mechanisms can start to work. In Sierra Leone, for instance, the international community felt obligated to include Foday Sankoh in the peace negotiations, even though there was heavy evidence that the leader of the Revolutionary United Front (RUF) was responsible for crimes against humanity and war crimes committed in the decade-long conflict. The Lomé Peace Agreement, signed on July 7, 1999 by the parties to the conflict and the Special Representative of the UN Secretary General, foresaw the establishment of a TRC to enable reconciliation in the country, but it also granted full amnesty to the members of the RUF, including Sankoh, and promised the latter the position of vice president in the Sierra Leonean government.[435] Although the general world opinion was

---

430 *Ibid.* at 159.

431 Gallagher, *supra* note 417 at 188.

432 *Ibid.* at 152.

433 *Ibid.* at 166.

434 See e.g. a report of the World Bank, "War-to-Peace Transition in Mozambique: The Provincial Reintegration Support Program" (July 1997), online: World Bank Group <http://www.worldbank.org/afr/findings/english/find90.htm>.

435 See article 5(2) of the agreement; article 9 states that "the Government of Sierra Leone shall take appropriate legal steps to grant corporate Foday

already moving towards "ending a climate of impunity", as manifested by the Rome Statute, a precarious peace agreement including blanket amnesties for notorious war criminals was concluded by the government. It was backed by the United Nations,[436] even if the UN Special Representative affirmed that the amnesty provisions should not apply to international crimes, such as genocide, crimes against humanity and war crimes.[437]

Mozambique's successful path following the 1992 peace agreement was often evoked to claim that amnesties could also work in other contexts, such as in Sierra Leone.[438] However, Sankoh demonstrated after the conclusion of the agreement that he could not be stopped by these "soft" means. Hostilities including attacks on the civilian population by the RUF continued without interruption, and it quickly became obvious that Sankoh's acceptance of the peace agreement had only been tac-

Sankoh absolute and free pardon." See *Lomé Peace Agreement*, UN Doc. S/1999/777 (7 July 1999). Another example where the United Nations opted against criminal investigations due to political considerations is Afghanistan. Even though, in September 2002, the UN High Commissioner for Human Rights, Mary Robinson, urged to investigate political leaders of the UN-backed Afghan government because of their alleged responsibility for war crimes, the UN administrator Lakhdar Brahimi argued that such investigations would only endanger peace and stability in the country; for more information, see Snyder & Vinjamuri, *supra* note 17 at 8.

436 Several representatives of the international community also signed the agreement, including the presidents of Burkina Faso, Liberia, Nigeria and Togo and international representatives from the UN, OAU, ECOWAS and the Commonwealth; see *Lomé Peace Agreement*, *supra* note 435 at 31.

437 As Gallagher notes, this reservation was added so late that it does not appear in early copies of the agreement, such as in the UN document cited above; see Gallagher, *supra* note 417 at 163, note 115. Kofi Annan also made it clear that it had been hard to accept this peace deal: "No one can feel happy about a peace accepted on such terms […] it is very hard to reconcile with the goal of ending the climate of impunity;" cited in Victoria Brittain, "Unrealistic Humanitarians" *The Guardian* (4 August 1999), online: Guardian Unlimited <http://www.guardian.co.uk/comment/story/0,,280229,00.html>.

438 Although Gallagher argues that the circumstances in Mozambique and Sierra Leone were remarkably similar, he also underlines that there are important differences. Due to the absence of natural resources in Mozambique, the RENAMO was more motivated to disarm and reintegrate itself in the political process than Foday Sankoh's RUF was; see Gallagher, *supra* note 417 at 188.

tical.[439] He was finally arrested in May 2000 and, in 2003, indicted by the Prosecutor of the newly established hybrid tribunal, the Special Court for Sierra Leone.[440]

Similarly, mediators in the Bosnian conflict had no better choice than to include Slobodan Milosevic in the negotiations, even though there was already considerable evidence at the time that Milosevic had either supported the ethnic cleansing carried out by the Bosnian Serbs or had, at least, not tried to avoid it.[441] In fact, the United States, as leading negotiator, had to rely on Milosevic because they did not want to deal directly with the Bosnian Serb leaders Radovan Karadzic and Ratko Mladic, who were already indicted by the ICTY Prosecutor at the time. Nevertheless, the result was "dealing with evil to end evil."[442] If the Dayton agreement ended the atrocities in Bosnia and drew a new map to divide the land between Bosnian Serbs and the Muslim-Croatian federation, it also strengthened the power of leading nationalists in the region, particularly of Milosevic himself and Croatian President Franjo Tudjman. Although the negotiators tried to maintain a high pressure on Milosevic while Dayton was implemented, the agreement inevitably empowered the "international statesman"[443] Milosevic and, in public opinion, confused his personal responsibility for the crimes committed during the Bosnian conflict. This power allowed him to orchestrate the ethnic cleansing of Albanians in Kosovo only a few years later. It has even been argued that "[t]he bloodshed of Kosovo is a symptom of the approach that strengthened Milosevic and Tudjman,"[444] and that Milosevic had received "de facto immunity"[445] in Dayton.

---

439 John L. Hirsch, *Sierra Leone: Diamonds and the Struggle for Democracy* (Boulder, Colo.: Lynne Rienner Publishers, 2001) at 89.

440 *Prosecutor v. Foday Sankoh* (2003), SCSL-03-02-I-001 (Indictment, 7 March 2003) (Special Court for Sierra Leone); due to Sankoh's death a few months later, the indictment was withdrawn.

441 Sadat, "Transformation", *supra* note 411 at 69.

442 Derek Chollet, *The Road to the Dayton Accords, A Study of American Statecraft* (New York: Palgrave Macmillan, 2005) at 199.

443 Adam LeBor, *Milosevic, A Biography* (New Haven: Yale University Press, 2004) at 253.

444 Warren Bass, "The Triage of Dayton" (1997) 77:5 Foreign Affairs 95 at 96. However, Bass later concedes to appreciate that Dayton, at least temporarily, stopped the fighting; see *ibid.* at 101.

445 Sadat, "Transformation", *supra* note 411 at 71. On the policy of the ICTY and

Arguments that indicting Milosevic would only persevere and prolong the conflict were reiterated during the Kosovo crisis. Although Milosevic had already been indicted by the ICTY for the additional crimes he was allegedly responsible for committing in Kosovo, the UN Human Rights Commission's Special Rapporteur for the former Yugoslavia nonetheless suggested in 2000 that promising immunity was the only way to remove Milosevic from power.[446] Although the activity of the ICTY was certainly not the only factor that must be taken into account, it is striking that a peace agreement was achieved shortly after Milosevic had been indicted for war crimes and crimes against humanity.[447] Milosevic was finally arrested in March 2001 by the Serbian police and surrendered to the ICTY. Unfortunately, the Kosovo crisis had been necessary to show that one of the key players in Dayton had had no intention to stop abusing his power. The threat of being indicted in The Hague did not seem to have a major influence on Milosevic as "he ignored Western diplomats' face-to-face warnings that he would be prosecuted if he failed to stop Serbian abuses in Kosovo."[448]

The examples of Sankoh and Milosevic both indicate that a climate of impunity does typically not contribute to settling an armed conflict and achieving lasting peace, in particular when the key players remain in power. In both cases, the offenders were able to carry on their criminal behavior. The international community, having recently established the first war crimes tribunals since Nuremberg and Tokyo and increasingly calling for international justice, seemed to have no better choice than to endorse the promising but dangerous peace agreements of Lomé and Dayton. Although it was considered impossible to remove both leaders from power without further bloodshed, trying to prosecute them earlier might have helped avoid a new outbreak of violence in Sierra Leone as well as the Kosovo crisis.

The agreement settling the conflict in southern Sudan is another recent example of a peace agreement that fell short on providing justice but was nevertheless approved by the international community. The peace process in Naivasha, Kenya, resulted in the Comprehensive Peace Agreement that was concluded between the Sudanese government and the Sudan

---

the "rumors" concerning Milosevic's possible amnesty, see Frédéric Mégret, "The Politics of International Criminal Justice" (2002) 13 E.J.I.L. 1261 at 1277.

446 See Sadat, "Transformation", *supra* note 411 at 71.

447 Robinson, *supra* note 399 at 496.

448 Snyder & Vinjamuri, *supra* note 17 at 20.

People's Liberation Army (SPLA) and signed in Nairobi on January 9, 2005. The agreement sought to end the 20 year-long conflict between the Islamic North and the Christian-dominated South, promising the SPLA an important share of political power and oil revenues. A referendum, to be held in 2011, will decide whether the South will remain in Sudan or become independent.[449]

The origins of the conflict in southern Sudan are similar to the one of the Darfur conflict.[450] Underneath the religious connotation, the conflict in the south is also marked by the center-periphery dichotomy typical for Sudan. Moreover, the north-south peace process also had a direct influence on the recent developments in Darfur. International negotiators put a lot of effort into the Naivasha peace process and were eager to have the peace agreement finally signed, even though it simply disregarded the question of prosecuting perpetrators, thus granting a *de facto* blanket amnesty for war criminals of all sides. As a result, the horrible crimes, including summary executions, rape, abductions, and forced recruitment,[451] committed by government troops and pro-government militias as well as the SPLA throughout the whole conflict will not be recalled, at least not officially. At a time when the Rome Statute had already entered into force and proclaimed in its preamble to end a climate of impunity, thus highlighting a world-wide tendency, "justice was quietly put aside".[452] The Naivasha agreement became the most recent case where the international community considered implicit impunity – not even a formally granted amnesty – a necessary prerequisite to make the warring parties, in particular the government in Khartoum, sign a peace agreement.

---

449 For an analysis of this provision, see Denis M. Tull, "Sudan after the Naivasha Peace Agreement, No Champagne Yet" (February 2005) German Institute for International and Security Affairs, SWP Comments 3, online: Stiftung Wissenschaft und Politik <http://swp-berlin.org/en/produkte/swp_aktuell_detail.php?id=4207> at 1.

450 It is interesting to note that the SPLA supported the nascent rebellion in Darfur by sending weapons to Darfur; see Res Publica, *supra* note 85 at 10. For more information on the ambiguous relationship between the SLA and the SPLA, see Flint & de Waal, *supra* note 86 at 81.

451 For more information on the conflict, see e.g. Marc Lavergne & Fabrice Weissman, "Sudan, Who Benefits from Humanitarian Aid?" in Fabrice Weissman, ed., *In the Shadow of 'Just Wars', Violence Politics and Humanitarian Action* (Ithaca, N.Y.: Cornell University Press, 2004) 137 at 147.

452 Flint & de Waal, *supra* note 86 at 129.

5.2. The ICC Prosecutor and the legal obligation to prosecute

5.2.1. Consequences for the ICC

As it has been argued above, a legal obligation for states to prosecute international crimes limits the ICC Prosecutor in his discretion to accept amnesties or, more generally, to remain inactive when facing certain situations of impunity. Where treaty law has created a clear duty for states to investigate and prosecute, the objective of the Rome Statute to end impunity for the worst crimes would be perverted if, given an admissible case, grave breaches of the 1949 Geneva Convention or genocide were not investigated and prosecuted by the Prosecutor. Although the wording of the Rome Statute does not distinguish between the various types of crimes but lists genocide, war crimes and crimes against humanity as equally punishable, the analysis made above shows that the discretion is larger concerning crimes against humanity as well as war crimes committed in non-international armed conflicts. For these crimes, the role of the ICC is comparable to a state acting in line with the principle of permissible universal jurisdiction: offenders can be prosecuted, but if they are not, international legal obligations are not violated.

The question to what degree or precisely through which means individuals must be held accountable in order to satisfy the requirements of the Rome Statute, especially in the context of national amnesty programs, has not been settled. Generally, amnesties and even blatant situations of impunity, such as in the situation of southern Sudan, are still accepted by the international community out of political considerations. Even though the ICC, due to its mandate, must be devoted to individual criminal accountability, it is clear that the acceptance of TRCs by the international community also increases the discretion of the Prosecutor to defer to non-prosecutorial accountability mechanisms, with the *caveat* that blanket amnesties, without any mechanism of individual accountability or truth-telling *à la* South Africa, seem to have largely been outlawed by states. Although the delegates at the Rome Conference could not find a consensus as to how the ICC should deal with amnesties or TRCs, the ICC can be expected to never accept blanket amnesties. In the words of Robinson, "blanket amnesties are the precise antithesis of the ICC."[453]

453 Robinson, *supra* note 399 at 497.

Other mechanisms, such as granting conditional amnesties through a commission after hearings that come close to judicial proceedings are, however, not equivalent to impunity and do not threaten the objective of delivering justice and holding individuals accountable. The acceptability of these mechanisms by the ICC is closely linked to the principle of complementarity and article 17 of the Rome Statute,[454] which stipulates that a case is inadmissible when it has been "*investigated* by a State which has jurisdiction over it and the State has *decided* not to prosecute the person concerned, unless the decision resulted from the unwillingness or inability of the State to *genuinely prosecute*."[455] If ordinary criminal investigations and prosecutions have not taken place, the first prerequisite to fulfill this provision is that a non-prosecutorial body, such as the TRC in South Africa, investigate the crimes. Although it has been argued that only criminal investigations can be subsumed under the term "investigations",[456] the ordinary sense of the word "investigation" suggests that a commission that systematically and objectively gathers the evidence can also meet this criterion.[457]

The second condition of article 17(1)(b) is that the state has discretion to decide whether or not to prosecute the person concerned. Unconditional amnesties must therefore be excluded, since, in the absence of a substantial decision, they do not leave open any other option but amnesty. The South African TRC, with its genuine power to grant amnesties or not, serves again as a possible example and stands in contrast to situations like the one in Uganda. The Ugandan Amnesty Act only requires a former combatant to report to an official and to surrender his weapons,[458] thus granting quasi-unconditional amnesty and leaving no option for the amnesty commission to refuse the issuance of an amnesty certificate.

As a third requirement of article 17(1)(b), the state must not be unable or unwilling "genuinely to prosecute", which refers to the provisions stipulated in article 17(2) and (3); above all, non-prosecutorial proceedings must not be undertaken with the "intent of shielding the person concerned from

---

454 For a more general analysis of article 17 and the principle of complementarity, see above, c. 3.5.1.

455 Article 17(1)(b) of the Rome Statute [emphasis added].

456 John T. Holmes, "The Principle of Complementarity" in Roy S. Lee, ed., *The International Criminal Court: The Making of the Rome Statute - Issues, Negotiations, Results* (The Hague: Kluwer Law International, 1999) 41 at 77.

457 See also Robinson, *supra* note 399 at 500.

458 See above, at note 287.

criminal responsibility."[459] If the main purpose of an amnesty program is to bring about reconciliation while uncovering the crimes committed, it would not appear to primarily shield the offenders from criminal responsibility. Those TRCs which come close to judicial proceedings, thanks to public hearings and the possibility of alternative sentences, would not be contradictory to article 17(2)(c), which states that the proceedings must not be "conducted in a manner which, in the circumstances, is inconsistent with an intent to bring the person concerned to justice."[460]

In sum, the discretion of the ICC Prosecutor to proceed with an investigation or prosecution in an admissible case chiefly depends on the type of crime committed, with international law significantly determining the prosecutorial discretion. Moreover, the efforts of the respective state to deal with the crimes committed also play an important role. In addition to the general question of complementarity, the way amnesties are granted and TRCs are established as well as what mandate they are given will decide whether the ICC could accept nationally granted amnesties or alternative justice mechanisms without infringing on its own principles.

In this context, it will be important for the ICC to determine who its primary constituencies are, an assessment that should be valid both generally and for a specific context. As a practical consequence, the prosecutorial discretion will be exercised differently if international prosecutions are considered to address mainly the international society as a whole or the "local constituencies"[461] of an armed conflict. This question is difficult to answer. Yet it is one of the key questions that determine the exercise of prosecutorial discretion. As it has been noted, although "[j]ustice for an entire society may mean individual injustices for victims, [...] ignoring or sacrificing the needs of individual victims may not serve the long-term interests of the society."[462]

---

459 Article 17(2)(a) of the Rome Statute.

460 Article 17(2)(c) of the Rome Statute.

461 Frédéric Mégret, "International Prosecutors: Accountability and Ethics", Leuven Centre for Global Governance Studies, Working Paper No. 18 (December 2008), online: SSRN <http://ssrn.com/abstract=1313691> at 35. Mégret lists three separate constituencies to which an international prosecutor can be symbolically accountable, namely the judicial constituency, the international constituencies and the local constituencies.

462 Avril McDonald & Roelof Haveman, "Prosecutorial Discretion – Some Thoughts on 'Objectifying' the Exercise of Prosecutorial Discretion by the Prosecutor of the ICC", Expert consultation process on general issues rele-

5.2.2. Significance for the conflicts in northern Uganda and Darfur

The conflict in northern Uganda is a non-international armed conflict. It is characterized by protracted armed violence between the Ugandan army and the LRA as well as by atrocious and wide-spread attacks on the civilian population. The long-lasting support of the Sudanese government for the LRA does not transform the conflict into an international conflict, since the level of support is clearly not high enough to speak of effective or overall control over the LRA by Khartoum. As the ICTY Appeals Chamber established in *Tadic*,

> "[i]n order to attribute the acts of a military or paramilitary group to a State, it must be proved that the State wields overall control over the group, not only by equipping and financing the group, but also by coordinating or helping in the general planning of its military activity."[463]

This means there is only one state, namely Uganda, directly involved in the conflict in northern Uganda. The facts that fighting has taken place on the territory of Sudan and that the LRA has used the territory of Southern Sudan and the DRC as its rear basis do not alter the situation; there is no armed conflict between two states according to international humanitarian law.[464] As a consequence, the Prosecutor only listed crimes with respect to a non-international armed conflict in his applications for arrest warrants against Joseph Kony and the other LRA commanders. The arrest warrants contain counts with respect to crimes against humanity, as listed in article 7 of the Rome Statute, and to war crimes, as listed in article 8(2)(c) and (e) of the Statute.

---

vant to the ICC Office of the Prosecutor (15 April 2003), online: International Criminal Court <http://www.icc-cpi.int/library/organs/otp/ mcdonald_haveman.pdf> at 8.

463 *Prosecutor v. Dusko*, *supra* note 301 at para. 131.

464 Article 2 common to the four Geneva Conventions speaks of an "armed conflict which may arise between two or more of the High Contracting Parties" compared to an "armed conflict not of an international character occurring in the territory of one of the High Contracting Parties" (common article 3); see e.g. *Geneva Convention Relative to the Protection of Civilian Persons in Time of War (Geneva IV)*, 12 August 1949, 75 U.N.T.S. 287 (entered into force 21 October 1950).

Similarly, the conflict in Darfur is clearly not of an international character either. The protracted armed violence between the Sudanese army, including its militia forces, and the various rebel groups, as well as the attacks on the civilian population are part of an internal armed conflict. The counts contained in the Prosecutor's application for the first arrest warrants in this case, against Ahmad Harun and Ali Kushayb confirm this view. According to the Prosecutor, crimes against humanity, as defined in article 7 of the Rome Statute, and war crimes, as defined in article 8(2)(c), have been committed.[465]

In the light of the analysis made above with respect to an international obligation to prosecute war crimes and crimes against humanity committed during a non-international armed conflict, this means that no state would be obliged under international law to prosecute these crimes. As a consequence, the legal discretion of the ICC Prosecutor whether to prosecute these crimes is considerably large in the situations of northern Uganda and Darfur compared to the situation of an international armed conflict. It is, however, likely that the massive crimes committed in Darfur and the shocking attacks of the LRA on the civilian population support a further shift towards a customary legal duty to prosecute crimes against humanity and war crimes other than grave breaches of the Geneva Conventions. The ICC itself might even try to accelerate the tendency towards a legal obligation to prosecute by arguing that such an obligation has already developed, in particular in the light of the establishment of several international criminal tribunals and the ICC itself. Only this role of the ICC will probably be approved by those states and non-governmental organizations[466] which advocated for the establishment of the ICC in order to close the loopholes where genocide, crimes against humanity and war crimes have not been prosecuted so far.

For the situation of Darfur, the question whether genocide has been committed is of particular concern, both from a legal-analytical and a human rights perspective. Even though this discussion is all but helpful for the victims,[467] it plays an important role to determine the legal discretion of the ICC Prosecutor. As concluded above, the prosecutorial discretion is

---

465 ICC, "Prosecutor's Application under Article 58(7)", *supra* note 121 at 6.

466 It has been suggested that the ICC Prosecutor may be accountable to NGOs; Alison M. Danner, "Enhancing the Legitimacy and Accountability of Prosecutorial Discretion at the International Criminal Court" (2003) 97 A.J.I.L. 510 at 532.

467 See above, note 115.

minimal in the case of genocide; perpetrators of genocide, considered as the worst of all crimes and specifically outlawed in a convention 60 years ago, must not go unpunished.

In 2005, the Commission of Inquiry reached the conclusion that "no genocidal policy has been pursued and implemented in Darfur by the Government authorities,"[468] but the Commission did not reject the possibility that some individuals, including government officials, may be acting with genocidal intent. In this case, states would have a legal obligation to prosecute. In such a situation of factual ambiguity, it is, however, not clear what degree of certainty regarding the offenders' intent is necessary in order to trigger a legal obligation for a state to carry out thorough investigations and bring the case before a competent tribunal. A sound approach might be the standard of proof required for the issuance of an arrest warrant under the Rome Statute, namely "reasonable grounds to believe".[469]

The importance of this deliberation in the situation of Darfur has radically changed since the Prosecutor's application for an arrest warrant against Omar al-Bashir. The Prosecutor concluded that there was enough evidence[470] showing that the Sudanese President has pursued a genocidal policy in Darfur and seeks to prosecute him for the crime of genocide according to article 6 of the Rome Statute, for which an international obligation to prosecute exists. This means that inactivity as well as a de-activation of the ICC would be inconsistent with international law. Although the Prosecutor's view on the question of genocidal intent is controversial, the degree to which a prosecution is required has nonetheless increased.

Conversely, the Sudanese government limits the discretion of the Prosecutor whether or not to proceed due to its minimal efforts of bringing the persons concerned to justice. As argued above,[471] the ICC and its approach to deal with the situation in Darfur can hardly be influenced by certain so-called judicial attempts of the Sudanese government. In the

468 UNCOI, *supra* note 96 at 4. On UNCOI's findings, see Schabas, "Darfur and the 'Odious Scourge'", *supra* note 115; for a comparison to the position of the United States, see Jamie A. Mathew, "The Darfur Debate: Whether the ICC Should Determine that the Atrocities in Darfur Constitute Genocide" (2006) 18 Fla. J. Int'l L. 517, demanding that the ICC hold the government of Sudan and the Janjaweed responsible for genocide.

469 See above, at note 253.

470 Article 53(2) of the Rome Statute speaks of a "sufficient basis for a prosecution."

471 See c. 3.5.3.

rather unlikely case that Khartoum start to seriously deal with the crimes committed in Darfur, thus showing itself willing and able to bring the persons concerned to justice, the principle of complementarity would fully apply and confer the primary competence to proceed to the national judicial system. National proceedings could still be examined by the OTP on their compliance with the standards set out in article 17 of the Rome Statute. Moreover, already indicted individuals would remain under the primary jurisdiction of the ICC, with the ICC itself deciding whether or not to hand over the cases to the Sudanese authorities.[472]

It is interesting to note that already several years ago, a consortium of Sudanese civil society organizations called for a broad truth commission, operating with the principles of amnesty, to achieve peace and democracy in Sudan.[473] If such a TRC and a workable amnesty program were set up in Sudan, something that might be considered particularly necessary in Darfur in order to stop the violence lastingly and to reconcile the largely divided society,[474] the discretion of the Prosecutor to defer to these nationally granted amnesties would be determined by the nature and functioning of the TRC, as explored above.

Similarly, the discussions on the situation in Uganda, and in particular the various announcements of the government to try the LRA leadership in local or "traditional" courts or provide for alternative mechanisms[475] show

---

472 Any other conclusion would appear unsound and inconsistent with the Rome Statute. If states could automatically regain (primary) jurisdiction over an individual already indicted by the ICC, proceedings before the ICC would constantly run high risks of being curtailed by states.

473 Yoanes Ajawin, "Human Rights Violations and Transitional Justice" in A.H. Abdel Salam & Alex de Waal, eds., *The Phoenix State: Civil Society and the Future of Sudan* (Lawrenceville, N.J.: Red Sea Press, 2001) 113 at 130.

474 A vague amnesty was already granted by Presidential Decree No.114 to members of the armed groups that signed the DPA and subsequent signatories. It is unclear whether this amnesty should also apply to members of the Sudanese army; see Human Rights Watch, "Sudan: National Courts Have Done Nothing on Darfur" (11 June 2007), online: Human Rights Watch <http://hrw.org/english/docs/2007/06/11/sudan16110.htm>. The possibility of a regime change in Khartoum, which might be combined with a self-amnesty for government officials, is currently rather unlikely and will, therefore, not be taken into account here.

475 In early 2008, for instance, President Museveni stated that "[w]hat we have agreed with our people is that they should face traditional justice, which is more compensatory than a retributive system," cited in Chris McGreal,

that complementarity and the kind and quality of domestic proceedings that can fulfill the requirements of article 17 are a major issue for the ICC. Uganda cannot simply de-activate the Court and invoke the principle of complementarity by investigating and prosecuting individuals already indicted by the ICC. However, it would be consistent with the objectives of the Rome Statute to opt for national proceedings, even if the situation had already been brought before the ICC. The Prosecutor could then monitor the domestic proceedings to ensure their genuineness and intervene if necessary. *A priori*, it is in the interests of the ICC that proceedings be carried out at the national level; trials in The Hague should always remain a second-best option. This assumption is based on two reasons. First, it is important to encourage national justice systems to react strongly and comprehensively if genocide, crimes against humanity or war crimes are committed. It is the responsibility of national prosecutors and judges to pursue alleged perpetrators; the ICC is only mandated to step in if they are unwilling or unable to do so. Second, very practical reasons, above all the limited financial and human resources of the Court, make it indispensable to favor national trials. Compared to the significant resources spent for an international trial,[476] domestic proceedings carried out by an already existing judicial system that has better and more immediate access to evidence material and witnesses simply cost less.

5.3. Prosecutorial discretion in the context of article 53 of the Rome Statute

The discretion of the ICC Prosecutor is not only guided by general norms of international law and the principle of complementarity but also by more specific provisions of the Rome Statute, which are distinct from the aforementioned line of reasoning. First, article 13 stipulates a very general dis-

---

"Museveni Refuses to Hand Over Rebel Leaders to War Crimes Court" *The Guardian* (13 March 2008), online: The Guardian <http://www.guardian.co.uk/world/2008/mar/13/uganda.internationalcrime>.

476 Both the ICTY and the ICTR have spent at least one billion US dollars each. However, the fact that international trials are comparatively costly should not represent a criticism against international criminal justice institutions *per se* and determine a preference for national trials in any case. The costs cannot be weighed up against the unique benefits of international trials. Moreover, thanks to the development of a body of international case law, the proceedings are likely to be faster and the costs lower in the future.

cretion for the ICC to exercise jurisdiction. "The Court *may* exercise its jurisdiction"[477] after having been activating through one of the triggering mechanisms, but it does not have to do so. Moreover, according to article 53(1)(c), the Prosecutor has to take into account the interests of justice when deciding on the initiation of investigations. A similar provision guides the decision whether there is a sufficient basis for a prosecution (article 53(2)(c)). These articles are the most important provisions of the Rome Statute which affirm the discretion of the Prosecutor not to proceed in some cases, independently from the manner in which the respective state acts.[478] Since these cases are not clearly defined, an interpretation of the vague provision "in the interests of justice" is necessary.

Generally, the ICC, and within the institution above all the Prosecutor, must be devoted to prosecuting international crimes, because of its determination "to put an end to impunity for the perpetrators of such crimes and thus to contribute to the prevention of such crimes."[479] The Rome Statute seems, however, to follow a broader notion of justice than the rather narrow definition in the sense of prosecutorial criminal justice. According to article 53(2)(c), not only the gravity of the crime, the age of the perpetrator, his role in the alleged crime, and other factors regularly found in general criminal law are to be taken into account, but also the interests of victims.[480] This provision, "the interests of victims," stands out as the most important one in the context of ongoing violence. These interests are not limited to the victims' opinion or preference, in other words whether they want to bring the perpetrators to justice, favor amnesties as an incentive to end violence, or have already forgiven the crimes and simply want to "move on". It has been convincingly argued that "[t]his aspect of prosecutorial discretion is particularly important when investigations or prosecutions may arguably prolong or aggravate an ongoing conflict or undermine a fragile peace

477 Article 13 of the Rome Statute [emphasis added].

478 The Prosecutor exercises this discretion under the supervision of the Pre-Trial Chamber. If the Pre-Trial Chamber does not approve the decision of the Prosecutor not to proceed it can, according to article 53(3)(b), oblige the Prosecutor to investigate and/or prosecute.

479 Preamble of the Rome Statute, para. 5.

480 As this list is not exhaustive, other factors can also be taken into consideration, thus enlarging the discretionary powers of the Prosecutor; see Philippa Webb, "The ICC Prosecutor's Discretion Not to Proceed in the 'Interest of Justice'" (2005) 50 Crim. L.Q. 305 at 326.

process."[481] As shown by the situation in northern Uganda, ICC indictments might be an obstacle to the conclusion of a peace agreement and therefore prolong an armed conflict and the suffering of victims. The situation in Darfur has experienced a similar development, in particular since the Prosecutor's application for an arrest warrant against Bashir and the subsequent increased problems regarding the deployment and work on the ground of the UN-AU peacekeeping operation and the work of humanitarian organizations in Darfur. In such a situation, the interests of victims probably do not consist in trying to achieve immediate retributive justice. Victims will primarily be interested in stopping the ongoing atrocities and ending their suffering as quickly as possible. In certain cases, it is obvious that this will only be possible to the detriment of instant indictments.

The arguments voiced by members of local peace initiatives in northern Uganda, who have been emphasizing the necessity of amnesties to bring the LRA leaders to the negotiating table, are a good example of an expression of the victims' concerns.[482] Most notably, people from the region, including those directly suffering under the LRA, asked the ICC to withdraw the indictments.[483] Asserting to express the interests of the victims, the Paramount Chief of the Acholi people in northern Uganda traveled to London, Washington DC, and Ottawa in July 2007 to convince Western governments to support a withdrawal of the ICC indictments.[484] Unfortunately, a withdrawal of the ICC could not bring about peace immediately, since the involvement of the ICC is clearly not the only obstacle to the conclusion of a peace agreement. It should, however, be emphasized once again that the provisions contained in article 53 are purposely directed at cases where armed groups are in principle willing to stop the fighting and agree to a peace accord, but, due to the prospect of criminal prosecutions in The Hague, develop a nothing-to-lose attitude and continue to commit atrocities. In short, investigations and/or prosecutions cannot be in the interests of the victims when the involvement of the ICC frustrates peace negotiations and prolongs human suffering.

---

481 Akhavan, "The LRA Case", *supra* note 40 at 416.

482 The Acholi Religious Leaders Peace Initiative has been particularly active; see Branch, "International Justice, Local Injustice", *supra* note 279.

483 Ross, *supra* note 280; see also OCHA, "UGANDA", *supra* note 281.

484 Erin Baines & Adrian Bradbury, "Peace in Northern Uganda, but Whose Justice?" *Sudan Tribune* (2 August 2007), online: Sudan Tribune <http://www.sudantribune.com/spip.php?article23087>.

On the one hand, since the interests of the victims must be taken into account, the ICC Prosecutor has the obligation to balance these practical considerations with the general insistence on prosecuting alleged perpetrators of crimes under the Rome Statute. Therefore, articles 53(1)(c) and 53(2)(c) underline not only the discretion of the Prosecutor not to proceed with investigations and prosecutions, at least temporarily, but also create an important *caveat*: the Prosecutor cannot act without considering the effects of investigations and indictments on the victims' situation. On the other hand, the Prosecutor should not simply yield to the interests of the victims and close the file. Even though the interests of the victims may put off proceedings because of a situation of imminent threat, the investigations and/or prosecutions should only be considered as postponed. Political situations can change rapidly, in particular when an armed conflict is still going on. The salient question will therefore often be how to determine the best timing to indict those who are most responsible for the crimes committed but who also influence the course of an armed conflict and a possible peace process.

In conclusion, the interests of victims might sometimes seem to obstruct the quest for justice. It should, however be kept in mind that not every mechanism of holding individuals accountable and deliver some form of justice to the victims is forever banned. This is highly relevant in a post-conflict period, when efficient reconciliation must take place as expeditiously as possible in order to avoid another outbreak of violence. A TRC, for instance, which does not automatically grant blanket amnesties but can be perceived as a true non-prosecutorial alternative to trials, might be perfectly consistent with the interests of the victims, while prosecutions might be too delicate and unnecessarily endanger a weak peace process or a newly established, still fragile democratic system.

5.4. The policy of the ICC Prosecutor concerning his discretion

So far, the policy and statements of the Prosecutor confirm the scope and nature of prosecutorial discretion and its exercise asserted above. Since it is obvious that the ICC cannot consecrate an important part of its work to political analyses and must avoid becoming a bargaining chip in negotiations between the warring parties, ICC officials cannot be expected to acknowledge that their decisions might depend on political deliberations.[485]

485 Philippe Kirsch clearly underlined this assumption after five years of the

The Prosecutor has even determinedly claimed to disregard political considerations when selecting situations and cases. In November 2008, for instance, Luis Moreno Ocampo declared before the ICC Assembly of States Parties: "I have to apply the law. Nothing more, nothing less. The decision that ending impunity will ensure lasting peace and security was taken in Rome. I should not, and I will not take into consideration political considerations."[486]

However, the Prosecutor has also suggested that he would not dogmatically proceed with prosecutions in all circumstances. Considering the interests of justice, the Prosecutor, for instance, stated in a 2005 report that he and his office would "remain sensitive to developments" in regards to the restoration of peace and security in Darfur.[487] Furthermore, the Prosecutor has repeatedly underlined the importance of protecting victims and witnesses. He declared, for instance, in a report in 2006 that, due to the ongoing violence in Darfur, his office had conducted the investigations from outside Darfur in order to avoid exposing victims and witnesses to additional risks.[488]

The Prosecutor's step-by-step strategy in Darfur also underlines this assumption. The Prosecutor first targeted Ali Kushayb, a militia leader, and Ahmad Harun, a member of the government who has had an important influence on the conflict in Darfur as former Minister of State for the Interior and current Minister of State for Humanitarian Affairs. These two individual are, however, clearly not on the top of the chain of com-

---

entry into force of the Rome Statute: "Pour parvenir à l'universalité, l'une des clés du succès de la Cour va être de se conduire en temps qu'organe judiciaire, de ne pas se comporter en tant qu'organe politique. Et j'estime qu'on ne peut pas trouver trace, dans les quatre années passées depuis la désignation des juges et du procureur, de politisation de la Cour;" cited in "Le long chemin de la Cour pénale internationale vers l'universalité" *Le Monde* (30 June 2007).

486 ICC, "Address to the ASP", *supra* note 36 at 6.

487 International Criminal Court, "Report of the Prosecutor of the International Criminal Court, Mr. Luis Moreno Ocampo, to the UN Security Council Pursuant to UNSCR 1593 (2005)" (29 June 2005), online: International Criminal Court <http://www.icc-cpi.int/library/cases/ICC_Darfur_UNSC_Report_29-06-05_EN.pdf> at 5. In a 2007 report, the Prosecutor affirmed that he would continue to seek dialogue with the victims "to ensure that their interests are well understood"; see ICC, "Fifth Report of the Prosecutor", *supra* note 120 at 9.

488 ICC, "Fourth Report of the Prosecutor", *supra* note 115 at 3.

mand. The policy of the Prosecutor suggests that simultaneous charges against several Sudanese leaders and an immediate stigmatization of higher-ranked Sudanese officials, including President Bashir and possibly also Vice-President Taha, was considered too risky from a political perspective.[489]

In the case of northern Uganda, the exercise of prosecutorial discretion to take into account political developments is even more apparent than in the situation of Darfur. Although the involvement of the ICC was heavily criticized by many sides and has even become an obstacle for the government of Uganda itself to conclude the peace negotiations, the ICC showed that it had considered the political situation before indicting the leaders of the LRA and issuing arrest warrants against them. The fact that the arrest warrants were not unsealed immediately after their issuance but only a few months later suggests that the ICC was conscious of the relatively promising looking peace negotiations in mid-2005 and did not want to endanger them by adding to the complexity of the process.[490] It has been argued that this delay was above all intended to ensure the protection of victims and witnesses.[491] A member of the OTP bluntly affirmed in late 2005 that "[w]e had intended to pull back if negotiations were completed."[492]

Moreover, by explicitly referring to the Ugandan Amnesty Act in a press release, the ICC indicated that the issue of national amnesties would not be disregarded, thus underlining the importance of this aspect for proceedings before the ICC:

489 On the other hand, it could be argued that in the most recent case the Prosecutor did not duly take into consideration the political risks of publicly applying for an arrest warrant against the Sudanese president. The concerns regarding this non-secret application have already been addressed above.

490 The arrest warrants, issued two months after the Prosecutor's application on July 8, 2005, were unsealed by the Pre-Trial Chamber on October 13, 2005, probably following an unplanned leak of information; see International Criminal Court, "Facts and Procedure Regarding the Situation in Uganda" (14 October 2005), online: International Criminal Court <http://www2.icc-cpi.int/NR/rdonlyres/4BCE015E-9F70-4CD1-8AC2-4CACDB6070B6/277312/ICC_20051410056I_English2.pdf>.

491 See e.g. Wasana Punyasena, "Conflict Prevention and the International Criminal Court: Deterrence in a Changing World" (2006) 14 Michigan State Journal of International Law 39 at 57.

492 Cited in Allen, *supra* note 37 at 193.

> "In a bid to encourage members of the LRA to return to normal life, the Ugandan authorities have enacted an amnesty law. President Museveni has indicated to the Prosecutor his intention to amend this amnesty so as to exclude the leadership of the LRA, ensuring that those bearing the greatest responsibility for the crimes against humanity committed in northern Uganda are brought to justice."[493]

This declaration confirms the assumption that the ICC takes due notice of nationally granted amnesties and might adapt its approach accordingly, with the decision of the Prosecutor not to proceed with investigations and/or prosecutions because of an amnesty becoming a veritable possibility.

5.5. Political discretion of the Prosecutor despite the powers of the Security Council

International indictments may have major political repercussions and may affect international relations significantly. In particular when it comes to indicting political and military leaders, who are regularly most responsible for the worst crimes and will therefore be primarily targeted by the ICC Prosecutor, international criminal justice is inherently linked to the immunity of state officials and the relations between sovereign states. This immunity *ratione personae*, which is built on the notion that the highest state representatives must be able to travel freely to ensure functioning inter-state relations, is one of the core concepts of customary international law, as affirmed by the International Court of Justice in its *Arrest Warrant* ruling.[494]

Since political deliberations are therefore unavoidable in the context of international criminal justice, the fundamental question is whether jurists should make the decisions that are likely to have such important political consequences. Eminent commentators have argued that "decisions to prosecute should be taken by political authorities, such as the UN Security Council or the governments of affected states, not by judges who remain politically unaccountable."[495] Although this statement did not specifically

493 ICC, "President of Uganda Refers Situation to the ICC", *supra* note 166.

494 *Democratic Republic of the Congo v. Belgium, Case Concerning the Arrest Warrant of 11 April 2000* (Judgement, 14 February 2002) (International Court of Justice) at para. 53.

495 Snyder & Vinjamuri, *supra* note 17 at 44. Similarly, Matthew R. Brubacher suggests that the Prosecutor will follow a complementary policy in regard

address the competence of the ICC, the result of its claim is clear: highly political decisions in the context of international criminal justice should be taken by political organs, such as the Security Council, and not by the ICC. Following this line of reasoning, the ICC should be able to proceed without worrying about the political situation or the political effects of its involvement. Since the Security Council can block a politically inopportune ICC involvement according to article 16 of the Rome Statute, the ICC should therefore not restrain itself because of political concerns.

The negotiators of the Rome Statute clearly acknowledged that the involvement of the ICC might not always be politically appropriate and that the Security Council, deciding that a threat to international peace and security exists, should be able to interfere by adopting a resolution under Chapter VII of the UN Charter. Article 16 of the Rome Statute stipulates that the Security Council can suspend the activity of the OTP for twelve months; this period is renewable, theoretically indefinitely, under the same circumstances, in other words if the threat to international peace and security persists. This has led to the conclusion that "[p]otentially, states and the Security Council have the ability to reduce the ICC to an ad hoc institution by limiting it to situations where there is international and political consensus."[496]

Article 16 was one of the most sensitive and controversial issues during the negotiations of the Rome Statute, as the states' opinions on the relationship between the Security Council and the ICC varied significantly. Some states wanted to follow the draft proposal of the International Law Commission (ILC)[497] to subordinate the ICC to the Security Council, thus making the judicial institution dependent on the political organ. This proposal would have automatically barred the ICC from situations dealt with by the Security Council. Other states wanted as much autonomy for the

---

to the Security Council; Matthew R. Brubacher, "Political Discretion within the International Criminal Court" (2004) 2 Journal of International Criminal Justice 71 at 83.

496 Jackson Nyamuya Maogoto, *State Sovereignty and International Criminal Law: Versailles to Rome* (Ardsley, N.Y.: Transnational Publishers, 2003) at 221.

497 Article 23(3) of the draft statute reads: "No prosecution may be commenced under this Statute arising from a situation which is being dealt with by the Security Council as a threat to or breach of the peace or an act of aggression under Chapter VII of the Charter, unless the Security Council otherwise decides." International Law Commission, *supra* note 181.

ICC as possible to avoid a politicization of the proceedings before the Court and to ensure its independence.[498] The final article 16 is a compromise, which recognizes the central position of the Security Council to deal with issues threatening international peace and security but limits its ability to block an ICC involvement. Contrary to the proposition made in the ILC draft, a permanent member of the Security Council cannot thwart ICC proceedings with its veto, since a positive vote is necessary to invoke article 16. In other words, each permanent member can veto an article 16 deferral and prevent that the ICC be requested not to commence or proceed with an investigation or prosecution.[499]

Article 16 is undoubtedly a powerful instrument in the hands of the highest political organ of the UN to control the activity of the ICC. However, conferring such powers to the Security Council does not automatically mean that it has exclusive authority to take decisions of political character. Several factors affirm this assumption.

First, the Rome Statute contains numerous provisions that indicate the intention of the drafters to make the ICC take into account political considerations. As argued above, particularly thanks to article 53 of the Rome Statute, the Prosecutor is clearly mandated to consider the political situation and the effects of publicizing the results of his investigations or of an application to issue warrants of arrest. The Prosecutor is not doomed to act as a prosecutorial organ *stricto sensu* that turns a blind eye to politics and deliberately overlooks the political impact of its decisions. Moreover, the Prosecutor has already shown, although to a varying degree, that he will act in line with this premise.[500] With respect to the ICC's relationship to the Security Council, it should also be noted that the Security Council's assessment that crimes under the Rome Statute appear to have been committed in a situation before the ICC does not pre-determine the

498 See Pietro Gargiulo, "The Controversial Relationship between the International Criminal Court and the Security Council" in Flavia Lattanzi & William A. Schabas, eds., *Essays on the Rome Statute of the International Criminal Court* (Ripa Fagnano Alto: il Sirente, 1999) 67 at 86.

499 For a more detailed analysis of the legal consequences of article 16, including the problem as to whether an already arrested person should be released in case of a Security Council deferral and other questions left open by article 16, see Mohamed El Zeidi, "The United States Dropped the Atomic Bomb of Article 16 of the Rome Statute: Security Council Power of Deferrals and Resolution 1422" (2002) 35 Vand. J. Transnat'l L. 1503 at 1512.

500 See above, c. 5.4.

Prosecutor. The Prosecutor, under the control of the Pre-Trial-Chamber according to article 53(3) of the Rome Statute, remains free to decide whether to initiate investigations.[501]

Second, the Court has the authority to determine whether a Security Council referral corresponds to the principles and purposes of the UN Charter. This means that the ICC can assess the legality of the Security Council's action, in particular "whether the Security Council had the power to invoke Chapter VII and thus whether it has preliminarily determined the existence of a threat to the peace, a breach of the peace, or an act of aggression as provided for in Article 39."[502] In other words, the ICC decides whether or not it has jurisdiction over a case according to the principle of *Kompetenz-Kompetenz*, as stipulated in article 19 of the Rome Statute. A precedent can be found in the ruling of the ICTY Appeals Chamber in *Tadic*.[503] However, the Court is limited to a legal analysis and cannot address the appropriateness or effectiveness of a Security Council referral.[504] This principle is equally applicable to the case of a deferral. Even though an article 16 deferral creates an obligation for the Court to suspend investigations and/or prosecutions, the ICC is also entitled to decide on the validity of the respective Security Council resolution and its conformity with Chapter VII.[505] This competence is an important mechanism to validate the decisions of the Security Council and limits the Security Council's apparent supremacy established by article 16.

Another imperative concern relates to the consequences of an article 16 deferral made in the belief that peace negotiations can be advanced significantly or that a peace agreement, which possibly contains a provision on amnesties, can be concluded more easily in the absence of an involvement of the ICC. Such a move has frequently been suggested as a possibility to deal more effectively with the conflict in northern Uganda, and more recently also with respect to Darfur. However, as it has been convincingly argued, this measure cannot realistically make the ICC respect nationally granted amnesties in the long run. "[D]eferring to a national amnesty implies (since amnesty laws are rarely overturned) a *permanent* respect for

501 Condorelli &Villalpandos, *supra* note 196 at 633.

502 *Ibid.* at 641.

503 *Prosecutor v. Dusko*, *supra* note 301 at para. 18.

504 Condorelli &Villalpando, *supra* note 196 at 641.

505 *Ibid.* at 648.

that amnesty."[506] Such a permanent respect is difficult to guarantee through article 16, since a repeated or perpetual renewal of the yearly postponement is, considering the political dynamics of the Security Council, highly unlikely. An article 16 deferral will therefore not make the ICC having to respect amnesties eternally. The analysis of such a scenario underlines the fact that article 16 was only intended as a delaying mechanism in order to temporarily suspend the work of the ICC and prevent it from interfering in peace negotiations.[507]

As a result, a Security Council deferral should only be an option of last resort, reserved for extreme situations. Article 16 is an emergency break.[508] Its mere existence does not support the argument that the Security Council should be in charge of political aspects of international criminal justice at the expense of political deliberations made in The Hague. Since there is enough room for political discretion, the ICC is not condemned to act as a narrow-minded judicial body.

5.6. The enforcement of ICC decisions and prosecutorial activism

The difficulty of implementing decisions of the ICC is one of the major obstacles to realizing the goals put forward in the Rome Statute as well as to a more immediate positive impact of the ICC involvement on ongoing conflicts. In this respect, the Rome Statute has created a system that generally resembles the structure of inter-state cooperation, rather than that of the *ad hoc* tribunals.[509] Although article 86 of the Rome Statute stipulates that "States Parties shall ... cooperate fully with the Court in its investigations and prosecutions of crimes within the jurisdiction of the Court," decisions of the ICC cannot be executed by the Court itself; it has no coercive powers. If the ICC does not want to become a toothless judicial body, it must find ways to have its decisions systematically enforced. Realistic sanctions for the case of non-compliance with ICC requests must be set up by the supportive community of international criminal justice.

506 Gavron, *supra* note 425 at 109 [emphasis added].

507 *Ibid.*

508 See similarly Condorelli & Villalpando, *supra* note 196 at 646.

509 For more information, see Bert Swart, "General Problems" in Antonio Cassese, Paola Gaeta & John R.W.D. Jones, eds., *The Rome Statute of the International Criminal Court: A Commentary* (Oxford: Oxford University Press, 2002) 1589 at 1595.

Otherwise, ICC indictments will not put any considerable pressure on current and future perpetrators of international crimes.

The current legal regime deals insufficiently with non-compliance. Non-States Parties to the Rome Statute are generally not obliged to cooperate with the Court. If a State Party does not comply with ICC decisions, it breaks international law by not respecting article 86 of the Rome Statute, which stipulates that States Parties must cooperate fully with the Court. If a State Party fails to cooperate, the Court can refer the matter to the Assembly of States Parties or, in case of a Security Council referral, to the Security Council.[510] Article 112(2)(f) only states that the Assembly of States Parties shall "consider [...] any question relating to non-cooperation." It has been suggested that the Assembly of States Parties could go as far as taking collective countermeasures, such as economic sanctions, against a non-compliant state.[511] This is, however, a rather unlikely scenario due to the manifest self-perception of the Assembly of States Parties as a mainly monitoring body which is not clearly mandated to take coercive measures against non-compliant States Parties. Moreover, under general public international law, a material breach of a multilateral treaty only allows the other states to suspend the operation of the treaty.[512] Such a measure will obviously not make uncooperative national authorities comply with the Rome Statute and transfer indictees to The Hague.

In other words, the ICC is dependent on the willingness of national governments to cooperate. Arrest warrants will regularly remain unenforceable without the approval of national authorities. State cooperation, which worked well in the case of the suspects arrested in the DRC, the first being Thomas Lubanga who was transferred to The Hague in March 2006,[513] has been a major obstacle in Darfur. Sudan is not a State Party to the Rome Statute and vigorously rejects ICC jurisdiction over crimes com-

510 Article 87(7) of the Rome Statute. In the latter case, it is then in the discretion of the Security Council whether or not to react to such information about non-cooperation.

511 Annalisa Ciampi, "The Obligation to Cooperate" in Antonio Cassese, Paola Gaeta & John R.W.D. Jones, eds., *The Rome Statute of the International Criminal Court: A Commentary* (Oxford: Oxford University Press, 2002) 1607 at 1635.

512 *Vienna Convention on the Law of the Treaties*, *supra* note 402 at article 60.

513 International Criminal Court, Press Release, "First Arrest for the International Criminal Court" (17 March 2006), online: International Criminal Court <http://www.icc-cpi.int/press/pressreleases/132.html>.

mitted on its territory. No substantial cooperation of Khartoum with the ICC can therefore be expected, even though the Security Council obliged the government of Sudan in Resolution 1593 to cooperate fully with the ICC. The regime governing the question of cooperation in the situation of Darfur is therefore similar to the one imposed by the Security Council regarding the *ad hoc* tribunals. However, as the precedents of the *ad hoc* tribunals have shown, the enforcement of decisions of international criminal tribunals, in particular of arrest warrants, can be frustrating and time-consuming even if the tribunal can count on the general collaboration of the respective state. Given Khartoum's stance on the ICC, it is obvious that the chances that any Sudanese indictee be arrested and surrendered to The Hague are minimal.

Interestingly, the Prosecutor himself indicated in various statements that he considers his role in Darfur to be similar to the one of the Prosecutor of the ICTY and the ICTR. In his December 2008 report to the Security Council, the Prosecutor requested that the Council take similar action as in 2003 to support the work of the *ad hoc* tribunals. The Prosecutor referred to resolution 1503, in which the Security Council had urged member states to "consider imposing measures against individuals and groups or organizations assisting indictees at large to continue to evade justice, including measures designed to restrict the travel and freeze the assets of such individuals, groups or organizations."[514] The ICC Prosecutor suggested that "[s]imilar action must be considered in the upcoming months in order to ensure the implementation of all the Court's arrest warrants in relation to Darfur."[515]

Security Council resolution 1593 stipulates an obligation to cooperate with the ICC only for Sudan but not for all UN member states.[516] With the exception of Sudan, non-States Parties to the Rome Statute may therefore, in full compliance with the resolution, ignore all requests of cooperation made by the ICC. This is likely to intensify the difficulties the ICC will encounter with respect to enforcing its requests. Since the Rome Statute is not universally ratified, the limited obligation of non-States Parties to cooperate with the ICC is a political setback for international criminal justice. Nevertheless, this *lacuna* will probably not have important practical effects in the case of Darfur. Most of the states that are likely to be signifi-

514 S/RES/1503 (2003), cited in ICC, "Eighth Report of the Prosecutor", *supra* note 116 at para. 98.

515 *Ibid.* at para. 99.

516 S/RES/1593 (2005) at para. 2.

cant for the work of the ICC in the course of investigations have ratified the Rome Statute: the Central African Republic, the DRC, Uganda and Chad.[517] However, since the Prosecutor's application for an arrest warrant against Bashir, the absence of an obligation for all member states of the United Nations to cooperate with the Court has proven to be a serious impediment. All non-States Parties to the ICC play at least potentially a role with respect to the arrest and surrender of indictees who travel abroad. If a sitting head of state had to fear his arrest in any jurisdiction, the impact of an international arrest warrant would be much more stringent than in the current situation where non-States Parties are not under a legal obligation to arrest the Sudanese President and surrender him to the ICC. Bashir might, of course, not feel entirely safe on the territory of non-States Parties, but a universal legal obligation to arrest him would clearly make his situation far more disquieting.

With respect to a voluntary state referral of a situation to the ICC Prosecutor, it can be assumed that the state has a true interest in facilitating the proceedings and therefore also an interest in cooperating with the Court. Yet Uganda has shown that the ICC remains dependent on the willingness of the referring government to cooperate in specific situation, which limits the Court's scope of action significantly. Although the Prosecutor tried to demonstrate relatively early in the proceedings that crimes committed by the Ugandan army would also by analyzed, it is obvious that the government would handle requests for cooperation regarding investigations into these crimes far less enthusiastically than requests with respect to investigations into crimes committed by the LRA.

As a consequence, the chances to ensure full cooperation by the respective state are not necessarily higher in the case of a Security Council referral or a self-referral by a State Party compared to a situation where

---

517 The only state in the region that has not ratified the Statute and is somehow linked to the conflict is Libya. For Libya's policy regarding Darfur, see Prunier, *The Ambiguous Genocide*, *supra* note 87 at 68. International players have repeatedly tried to encourage Libya to exercise pressure on Sudan, for instance to allow the deployment of a joint UN-AU force, which underlines Libya's important role; see "US Seeks Libyan Help on Darfur force" *Sudan Tribune* (10 March 2007), online: Sudan Tribune <http://www.sudantribune.com/spip.php?article20692>; in 2007, several international meetings on the situation in Darfur took place in Libya. Egypt, Eritrea and Ethiopia are not States Parties to the Rome Statute either; their role regarding cooperation with the Court is, however, less significant with respect to the situation of Darfur.

the Prosecutor uses his *proprio motu* powers. These powers were considered a crucial novelty in international criminal law, intended to give the Prosecutor the means to act as independently as possible and to be active in precisely those situations where impunity is most likely, namely when states fail to act. So far, the Prosecutor has, however, tried to pursue a "safer" strategy regarding cooperation by accepting and soliciting self-referrals. This strategy cannot be considered successful, since the risks for the Prosecutor to become too dependent on the "voluntary" state outweigh the potential to gather information more easily; the added value of this strategy does not outweigh the costs. From a practical point of view, and as the situation in Uganda has shown, the problem of enforcing ICC requests cannot be solved by relying on self-referrals based on article 13(a) of the Rome Statute. Similarly, Darfur has shown that a Security Council referral according to article 13(b) is not a powerful basis for the Prosecutor, since the Security Council clearly does not support the ICC unconditionally. Backing of the ICC is limited to specific circumstances and depends on the political and diplomatic feasibility as determined by the five permanent members.

To avoid such unconstructive situations and to raise the profile of the Court and of international criminal justice in general, the Prosecutor could make use of his *proprio motu* powers according to article 13(c). First, the Court would not appear as a sub-organ of the Security Council, to which the Prosecutor has to report periodically without generating any meaningful reaction. Second, the image of the Court as a truly independent institution and of the Prosecutor as an international prosecutorial organ that is absolutely uninfluenced by the political dynamics governing international relations would improve.[518] The risk that certain requests cannot be enforced exists in each situation, but this risk will always impinge on the work of the Court and should not be the decisive criterion for giving preference to a certain trigger mechanism.

518 See also HRW, "Courting History", *supra* note 291.

Conclusion

The ICC is a young institution. It faces numerous challenges, some new and others comparable to those faced by the *ad hoc* tribunals. At the same time, its existence offers novel opportunities to fight impunity for genocide, war crimes and crimes against humanity and contribute to international peace and security.

The policy of the Security Council and several States Parties mirrors the somewhat short-sighted reasoning of achieving peace first and justice afterwards. The decisions to activate the ICC in the situations of northern Uganda and Darfur were, however, not driven by a wish to pursue the primary objective of the Rome Statute, namely to end impunity for the core crimes. The best illustration of this shift is the reluctance of the two referring authorities, the Ugandan government and the Security Council, to support the ICC in politically challenging situations. In short, the attempt of achieving justice in midst of an ongoing armed conflict and bringing about peace by involving an international criminal justice institution has failed. The re-election of President Bashir in April 2010, at a time when he was already indicted by the ICC, and the continued violence committed by the LRA are gloomy manifestations of the Court's limited potential to bring about immediate and measurable change in a conflict situation.

Despite this lack of crucial support from key players, the ICC should not be considered a weak and politically manipulated institution. There is scope for legal action to counter such politicization. Moreover, there should be no room for a politically shaped pick-and-chose-strategy of the international community *vis-à-vis* the ICC. Internal checks and balances, in other words the judicial oversight of the Pre-Trial-Chamber over the Prosecutor, as well as article 16 powers of the Security Council in extreme situations should be sufficient to counterbalance politically risky investigations and prosecutions. Unfortunately, the ICC, in particular because of the policy decisions of the Prosecutor, conforms to certain political expectations and does not respond vigorously enough – and within the legal framework of the Rome Statute – to the tendency of being misused as a political institution.

The Rome Statute stipulates in paragraph three of its preamble that "grave crimes threaten the peace, security and well-being of the world", which means that contributing to peace and security is clearly one of the objectives of the ICC. This objective seems to have been partly achieved in the situation of northern Uganda by indicting the LRA leaders and also to some extent in the situation of Darfur, although the long-term potential of the ICC's involvement in these situations is more significant than a specific and measurable immediate outcome. Contributing to or even ensuring peace and security *per se* was not intended to be the main objective of the ICC when the Rome Statute was signed. The role and purpose of the Security Council as highest political organ of the United Nations was never challenged. Rather, the focus was put on ending impunity for the core crimes, *through which* international peace and security are to be strengthened. The ICC was therefore not meant to be a political institution but primarily a legal one, which was set up to ensure that those responsible for the most serious crimes of concern to the international community as a whole[519] do not go unpunished.

This reasoning seems to have been reversed. The involvement of the ICC has been considered a partial success, precisely because it has contributed or can contribute to weakening political and military leaders, who might eventually be tried in The Hague. It is striking that the ICC now seems to have its most crucial role to play in the pre-trial phase; stigmatizing allegedly criminal leaders appears to have become the main purpose of the ICC. A fundamental principle of criminal justice, namely the presumption of innocence as stipulated in article 14(2) of the International Covenant on Civil and Political Rights,[520] therefore plays an inferior role compared to generating political effects. The primary mission of the ICC now seems to be to first exercise political pressure on leaders *in order* to deliver, sooner or later, justice.

519 As stipulated in para. 4 of the preamble.

520 "Everyone charged with criminal offences shall have the right to be presumed innocent until proved guilty according to law." *International Covenant on Civil and Political Rights,* 16 December 1966, 999 U.N.T.S. 171 (entered info force on 23 March 1976), article 14(2).

This logic cannot easily be reconciled with an exclusively legal perception of the ICC. As has been shown, the Court must also be considered a political institution with the Prosecutor as its key player, whose decisions do not only have political effects, but who also acts to a certain extent according to political calculations. It can, therefore, be concluded that the ICC has not contributed to the developments in northern Uganda and Darfur as a judicial institution but foremost as a political one. The initial, more limited mandate of the ICC has changed. Yet the ICC has not received additional tools to properly fulfill such a political mandate.

Increased prosecutorial activism might be necessary to focus on the original, legal mandate of the ICC and to maintain the independence and credibility of the Court. The use of the Prosecutor's *proprio motu* powers has been proposed as a key measure. Initiating proceedings on the basis of article 13(c) of the Rome Statute independent of the stance of the territorial state towards ICC proceedings would decrease the weight of redundant and inevitably politicized self-referrals and of Security Council referrals, which have shown that the pursuit of justice is not the main concern of the Security Council and which make the ICC unnecessarily dependent on the volatile will of a political organ.

The ICC can still have important beneficial effects on ongoing armed conflicts by targeting and isolating allegedly criminal leaders. Referring a situation to the ICC Prosecutor or supporting *proprio motu* proceedings remains a vital strategy for the Security Council and States Parties to deal with genocide, crimes against humanity and war crimes. However, the ICC is first of all a judicial institution that should not be expected to resolve armed conflicts and humanitarian crises on its own. Clearly, the international community cannot rely exclusively on a court to stop mass violence. The primary *raison d'être* of the ICC should not be to have immediate political effects but to contribute to a durable, global fight against impunity for international crimes.

Bibliography

1. Documents of the United Nations

Treaties (in chronological order)

Convention on the Prevention and Punishment of the Crime of Genocide, 9 December 1948, 78 U.N.T.S. 277 (entered into force 12 January 1951).

Geneva Convention Relative to the Treatment of Prisoners of War (Geneva III), 12 August 1949, 75 U.N.T.S. 135 (entered into force 21 October 1950).

Geneva Convention Relative to the Protection of Civilian Persons in Time of War (Geneva IV), 12 August 1949, 75 U.N.T.S. 287 (entered into force 21 October 1950).

Vienna Convention on the Law of the Treaties, 23 May 1969, 1155 U.N.T.S. 331 (entered into force 27 January 1980).

International Law Commission, *Draft Statute for an International Criminal Court*, in *Report of the International Law Commission on the work of its forty-sixth session (2 May–22 July 1994)*, UN GAOR, 49th Session, Supp. No. 10, UN Doc. A/49/10 (1994).

International Criminal Tribunal for the Former Yugoslavia, *Rules of Procedure and Evidence* (adopted 11 February 1994, as amended on 25 June and 5 July 1996), UN Doc. IT/32/Rev.9 (1996).

Rome Statute of the International Criminal Court, 17 July 1998, UN Doc. A/CONF.183/9.

Security Council Resolutions (in chronological order)

UN SCOR, 48th Year, 3217th Mtg., UN Doc. S/RES/827 (1993).

UN SCOR, 49th Year, 3453rd Mtg., UN Doc. S/RES/955 (1994).

UN SCOR, 51st Year, 3660th Mtg., UN Doc. S/RES/1054 (1996).

UN SCOR, 54th Year, 4076th Mtg., UN Doc. S/RES/1279 (1999).

UN SCOR, 55th Year, 4104th Mtg., UN Doc. S/RES/1291 (2000).

UN SCOR, 59th Year, 5015th Mtg., UN Doc. S/RES/1556 (2004).

UN SCOR, 59th Year, 5040th Mtg., UN Doc. S/RES/1564 (2004).

UN SCOR, 60th Year, 5153rd Mtg., UN Doc. S/RES/1591 (2005).

UN SCOR, 60th Year, 5158th Mtg., UN Doc. S/RES/1593 (2005).

UN SCOR, 60th Year, 5304th Mtg., UN Doc. S/RES/1638 (2005).

UN SCOR, 61st Year, 5423rd Mtg., UN Doc. S/RES/1672 (2006).

UN SCOR, 61st Year, 5519th Mtg., UN Doc. S/RES/1706 (2006).

UN SCOR, 62nd Year, 5727th Mtg., UN Doc. S/RES/1769 (2007).

UN SCOR, 63rd Year, 5947th Mtg., UN Doc. S/RES/1828 (2008).

Reports, statements, press releases (in chronological order)

UN GAOR, 50th Session, Supp. No. 22, "Report of the Ad Hoc Committee on the Establishment of an International Criminal Court", UN Doc. A/50/22 (1995).

UN Commission on Human Rights, "Report of the United Nations High Commissioner for Human Rights on the mission undertaken by her Office, pursuant to Commission resolution 2000/60, to assess the situation on the ground with regard to the abduction of children from northern Uganda", UN Doc. E/CN.4/2002/86 (9 November 2001).

UN News Centre, "Sudan: Envoy Warns of Ethnic Cleansing as Security Council Calls for Ceasefire" (2 April 2004), online: UN News Centre <http://www.un. org/apps/news/storyAr.asp?NewsID=10307&Cr=sudan&Cr1=>.

"Report of the International Commission of Inquiry on Darfur Pursuant to Security Council Resolution 1564 of 18 September 2004", UN Doc. S/2005/60 (Geneva, 25 January 2005).

UN Security Council, "Report of the Secretary-General pursuant to resolutions 1653 (2006) and 1663 (2006)", UN Doc. S/2006/478 (26 June 2006), online: United Nations <http://daccessdds.un.org/doc/UNDOC/GEN/N06/415/40/PDF/N0641540.pdf?OpenElement>.

"Report of the Panel of Experts established pursuant to resolution 1591 (2005) concerning the Sudan prepared in accordance with paragraph 2 of resolution 1665 (2006)", UN Doc. S/2006/795 (3 October 2006).

UN Security Council, 5566th Mtg., SC/8869, "Security Council Presidential Statement Demands Release of Women, Children by Lord's Resistance Army, Expeditious Conclusion of Peace Process", UN Doc. SC/8869 (16 November 2006), online: United Nations <http://www.un.org/News/Press/docs/2006/sc8869.doc.htm>.

Human Rights Council, "Report of the High-Level Mission on the Situation of Human Rights in Darfur pursuant to Human Rights Council Decision S-4/101", UN Doc. A/HRC/4/80 (7 March 2007).

"UNAMID Deployment, Background Fact Sheet" (September 2007), online: United Nations <http://www.un.org/depts/dpko/missions/unamid/UNAMID_Deployment.pdf>.

"Darfur - UNAMID - Background", online: United Nations <http://www.un.org/Depts/dpko/missions/unamid/background.html>.

"Darfur – UNAMID – Facts and Figures", online: United Nations <http://www.un.org/depts/dpko/missions/unamid/facts.html>.

UN News Centre, "Security Council Slates Weekend Attacks by Darfur Rebels near Sudanese Capital" (13 May 2008), online: UN News Centre <http://www.un.org/apps/news/story.asp?NewsID=26661&Cr=darfur&Cr1=>.

UN Security Council, Press Release, "Darfur Mission Deployment Slowed by Deteriorating Security, Harsh Conditions", UN Doc. SC/9330 (14 May 2008).

UN Security Council, "Statement by the President of the Security Council", UN Doc. S/PRST/2008/21 (16 June 2008), online: United Nations <http://daccessdds.un.org/doc/UNDOC/GEN/N08/384/05/PDF/N0838405.pdf?OpenElement>.

UN Security Council, "Additional report of the Secretary-General on children and armed conflict in Uganda", UN Doc. S/2008/409 (23 June 2008).

UN Security Council, "Report of the Secretary-General on the Deployment of the African Union-United Nations Hybrid Operation in Darfur", UN Doc. S/2008/443 (7 July 2008), online: United Nations <http://daccessdds.un.org/doc/UNDOC/GEN/N08/409/84/PDF/N0840984.pdf?OpenElement>.

UN News Centre, "Darfur: UN-African peacekeeper shot, as concern grows over humanitarian aid" (10 March 2009), online: UN News Centre <http://www.un.org/apps/news/story.asp?NewsID=30142&Cr=darfur&Cr1>.

UN Agencies (in chronological order)

UN Office for the Coordination of Humanitarian Affairs, "UGANDA: Peace Groups and Government Officials Worried about ICC Probe into LRA" (30 January 2004), online: IRIN <http://www.irinnews.org/Report.aspx?ReportId=48356>.

___. "UGANDA: Locals want rebel leader forgiven" (7 December 2006), online: IRIN <http://www.irinnews.org/report.aspx?reportid=59805>.

___. "Somalia: Impunity 'the Root Cause of Crisis" (27 February 2007), online: IRIN <http://www.irinnews.org/report.aspx?ReportId=76993>.

___. "Darfur Humanitarian Profile No. 30" (1 January 2008) online: OCHA <http://www.unsudanig.org/docs/DHP%2030%20-%201%20January%20 2008%20-%20narrative.pdf >.

Office of the United Nations High Commissioner for Human Rights, "Ninth periodic report of the United Nations High Commissioner for Human Rights on the situation of human rights in the Sudan, Attacks on civilians in Saraf Jidad, Sirba, Silea and Abu Suruj in January and February 2008" (20 March 2008), online: OHCHR <http://www.ohchr.org/Documents/Press/WestDarfurreport2003.pdf>.

___. "Eleventh periodic report of the United Nations for Human Rights on the situation of human rights in the Sudan, Killing and injuring of civilians on 25 August 2008 by government security forces: Kalma IDP camp, South Darfur, Sudan" (23 January 2009), online: OHCHR <http://www.ohchr.org/Documents/Countries/11thOHCHR22jan09.pdf>.

UN Office for the Coordination of Humanitarian Affairs, "Sudan, Situation Report #2" (13 March 2009), online: ReliefWeb <http://www.reliefweb.int/rw/rwb.nsf/db900SID/MUMA-7Q52WN?OpenDocument>.

2. Documents of the International Criminal Court (in chronological order)

"Informal Expert Paper: The Principle of Complementarity in Practice" (2003), online: International Criminal Court <http://www.icc-cpi.int/iccdocs/doc/doc656350.PDF>

"Background Information on the Situation in Uganda" (29 January 2004), online: International Criminal Court <http://www.icc-cpi.int/library/press/ press-releases/Uganda_200401_EN.doc>.

Press Release, "President of Uganda refers situation concerning the Lord's Resistance Army (LRA) to the ICC" (29 January 2004), online: International Criminal Court <http://www.icc-cpi.int/pressrelease_details&id=16&l=en.html>.

Press Release, "Prosecutor of the International Criminal Court Opens an Investigation into Northern Uganda" (29 July 2004), online: International Criminal Court <http://www.icc-cpi.int/pressrelease_details&id=33&l=en.html>.

Press Release, "Statements by ICC Chief Prosecutor and the Visiting Delegation of Acholi Leaders from northern Uganda" (18 March 2005), online: International Criminal Court <http://www2.icc-cpi.int/NR/exeres/2B9064A4-9944-4A55-8123-1B62B0634239.htm>.

"Report of the Prosecutor of the International Criminal Court, Mr. Luis Moreno Ocampo, to the UN Security Council Pursuant to UNSCR 1593 (2005)" (29 June 2005), online: International Criminal Court <http://www.icc-cpi.int/library/cases/ICC_ Darfur_UNSC_Report_29-06-05_EN.pdf>.

Pre-Trial Chamber II, "Warrant of Arrest for Joseph Kony Issued on 8 July 2005 as Amended on 27 September 2005" (27 September 2005), ICC-02/04-01/05-53.

"Facts and Procedure Regarding the Situation in Uganda" (14 October 2005), online: International Criminal Court <http://www2.icc-cpi.int/NR/rdonlyres/4BCE015E-9F70-4CD1-8AC2-4CACDB6070B6/277312/ICC_20051410056I_English2.pdf>.

"Statement by the Chief Prosecutor on the Uganda Arrest Warrants" (14 October 2005), online: International Criminal Court <http://www2.icc-cpi.int/NR/rdonlyres/3255817D-FD00-4072-9F58-FDB869F9B7CF/143834/LMO_20051014_English1.pdf>.

"The Investigation in Northern Uganda" (14 October 2005), online: International Criminal Court <http://www2.icc-cpi.int/NR/rdonlyres/2919856F-03E0-403F-A1A8-D61D4F350A20/277306/Uganda_PPpresentation6.pdf>.

"Statement by Luis Moreno-Ocampo, Prosecutor of the International Criminal Court, Informal meeting of Legal Advisors of Ministries of Foreign Affairs" (24 October 2005), online: International Criminal Court <http://www.icc-cpi.int/library/organs/otp/speeches/LMO_20051024_English.pdf>.

"Decision to Convene a Status Conference on the Investigation in the Situation in Uganda in Relation to the Application of Article 53" (2 December 2005), ICC-02/04-01/05-68, online: International Criminal Court <http://www2.icc-cpi.int/iccdocs/doc/doc97225.PDF>.

"Second Report of the Prosecutor of the International Criminal Court, Mr. Luis Moreno Ocampo, to the UN Security Council Pursuant to UNSCR 1593 (2005)" (13 December 2005), online: International Criminal Court <http://www.icc-cpi.int/library/organs/otp/LMO_UNSC_ReportB_En.pdf>.

"Update on Communications Received by the Office of the Prosecutor of the ICC" (10 February 2006), online: International Criminal Court <http://www2.icc-cpi.int/NR/rdonlyres/F596D08D-D810-43A2-99BB-B899B9C5BCD2/277421/OTP_Update_on_Communications_10_February_2006.pdf>.

Press Release, "First Arrest for the International Criminal Court" (17 March 2006), online: International Criminal Court <http://www.icc-cpi.int/press/pressreleases/132.html>.

"Fourth Report of the Prosecutor of the International Criminal Court, Mr. Luis Moreno Ocampo, to the UN Security Council Pursuant to UNSCR 1593 (2005)" (14 December 2006), online: International Criminal Court <http://www.icc-cpi.int/library/organs/otp/OTP_ReportUNSC4-Darfur_English.pdf>.

"Situation in Darfur, the Sudan, Prosecutor's Application under Article 58(7)" (27 February 2007), online: International Criminal Court <http://www.icc-cpi.int/library/cases/ICC-02-05-56_English.pdf>.

"Fact Sheet, The Situation in Darfur, the Sudan" (27 February 2007), online: International Criminal Court <http://www2.icc-cpi.int/NR/rdonlyres/08D1428F-62DA-4C0F-AF47-17FABFFAF995/143641/ICCOTP_FactSheetDarfur20070227_en.pdf>.

Pre-Trial Chamber I, "Warrant of Arrest for Ahmad Harun" and "Warrant of Arrest for Ali Kushayb" (27 April 2007), ICC-02/05-01/07-2 and ICC-02/05-01/07-3, online: International Criminal Court <http http://www.icc-cpi.int/iccdocs/doc/doc279813.PDF> and <http://www.icc-cpi.int/iccdocs/doc/doc279858.PDF>.

"Fifth Report of the Prosecutor of the International Criminal Court, Mr. Luis Moreno Ocampo, to the UN Security Council Pursuant to UNSCR 1593 (2005)" (7 June 2007), online: International Criminal Court <http://www.icc-cpi.int/library/organs/otp/OTP_ReportUNSC5-Darfur_English.pdf>.

Pre-Trial Chamber II, "Decision to Terminate the Proceedings Against Raska Lukwiya" (11 July 2007), ICC-02/04-01/05-348, online: International Criminal Court <http://www2.icc-cpi.int/iccdocs/doc/doc297945.pdf>.

Press Release, "ICC Arrest Jean-Pierre Bemba – massive sexual crimes in Central African Republic will not go unpunished" (24 May 2008), online: International Criminal Court <http://www2.icc-cpi.int/menus/icc/situations%20and%20cases/situations/situation%20icc%200105/related%20cases/icc%200105%200108/press%20releases/icc%20arrest%20jean_pierre%20bemba%20%E2%80%93%20massive%20sexual%20crimes%20in%20central%20african%20republic%20will%20not%20go%20unpunis>.

"Prosecutor's Application for Warrant of Arrest under Article 58 Against Omar Hassan Ahmad Al Bashir, Summary of the Case" (14 July 2008), online: International Criminal Court <http://www2.icc-cpi.int/NR/rdonlyres/64FA6B33-05C3-4E9C-A672-3FA2B58CB2C9/277758/ICCOTPSummary20081704ENG.pdf>.

"Address to the Assembly of States Parties by Mr Luis Moreno-Ocampo" (14 November 2008), online: International Criminal Court <http://www2.icc-cpi.int/NR/rdonlyres/50F9D0FA-33A0-48B3-942E-4CFF88CA3A27/0/ICCASPASP7StatementProsecutor.pdf>.

"Eighth Report of the Prosecutor of the International Criminal Court, Mr. Luis Moreno Ocampo, to the UN Security Council Pursuant to UNSCR 1593 (2005)" (3 December 2008), online: International Criminal Court <http://www.icc-cpi.int/library/organs/otp/8thUNSCreportsenttoUN-ENG.pdf>.

Pre-Trial Chamber I, "Warrant of Arrest for Omar Hassan Ahmad Al Bashir", ICC-02/05-01/09-1 (4 March 2009), online: International Criminal Court <http://www.icc-cpi.int/iccdocs/doc/doc639078.pdf>.

Pre-Trial Chamber I, "Decision on the Prosecution's Application for a Warrant of Arrest against Omar Hassan Ahmad Al Bashir", ICC-02/05-01/09-3 (4 March 2009), online: International Criminal Court <http://www.icc-cpi.int/iccdocs/doc/doc639096.pdf>.

Pre-Trial Chamber I, "Prosecutor's Application for Leave to Appeal the 'Decision on the Prosecution's Application for a Warrant of Arrest against Omar Hassan Ahmad Al Bashir'", ICC-02/05-01/09-12 (13 March 2009), online: International Criminal Court <http://www.icc-cpi.int/iccdocs/doc/doc644001.pdf>.

"Case Information Sheet, The Prosecutor v. Bahr Idriss Abu Garda", ICC-02/05-02/09 (16 October 2009), online: International Criminal Court <http://www.icc-cpi.int/NR/rdonlyres/BF7BC998-49F6-4588-A9ED-16413A750D14/280960/CISAbu_GardaEn2.pdf>.

Appeals Chamber, "Judgment on the Appeal of Mr. Germain Katanga against the Oral Decision of Trial Chamber II of 12 June 2009 on the Admissibility of the Case", ICC-01/04-01/07-1497 (25 September 2009), online: International Criminal Court <http://www.icc-cpi.int/iccdocs/doc/doc746819.pdf>.

Assembly of States Parties, "Resolution RC/Res.6" (adopted at the 13th plenary meeting, on 11 June 2010), online: International Criminal Court <http://www.icc-cpi.int/iccdocs/asp_docs/Resolutions/RC-Res.6-ENG.pdf>.

Pre-Trial Chamber I, "Second Warrant of Arrest for Omar Hassan Ahmad Al Bashir", ICC-02/05-01/09-95 (12 July 2010), online: International Criminal Court <http://www.icc-cpi.int/iccdocs/doc/doc907140.pdf>.

3. Legislation and agreements (in chronological order)

Constitution of the Republic of Sudan 1998, trans. by Curtis Francis Doebbler, online: International Committee of the Red Cross <http://www.icrc.org/ihl-nat.nsf/162d151af444ded44125673e00508141/d728f18be88d9482c1256dc600507f33/$FILE/Constitution%20Sudan%20-%20EN.pdf>.

Lomé Peace Agreement, UN Doc. S/1999/777 (7 July 1999).

The Amnesty Act, 2000, available online: Website of International Humanitarian Law <http://www.wihl.nl/finals/Uganda/UG.%20T-TR.Agreement%20on%20Amnesty%20Commission.pdf>.

Constitution of the Republic of Sudan 2005, available online: Sudan Tribune <http://www.sudantribune.com/IMG/pdf/20050316_SUDAN_DRAFT_CONSTITUTIONAL_TEXT.pdf>.

Annexure to the Agreement on Accountability and Reconciliation (19 February 2008), available online: Coalition for the International Criminal Court <http://www.iccnow.org/documents/Annexure_to_agreement_on_Accountability_signed_today.pdf>.

4. Other jurisprudence (in chronological order)

Bleier v. Uruguay, U.N. Human Rights Committee, UN Doc. A/37/40 (1982).

Velasquez-Rodriguez Case (Honduras) (1988), Inter-Am. Ct. H.R. (Ser. C) No. 4, Annual Report of the Inter-American Court of Human Rights: OAS/ser. L/V/III, doc.13, app. IV (1988).

Mojica v. Dominican Republic, U.N. Human Rights Committee, UN Doc. CCPR/C/51/D/449/1991 (1994).

Kurt v. Turkey (1998), 74 E.C.H.R. (Ser. A) 1152, 27 E.H.R.R. 373.

Prosecutor v. Zejnil Delalic et al. (Celebici), IT-96-21-T (Judgment, 16 November 1998) (International Criminal Tribunal for the former Yugoslavia, Trial Chamber).

Prosecutor v. Kayishema and Ruzindana (1999), ICTR-95-1-T (Judgment, 21 May 1999) (International Criminal Tribunal for Rwanda, Trial Chamber).

Prosecutor v. Dusko Tadic, IT-94-1-A (Judgment, 15 July 1999) (International Criminal Tribunal for the former Yugoslavia, Appeals Chamber).

Democratic Republic of the Congo v. Belgium, Case Concerning the Arrest Warrant of 11 April 2000 (Judgement, 14 February 2002) (International Court of Justice).

Prosecutor v. Foday Sankoh (2003), SCSL-03-02-I-001 (Indictment, 7 March 2003) (Special Court for Sierra Leone).

5. Secondary materials

Books (in alphabetical order)

Allen, Tim. *Trial Justice, The International Criminal Court and The Lord's Resistance Army* (London: International African Institute, 2006).

Bass, Gary Jonathan. *Stay the Hand of Vengeance: the Politics of War Crimes Tribunals* (Princeton: Princeton University Press, 2000).

Beigbeder, Yves. *Judging War Criminals* (New York: St. Martin's Press, 1999).

Center of International Cooperation. *Annual Review of Global Peace Operations 2006* (Boulder, Colo.: Lynne Rienner Publishers, 2006).

Cheadle, Don & John Prendergast. *Not on Our Watch, The Mission to End Genocide in Darfur and Beyond* (New York: Hyperion, 2007).

Chollet, Derek. *The Road to the Dayton Accords, A Study of American Statecraft* (New York: Palgrave Macmillan, 2005).

Cobban, Helena. *Amnesty after Atrocity? Healing Nations after Genocide and War Crimes* (Boulder, Colo.: Paradigm Publishers, 2007).

Fatić, Aleksandar. *Reconciliation via the War Crimes Tribunal?* (Aldershot: Ashgate, 2000).

Fawzy-Rossano, Didar. *Le Soudan en question* (Paris: Éditions de la Table Ronde, 2002).

Flint, Julie & Axel de Waal. *Darfur, A Short History of a Long War* (London: Zed Books, 2005).

Hirsch, John L. *Sierra Leone: Diamonds and the Struggle for Democracy* (Boulder, Colo.: Lynne Rienner Publishers, 2001).

International Commission on Intervention and State Sovereignty. *The Responsibility to Protect* (Ottawa: International Development Research Centre, 2001).

Iyob, Ruth & Gilbert M. Khadiagala. *Sudan, The Elusive Quest for Peace* (Boulder, Colo.: Lynne Rienner Publishers, 2006).

LeBor, Adam. *Milosevic, A Biography* (New Haven: Yale University Press, 2004).

Maogoto, Jackson Nyamuya. *State Sovereignty and International Criminal Law: Versailles to Rome* (Ardsley, N.Y.: Transnational Publishers, 2003).

Medani, Armin Mekki. *Crimes Against International Humanitarian Law in Sudan, 1989-2000* (Cairo: Dar El Mostaqbal El Arabi, 2001).

Minow, Martha. *Between Vengeance and Forgiveness, Facing History after Genocide and Mass Violence* (Boston: Beacon Press, 1998).

Moghalu, Kingsley Chiedu. *The Politics of War Crimes Trials* (Westport, C.T.: Praeger Security International, 2006).

Niblock, Tim. *"Pariah States" & Sanctions in the Middle East, Iraq, Libya, Sudan* (Boulder, Colo.: Lynne Rienner Publishers, 2001).

Niemeyer, Lucian. *Africa, the Holocausts of Rwanda and Sudan* (Albuquerque: University of New Mexico Press, 2006).

Olásolo, Héctor. *The Triggering Procedure of the International Criminal Court* (Leiden: Martinus Nijhoff Publishers, 2006).

Prunier, Gérard. *Darfur, The Ambiguous Genocide* (Ithaca, N.Y.: Cornell University Press, 2005).

Roper, Steven D. & Lilian A. Barria. *Designing Criminal Tribunals, Sovereignty and International Concerns in the Protection of Human Rights* (Aldershot: Ashgate, 2006).

Sadat, Leila Nadya. *The International Criminal Court and the Transformation of International Law, Justice for the New Millennium* (Ardsley, N.Y.: Transnational Publishers, 2002).

Journal articles (in alphabetical order)

Ajawin, Yoanes. "Human Rights Violations and Transitional Justice" in A.H. Abdel Salam & Alex de Waal, eds., *The Phoenix State: Civil Society and the Future of Sudan* (Lawrenceville, N.J.: Red Sea Press, 2001) 113.

Akande, Dapo. "International Law Immunities and the International Criminal Court" (2004) 98:3 A.J.I.L. 407.

Akhavan, Payam. "The Yugoslav Tribunal at a Crossroads: The Dayton Peace Agreement and Beyond" (1996) 18:2 Hum. Rts. Q. 259.

___. "Justice in The Hague, Peace in the Former Yugoslavia? A Commentary on the United Nations War Crimes Tribunal" (1998) 20:4 Hum. Rts. Q. 737.

___. "Beyond Impunity: Can International Criminal Justice Prevent Future Atrocities?" (2001) 95 A.J.I.L. 7.

___. "The Lord's Resistance Army Case: Uganda's Submission of the First State Referral to the International Criminal Court" (2005) 99 A.J.I.L. 403.

Ambos, Kai. "Superior Responsibility" in Antonio Cassese, Paola Gaeta & John R.W.D. Jones, eds., *The Rome Statute of the International Criminal Court: A Commentary* (Oxford: Oxford University Press, 2002) 823.

Anonymous. "Human Rights in Peace Negotiations" (1996) 18:2 Hum. Rts. Q. 249.

Baldo, Suliman. "La paix, arme de guerre" (2006) 14 Enjeux Internationaux 21.

Bass, Warren. "The Triage of Dayton" (1997) 77:5 Foreign Affairs 95.

Bassiouni, M. Cherif. "The ICC – *Quo Vadis*?" (2006) 4 Journal of International Criminal Justice 421.

Bergsmo, Morten, Catherine Cissé & Christopher Staker. "The Prosecutor of the Nuremberg and Tokyo Tribunals, the ICTY and the ICTR, and the ICC Compared" in Louise Arbour *et al.*, eds., *The Prosecutor of a Permanent International Criminal Court* (Freiburg im Breisgau: edition iuscrim, 1998) 121.

Branch, Adam. "International Justice, Local Injustice" *Dissent Magazine* (Summer 2004), online: Dissent Magazine <http://www.dissentmagazine.org/article/?article=336>.

___. "Uganda's Civil War and the Politics of ICC Intervention" (2007) 21:2 Ethics & International Affairs 179, online: Wiley InterScience <http://www3.interscience.wiley.com/journal/117999022/abstract>.

___. "Against Humanitarian Impunity: Rethinking Responsibility for Displacement and Disaster in Northern Uganda" (2008) 2:2 Journal of Intervention and Statebuilding 151.

Brubacher, Matthew R. "Political Discretion within the International Criminal Court" (2004) 2 Journal of International Criminal Justice 71.

Castillo, Pablo. "Rethinking Deterrence: The International Criminal Court in Sudan" (2007) 13 UNISCI Discussion Papers 167.

Ciampi, Annalisa. "The Obligation to Cooperate" in Antonio Cassese, Paola Gaeta & John R.W.D. Jones, eds., *The Rome Statute of the International Criminal Court: A Commentary* (Oxford: Oxford University Press, 2002) 1607.

Cobban, Helena. "Think Again: International Courts" *Foreign Policy* (March/ April 2006).

Collins, Robert O. "Disaster in Darfur: Historical Overview" in Samuel Totten & Eric Markusen, *Genocide in Darfur, Investigating the Atrocities in the Sudan* (New York: Routledge, 2006) 3.

Condorelli, Luigi & Santiago Villalpando. "Referral and Deferral by the Security Council" in Antonio Cassese, Paola Gaeta & John R.W.D. Jones, eds., *The Rome Statute of the International Criminal Court: A Commentary* (Oxford: Oxford University Press, 2002) 627.

Danner, Alison M. "Enhancing the Legitimacy and Accountability of Prosecutorial Discretion at the International Criminal Court" (2003) 97 A.J.I.L. 510 at 532.

De Waal, Alex. "Who are the Darfurians? Arab and African Identities, Violence and External Engagement" (2005) 104:415 African Affairs 181.

De Waal, Alex & A.H. Abdel Salam. "Islamism, State Power and *Jihad* in Sudan" in Alex de Waal, ed., *Islamism and Its Enemies in the Horn of Africa* (Bloomington: Indiana University Press, 2004) 71.

El Zeidi, Mohamed. "The United States Dropped the Atomic Bomb of Article 16 of the Rome Statute: Security Council Power of Deferrals and Resolution 1422" (2002) 35 Vand. J. Transnat'l L. 1503.

Fowler, Jerry. "A New Chapter of Irony: The Legal Definition of Genocide and the Implications of Powell's Determination" in Samuel Totten & Eric Markusen, *Genocide in Darfur, Investigating the Atrocities in the Sudan* (New York: Routledge, 2006) 127.

Frulli, Micaela. "A Turning Point in International Efforts to Apprehend War Criminals, The UN Mandates Taylor's Arrest in Liberia" (2006) 4 Journal of International Criminal Justice 351.

Gaeta, Paula. "Is NATO Authorized or Obliged to Arrest Persons Indicted by the International Criminal Tribunal for the Former Yugoslavia?" (1998) 9 E.J.I.L. 174.

Gallagher, Karen. "No Justice, no Peace: The Legalities and Realities of Amnesty in Sierra Leone" (2000) 23 Thomas Jefferson L. Rev. 149.

Gargiulo, Pietro. "The Controversial Relationship between the International Criminal Court and the Security Council" in Flavia Lattanzi & William A. Schabas, eds., *Essays on the Rome Statute of the International Criminal Court* (Ripa Fagnano Alto: il Sirente, 1999) 67.

Gavron, Jessica. "Amnesties in the Light of Developments in International Law and the Establishment of the International Criminal Court" (2002) 51 I.C.L.Q. 91.

Gebrewold, Belachew. "Civil Militia and Militarisation of Society in the Horn of Africa" in David J. Francis, ed., *Civil Militia, Africa's Intractable Security Menace?* (Hants: Ashgate, 2005) 189.

Grono, Nick. "The International Community's Failure to Protect" (2006) 105:421 African Affairs 625.

Happold, Matthew. "Darfur, The Security Council, and the International Criminal Court" (2006) 55 I.C.L.Q. 226.

Hewett, Dawn Yamene. "Sudan's Court and Complementarity in the Face of Darfur" (2006) 31 Yale J. Int'l L. 276.

Holmes, John T. "The Principle of Complementarity" in Roy S. Lee, ed., *The International Criminal Court: The Making of the Rome Statute - Issues, Negotiations, Results* (The Hague: Kluwer Law International, 1999) 41.

___. "Complementarity: National Courts versus the ICC" in Antonio Cassese, Paola Gaeta & John R.W.D. Jones, eds., *The Rome Statute of the International Criminal Court: A Commentary* (Oxford: Oxford University Press, 2002) 667.

Jacobs, Dov. "Puzzling Over Amnesties: Defragmenting the Debate for International Criminal Tribunals", online: SSRN <http://papers.ssrn.com/sol3/papers.cfm?abstract_id=1562088>.

Kaufman, Zachary D. "Justice in Jeopardy: Accountability for the Darfur Atrocities" (2006) 16 Criminal Law Forum 343.

Kheiltash, Golzar. "ICC Arrest Warrants Hang in the Balance as Ugandans Prepare for Second Round of Peace Talks" (2006) 8 International Law Enforcement Reporter 317.

Kirsch, Philipp. "Keynote Address by Ambassador Philippe Kirsch" (1999) 32 Cornell International Law Journal 438.

Kirsch, Philippe & Darryl Robinson. "Referral by States Parties" in Antonio Cassese, Paola Gaeta & John R.W.D. Jones, eds., *The Rome Statute of the International Criminal Court: A Commentary* (Oxford: Oxford University Press, 2002) 619.

Lansing, Paul & Julie C. King. "South Africa's Truth and Reconciliation Commission: The Conflict Between Individual Justice and the National Healing in the Post-Apartheid Age" (1998) 15 Ariz. J. Int'l & Comp. L. 753.

Lavergne, Marc & Fabrice Weissman. "Sudan, Who Benefits from Humanitarian Aid?" in Fabrice Weissman, ed., *In the Shadow of 'Just Wars', Violence Politics and Humanitarian Action* (Ithaca, N.Y.: Cornell University Press, 2004) 137.

Lemarchand, René. "Unsimplifying Darfur" (2006) 1:1 Genocide Studies and Prevention 1.

Levitt, Jeremy I. "The Peace and Security Council of the African Union and the United Nations Security Council: The Case of Darfur, Sudan" in Niels Blokker & Nico Schrijver, *The Security Council and the Use of Force, Theory and Reality – A Need for Change?* (Leiden: Martinus Nijhoff Publishers, 2005) 213.

Lipscomb, Rosanna. "Restructuring the ICC Framework to Advance Transitional Justice: A Search for a Permanent Solution in Sudan" (2006) 106 Colum. L. Rev. 182.

Marchal, Roland. "Le conflit de toutes les ambivalences" (2006) 14 Enjeux Internationaux 34.

Marthoz, Paul. "Le Soudan, pays de tous les enjeux" (2006) 14 Enjeux Internationaux 13.

Mathew, Jamie A. "The Darfur Debate: Whether the ICC Should Determine that the Atrocities in Darfur Constitute Genocide" (2006) 18 Fla. J. Int'l L. 517.

McGoldrick, Dominic. "Legal and Political Significance of a Permanent ICC" in Dominic McGoldrick, Peter Rowe & Eric Donnelly, eds., *The Permanent International Criminal Court, Legal and Policy Issues* (Portland: Hart, 2004) 453.

Mégret, Frédéric. "The Politics of International Criminal Justice" (2002) 13 E.J.I.L. 1261.

___. "International Prosecutors: Accountability and Ethics", Leuven Centre for Global Governance Studies, Working Paper No. 18 (December 2008), online: SSRN <http://ssrn.com/abstract=1313691>.

Mennecke, Martin. "What's in a Name? Reflections on Using, Not Using, and Overusing the "G-Word"" (2007) 2:1 Genocide Studies and Prevention 57.

Miles, William F.S. "Labeling "Genocide" in Sudan: A Constructionist Analysis of Darfur" (2006) 1:3 Genocide Studies and Prevention 251.

Morris, Madeleine H. "Democracy, Global Governance and the International Criminal Court" in Ramesh Thakur & Peter Malcontent, eds., *From Sovereign Impunity to International Accountability* (Tokyo: United Nations Press, 2004) 187.

Natsios, Andrew S. "Moving Beyond the Sense of Alarm" in Samuel Totten & Eric Markusen, *Genocide in Darfur, Investigating the Atrocities in the Sudan* (New York: Routledge, 2006) 25.

___. "Beyond Darfur, Sudan's Slide Toward Civil War" (2008) 87:3 Foreign Affairs.

Newman, Dwight G. "The Rome Statute, Some Reservations Concerning Amnesties, and a Distributive Problem" (2005) 20 Am. U. Int'l L. Rev. 293.

O'Brien, Kevin A. "Truth and Reconciliation in South Africa: Confronting the Past, Building the Future?" (2000) 15:2 International Relations 1.

Orentlicher, Diane. "Settling Accounts: the Duty to Prosecute Human Rights Violations of a Prior Regime" (1990) 100 Yale L. J. 2537.

Prendergast, John. "Resolving the Three Headed War from Hell in Southern Sudan, Northern Uganda, and Darfur" (February 2005) 3 Woodrow Wilson International Center for Scholars, Africa Program Occasional Paper Series.

Prunier, Gérard. "La paix reste incertaine" (2006) 14 Enjeux Internationaux 28.

___. "Darfur, La Chronique d'un « Génocide Ambigu »" *Le Monde Diplomatique* (Mars 2007) 16.

Punyasena, Wasana. "Conflict Prevention and the International Criminal Court: Deterrence in a Changing World" (2006) 14 Michigan State Journal of International Law 39.

Reeves, Eric. "Darfur: Genocide Before Our Eyes" in Joyce Apsel, ed., *Darfur: Genocide Before Our Eyes* (New York: Institute for Study of Genocide, 2005) 26.

Roberts, Adam. "Implementing the Laws of Wars in Late 20th-Century Conflicts, Part II" (1998) 29:3 Security Dialogue 265.

Robinson, Darryl. "Serving the Interests of Justice: Amnesties, Truth Commissions and the International Criminal Court" (2003) 14 E.J.I.L. 481.

Sadat, Leila Nadya. "Exile, Amnesty and International Law" (2006) 81 Notre Dame L. Rev. 955.

Schabas, William A. "Darfur and the 'Odious Scourge': The Commission of Inquiry's Findings on Genocide" (2005) 18 Leiden J. Int'l L. 871.

___. "First Prosecutions at the International Criminal Court" (2006) 27 Human Rights Law Journal 25.

___. "Prosecutorial Discretion v. Judicial Activism at the International Criminal Court" (2008) 6 Journal of International Criminal Justice 731.

Scharf, Michael P. "The Letter of the Law: The Scope of the International Obligation to Prosecute Human Rights Crimes" (1996) 59 Law & Contemp. Probs. 41.

___. "The Amnesty Exception to the Jurisdiction of the International Criminal Court" (1999) 32 Cornell Int'l L.J. 507.

Shinoda, Hideaki. "Peace-Building by the Rule of Law: An Examination of Intervention in the Form of International Tribunals" (2002) 7 International Journal of Peace Studies 41.

Smith, Thomas W. "Moral Hazard and Humanitarian Law: The International Criminal Court and the Limits of Legalism" (2002) 39 International Politics 175.

Snyder, Jack & Leslie Vinjamuri. "Trials and Errors, Principle and Pragmatism in Strategies of International Justice" (2004) 28:3 International Security 5.

Stahn, Carsten. "Complementarity: A Tale of Two Notions" (2008) 19 Criminal Law Forum 87.

Strauss, Scott. "Darfur and the Genocide Debate" (2005) 84 Foreign Affairs 123.

Swart, Bert. "General Problems" in Antonio Cassese, Paola Gaeta & John R.W.D. Jones, eds., *The Rome Statute of the International Criminal Court: A Commentary* (Oxford: Oxford University Press, 2002) 1589.

Tar, Usman. "Counter-Insurgents or Ethnic Vanguards? Civil Militia and State Violence in the Darfur Region, Western Sudan" in David J. Francis, ed., *Civil Militia, Africa's Intractable Security Menace?* (Hants: Ashgate, 2005) 134.

Tubiana, Jérôme. "Le Darfur: un conflit identitaire?" (2005) 214 Afrique Contemporaine 165.

___. "Le Darfour, un conflit pour la terre?" (2006) 101 Politique africaine 111.

Tull, Denis M. "Sudan after the Naivasha Peace Agreement, No Champagne Yet" (February 2005) German Institute for International and Security Affairs, SWP Comments 3, online: Stiftung Wissenschaft und Politik <http://swp-berlin.org/en/produkte/swp_aktuell_detail.php?id=4207>.

Turone, Giuliano. "Powers and Duties of the Prosecutor" in Antonio Cassese, Paola Gaeta & John R.W.D. Jones, eds., *The Rome Statute of the International Criminal Court: A Commentary* (Oxford: Oxford University Press, 2002) 1137.

Vetter, Greg R. "Command Responsibility of Non-Military Superiors in the International Criminal Court (ICC)" (2000) 25 Yale J. Int'l L. 89.

Webb, Philippa. "The ICC Prosecutor's Discretion Not to Proceed in the "Interest of Justice"" (2005) 50 Crim. L.Q. 305.

Wedgwood, Ruth, Harold K. Jacobson & Allan Gerson. "Peace Building, The Private Sector's Role" (2001) 95 A.J.I.L. 102.

Wilson, Richard A. "Reconciliation and Revenge in Post-Apartheid South Africa: Rethinking Legal Pluralism and Human Rights" (2000) 41:1 Current Anthropology 75

Wippman, David. "Atrocities, Deterrence, and the Limits of International Justice" (1999) 23 Fordham Int'l L.J. 473.

Conferences, interviews and theses (in chronological order)

Le Fort, Olivia. "The Politics of Amnesty" (LL.M. Thesis, McGill University Faculty of Law, 2005) [unpublished].

Medani, Khalid. "The Darfur Crisis and the Challenge of Democracy in Sudan" (Paper presented to the Conference *The Challenge of Development in Sub-Saharan Africa: Conflict Resolution, Democratic Governance and Education*, Centre for Developing-Area Studies, McGill University, 29 March 2007) [unpublished].

Interview of Annette Weber, researcher at the German Institute for International and Security Affairs (3 July 2007).

News sources (in alphabetical order by title / author if available)

"Aid Group's Expulsion, Fears of More Misery" *New York Times* (22 March 2009).

"Darfur mediator says Bashir warrant imperils talks" *Reuters* (26 March 2009), online: Reuters <http://www.reuters.com/article/NewsMaps/idUS-TRE52P7FO20090326>.

"EU in Kenya Poll Tribunal Threat" *BBC News* (18 November 2008), online: BBC <http://news.bbc.co.uk/go/pr/fr/-/2/hi/africa/7736011.stm>.

"ICC Prosecutor says he received 'zero' information from NGO's in Sudan" *Sudan Tribune* (21 March 2009), online: Sudan Tribune <http://www.sudan-tribune.com/spip.php?article30580>.

"In Darfur gibt es keinen Frieden zu sichern" [There is no peace to be kept in Darfur] *Der Standard* (4 July 2008).

"Khartoum under Curfew as 3,000 Darfur Rebels Advance on Capital" *The Guardian* (11 May 2008), online: The Guardian <http://www.guardian.co.uk/world/2008/may/11/sudan?gusrc=rss&feed=fromtheobserver>.

"Le long chemin de la Cour pénale internationale vers l'universalité" *Le Monde* (30 June 2007), online: Le Monde <http://www.lemonde.fr>.

"Le Soudan rejette la légitimité de la CPI sur le Darfour" *Le Monde* (27 February 2007), online: Le Monde <http://www.lemonde.fr>.

"Peace or Justice?" *Guardian Weekly* (10 January 2007), online: Guardian Unlimited <http://www.guardian.co.uk/guardianweekly/story/0,,1987173,00.html>.

"President Omar al-Bashir declared winner of Sudan poll" *BBC News* (26 April 2010), online: BBC <http://news.bbc.co.uk/2/hi/africa/8643602.stm>.

"Q&A: Sudan's Darfur Conflict" *BBC News* (15 November 2007), online: BBC <http://news.bbc.co.uk/2/hi/africa/3496731.stm>.

"Sudan 'Backs UN-led Darfur Force'" *BBC News* (18 June 2007), online: BBC <http://news.bbc.co.uk/2/hi/africa/6760781.stm>.

"Sudan 'Blocking' Darfur Mission" *BBC News* (28 November 2007), online: BBC <http://news.bbc.co.uk/2/hi/africa/7116284.stm>.

"Sudanese Official Arrested in Connection with Rebel Assault on Capital" *Sudan Tribune* (19 May 2008), online: Sudan Tribune <http://sudantribune.com/spip.php?article27203>.

"Sudan Hints at Involvement of Libya & France in Rebel Attack on Capital" *Sudan Tribune* (14 May 2008), online: Sudan Tribune <http://www.sudantribune.com/spip.php?article27137>.

"Sudan rejects calls to hand over 2 wanted by ICC for their role in Darfur crisis" *Associated Press* (7 June 2008), available online at: Sudan.Net <http://www.sudan.net/news/posted/16044.html>.

"Sudan-US Talks to Resume Next Week after Brief Delay" *Sudan Tribune* (25 May 2008), online: Sudan Tribune <http://www.sudantribune.com/spip.php?article27273>.

"Sudan Vows 'Strong' Response to ICC Arrest Attempts of Darfur Suspect" *Sudan Tribune* (9 June 2008), online: Sudan Tribune <http://www.sudantribune.com/spip.php?article27457>.

"Uganda's President Hopes Rebels Choose 'Soft Landing'" *Reuters* (4 June 2007), online: Reuters <http://www.reuters.com/articles/latestCrisis/idUSL04425927>.

"UN Fury at Darfur Militia Ambush" *BBC* News (9 July 2008), online: BBC <http://news.bbc.co.uk/2/hi/africa/7498811.stm>.

"US Seeks Libyan Help on Darfur force" *Sudan Tribune* (10 March 2007), online: Sudan Tribune <http://www.sudantribune.com/spip.php?article20692>.

Ali, Wasil. "Feature: Justice a Threat to Peace in Darfur?" *Sudan Tribune* (30 June 2008), online: Sudan Tribune <http://sudantribune.com/spip.php?article27689>.

Baines, Erin & Adrian Bradbury. "Peace in Northern Uganda, but Whose Justice?" *Sudan Tribune* (2 August 2007), online: Sudan Tribune <http://www.sudantribune.com/spip.php?article23087>.

Besheer, Margaret. "Concern Grows at UN for Peacekeepers, Stuff in Sudan" *VOA News* (11 July 2008), online: VOA News <http://www.voanews.com/english/2008-07-11-voa65.cfm>.

Brittain, Victoria. "Unrealistic Humanitarians" *The Guardian* (4 August 1999), online: Guardian Unlimited <http://www.guardian.co.uk/comment/story/0,,280229,00.html>.

Cassese, Antonio. "Il colpo di scena del procuratore" *La Repubblica* (15 July 2008) [an English translation, "Flawed International Justice for Sudan", is available at <www.mediafire.com/?zyzjnofumlz>].

___. "The Decision on Darfur has been Tactically Mishandled" *The Daily Star* (18 July 2008).

Clifford, Lisa. "ICC Risks Losing the Plot in Congo" *Institute for War and Peace Reporting* (21 November 2008), online: Institute for War & Peace Reporting <http://www.iwpr.net/?p=acr&s=f&o=347941&apc_state=henh>.

Farley, Maggie. "Darfur War Crimes Suspect Has Free Rein Despite ICC Warrants" *Los Angeles Times* (5 August 2007).

Glassborow, Katy & Joe Wacha. "ICC Judges to Review LRA Cases" *Institute for War & Peace Reporting* (19 November 2008), online: Institute for War & Peace Reporting <http://www.iwpr.net/?p=acr&s=f&o=347885&apc_state=henh>.

Gruda, Agnès. "Le Darfour n'est pas le Rwanda" *La Presse* (13 April 2007).

Idris, Amir. "Making Sense of JEM Attack on Sudan's Capital" *Sudan Tribune* (27 May 2008), online: Sudan Tribune <http://www.sudantribune.com/spip.php?article27285>.

Miller, Greg & Josh Meyer. "U.S. Relies on Sudan Despite Condemning it" *Los Angeles Times* (11 June 2007), online: Los Angeles Times <www.latimes.com>.

Perry, Alex. "Defections in Darfur?" *Time* (21 March 2007), online: Time Inc. <http://www.time.com/time/world/article/0,8599,1601495,00.html>.

Polgreen, Lydia. "Militia Talks Could Reshape Conflict in Darfur" *New York Times* (15 April 2007).

Reeves, Eric. "Darfur Peace Talks in Libya Produce Only an Emboldened Khartoum" *Sudan Tribune* (13 November 2007), online: Sudan Tribune <http://www.sudantribune.com/spip.php?article24721>.

___. "Sudanese Government Responsible of Attack on Darfur Peacekeepers" *Sudan Tribune* (14 July 2008), online: Sudan Tribune <http://sudantribune.com/spip.php?article27838>.

Ross, Will. "Ugandans Ask ICC to Spare Rebels" *BBC News* (16 March 2005), online: BBC <http://news.bbc.co.uk/2/low/africa/4352901.stm>.

Sengupta, Somini. "Besieged Liberian" *New York Times* (11 July 2003).

Stahnke, Jochen. "Erste Kriegsverbrecher benannt" [First War Criminals Named] *Die Zeit* (28 February 2007), online: Die Zeit <http://www.zeit.de/online/2007/09/ICC-Darfur>.

Storey, Peter. "A Different Kind of Justice: Truth and Reconciliation in South Africa" *Christian Century* (10 September 1997), online: FindArticles <http://www.findarticles.com/p/articles/mi_m1058/is_n25_v114/ai_19844884>.

Wacha, Joe. "Kony Meeting Request Raises Hopes" *Institute for War & Peace Reporting* (21 August 2008), online: Institute for War & Peace Reporting <http://www.iwpr.net/?p=acr&s=f&o=346316&apc_state=henh>.

Electronic resources (in alphabetical order)

Akande, Dapo. "The Bashir Indictment: Are Serving Heads of State Immune from ICC Prosecution?" Oxford Transitional Justice Research Working Paper Series (30 July 2008), online: University of Oxford <http://www.csls.ox.ac.uk/documents/Akande.pdf>.

Allen, Tim. "War and Justice in Northern Uganda: An Assessment of the International Criminal Court's Intervention" (February 2005), online: Crisis States Research Centre, London School of Economics <http://www.crisis-states.com/download/others/AllenICCReport.pdf>

Amnesty International. "Sudan: National court for Darfur crimes lacks credibility, and is no replacement for ICC investigations" (14 June 2005), online: Amnesty International <http://www.amnesty.org.uk/news_details.asp?NewsID=16169>.

___. "Chad, 'Are we citizens of this country?' Civilians in Chad unprotected from Janjaweed attacks" (29 January 2007), online: Amnesty International <http://www.amnesty.org/en/library/info/AFR20/001/2007>.

___. "Sudan: Arms Continuing to Fuel Serious Human Rights Violations in Darfur, (8 May 2007), online: Amnesty International <http://www.amnesty.org/fr/library/info/AFR54/019/2007/en>.

___. "Uganda: Agreement and Annex on Accountability and Reconciliation Falls Short of a Comprehensive Plan to End Impunity" (March 2008), online: reliefweb <http://www2.reliefweb.int/rw/RWFiles2008.nsf/FilesByRWDocUnidFilename/LRON-7CTEZN-full_report.pdf/$File/full_report.pdf>.

___. "Darfur Crisis Reaches Sudanese Capital" (23 May 2008), online: Amnesty International <http://www.amnesty.org/en/news-and-updates/darfur-crisis-reaches-sudanese-capital-20080523>.

___. "Left to Their Own Devices, The Continued Suffering of Victims of the Conflict in Northern Ugandan and the Need for Reparations" (17 November 2008), online: Amnesty International <http://www.amnesty.org/fr/library/info/AFR59/009/2008/en>.

Global Policy Forum. "Sudan: Judiciary Challenges ICC over Darfur Case" (24 June 2005), online: Global Policy Forum <http://www.globalpolicy.org/intljustice/icc/2005/0624collaborate.htm>.

Grono, Nick & Caroline Flintoft. "Negotiating Justice to Understand Accountability", Expert Paper for Workshop 6 – Negotiating Justice", Nuremberg Conference: Building a Future on Peace and Justice (25 June 2007), online: International Crisis Group <http://www.crisisgroup.org/home/index.cfm?id=4912>.

Grono Nick, & David Mozersky. "Sudan and the ICC: A Question of Accountability" (31 January 2007), online: International Crisis Group <http://www.crisisgroup.org/home/index.cfm?id=4640&l=1>.

Human Rights Watch. "Q & A: Crisis in Darfur", online: Human Rights Watch <http://hrw.org/english/docs/2004/05/05/darfur8536.htm>.

___. "Stolen Children" (March 2003), online: Human Rights Watch <http://www.hrw.org/reports/2003/uganda0303/uganda0403.pdf>.

___. "Entrenching Impunity, Government Responsibility for International Crimes in Darfur" (December 2005), online: Human Rights Watch <http://hrw.org/reports/2005/darfur1205/>.

___. "The Lack of Conviction, The Special Criminal Court on the Events in Darfur" (June 2006), online: Human Rights Watch <http://hrw.org/backgrounder/ij/sudan0606/sudan0606.pdf>.

___. "Sudan: National Courts Have Done Nothing on Darfur" (11 June 2007), online: Human Rights Watch <http://hrw.org/english/docs/2007/06/11/sudan16110.htm>.

___. "Courting History, The Landmark International Criminal Court's First Five Years" (July 2008), online: Human Rights Watch <http://hrw.org/reports/2008/icc0708/icc0708web.pdf>.

___. "Sudan, justice and peace" (16 July 2008), online: Human Rights Watch <http://www.hrw.org/en/news/2008/07/15/sudan-justice-and-peace>.

___. "DR Congo: LRA Slaughters 620 in 'Christmas Massacre'" (17 January 2009), online: Human Rights Watch <http://www.hrw.org/en/news/2009/01/17/dr-congo-lra-slaughters-620-christmas-massacres>.

___. "DR Congo: Lord's Resistance Army Rampage Kills 321" (28 March 2010), online: Human Rights Watch <http://www.hrw.org/en/news/2010/03/28/dr-congo-lord-s-resistance-army-rampage-kills-321>.

___. "Sudan: ICC Warrant for Al-Bashir on Genocide" (13 July 2010), online: Human Rights Watch <http://www.hrw.org/en/news/2010/07/13/sudan-icc-warrant-al-bashir-genocide>.

Human Rights Watch & International Crisis Group. "Security Council Must Take Action to Protect Civilians in Darfur, Joint Human Rights Watch and International Crisis Group Letter to the Members of the U.N. Security Council Regarding Darfur" (31 January 2006), online: Human Rights Watch <http://hrw.org/english/docs/2006/01/31/sudan12577.htm>.

International Committee of the Red Cross. Press Release, "On his Return from Darfur, ICRC President Deplores Worsening Conditions for the Region's Population" (21 February 2007), online: International Committee of the Red Cross <http://www.icrc.org/web/eng/siteengo.nsf/html/sudan-news-210207>.

International Crisis Group. "Conflict History: Uganda", online: International Crisis Group <http://www.crisisgroup.org/home/index.cfm?action=conflict_search&l=1&t=1&c_country=111>.

___. "Shock Therapy for Northern Uganda's Peace Process" (11 April 2005), online: International Crisis Group <http://www.crisisgroup.org/home/index.cfm?id=3366&l=1>.

___. "Peace in Northern Uganda?" (13 September 2006), online: International Crisis Group <http://www.crisisgroup.org/home/index.cfm?id=4374&l=1>.

___. "Northern Uganda: Seizing the Opportunity for Peace" (26 April 2007), online: International Crisis Group <http://www.crisisgroup.org/home/index.cfm?id=4791>.

___. "Darfur: Revitalising the Peace Process" (30 April 2007), online: International Crisis Group <http://www.crisisgroup.org/home/index.cfm?id=4769>.

___. "A Strategy for Comprehensive Peace in Sudan" (26 July 2007), online: International Crisis Group <http://www.crisisgroup.org/home/index.cfm?id=4961&l=1>.

Kiranda, Yusuf. "Juba Peace Talks Collapse, A Golden Opportunity for Peace is Slipping through our Hands", Konrad-Adenauer-Stiftung (12 June 2008), online: Konrad-Adenauer-Stiftung <http://www.kas.de/proj/home/pub/36/1/dokument_id-13956/index.html>.

McDonald, Avril & Roelof Haveman. "Prosecutorial Discretion – Some Thoughts on 'Objectifying' the Exercise of Prosecutorial Discretion by the Prosecutor of the ICC", Expert consultation process on general issues relevant to the ICC Office of the Prosecutor (15 April 2003), online: International Criminal Court <http://www.icc-cpi.int/library/organs/otp/mcdonald_haveman.pdf>.

Médecins Sans Frontières. "A cause de l'insécurité, des zones inaccessibles, des personnes sans assistance" (25 October 2006), online: Médecins Sans Frontières <http://www.msf.fr/site/actu.nsf/actus/darfouritvjs251006>.

___. "De mauvaises réponses à de bonnes questions" (23 March 2007), online: Médecins Sans Frontières <http://www.msf.fr/site/actu.nsf/actus/darfourit-wgab230307>.

Opinio Juris. online: Opinio Juris <http://opiniojuris.org/2008/07/11/icc-prosecutor-to-charge-sudans-president-with-genocide/>.

Parliamentarians for Global Action. "A Deterrent International Criminal Court - The Ultimate Objective", (6-7 December 2004), online: Parliamentarians for Global Action <http://www.pgaction.org/uploadedfiles/deterrent%20 paper% 20for%20NZ_panel%201_.pdf>.

Prendergast, John. "The Answer to the Lord's Resistance Army" (June 2007), online: Center for American Progress <http://www.enoughproject.org/files/publications/answer_lra.pdf>.

Prunier, Gérard. "Darfur's Sudan Problem", openDemocracy (15 September 2006), online: opendemocracy <http://www.opendemocracy.net/democracy-africa_democracy/darfur_conflict_3909.jsp>.

Refugee Law Project. "Whose Justice? Perceptions of Uganda's Amnesty Act 2000: The Potential for Conflict Resolution and Long-Term Reconciliation" (February 2005), online: Refugee Law Project <http://www. refugeelawproject.org/resources/papers/workingpapers/RLP.WP15.pdf>.

Reporters Without Borders. "Darfur: An Investigation into a Tragedy's Forgotten Actors" (April 2007), online: Reporters Without Borders <http://www.rsf.org/IMG/pdf/RSF_Sudan_ENG.pdf>.

Resolve Uganda. "Seizing the Second Chance: Peace on the Horizon for Uganda?" (26 April 2007), online: Resolve Uganda <http://www.resolveuganda.org/seizing-the-second-chance>.

___. "The Peace Process Must Live On: Juba's Lessons and Its Legacy" (June 2008), online: Resolve Uganda <https://salsa.democracyinaction.org/o/2241/images/Resolve%20Uganda%20Policy%20Brief%20June%202008.pdf>.

Res Publica. "The Darfur Resistance, *Who They Are, What They Want, and What They Need to Create a New Sudan*", online: Res Publica <http://www.darfurgenocide.org/ResPublicaDarfurTripReport.pdf>.

Save Darfur Coalition. "Background" (25 October 2006), online: SaveDarfur <http://www.savedarfur.org>.

Schabas, William. "A Major Complementary Ruling by the Appeals Chamber of the International Criminal Court" (27 September 2009), online: PhD studies in human rights <http://humanrightsdoctorate.blogspot.com/2009_09_01_archive.html>.

Security Council Report. "Uganda/LRA, Update Report No.1" (11 April 2008), online: Security Council Report <http://www.securitycouncilreport.org/site/c.glKWLeMTIsG/b.4018489/>.

The White House. Press Release, "President's Statement on Violence in Darfur, Sudan" (9 September 2004), online: The White House <http://www.whitehouse.gov/news/releases/2004/09/20040909-10.html>.

Wolfe, Adam. "China Claims Success on Darfur", Power and Interest News Report (24 April 2007), online: PINR: <http://www.pinr.com/report.php?ac=view_report &report_id=643&language_id=1>.

World Bank. "War-to-Peace Transition in Mozambique: The Provincial Reintegration Support Program" (July 1997) online: World Bank Group <http://www.worldbank.org/afr/findings/english/find90.htm>.

Index

I

J

K

L

R

S

www.ingramcontent.com/pod-product-compliance
Lightning Source LLC
LaVergne TN
LVHW081515300926
849161LV00006B/1190